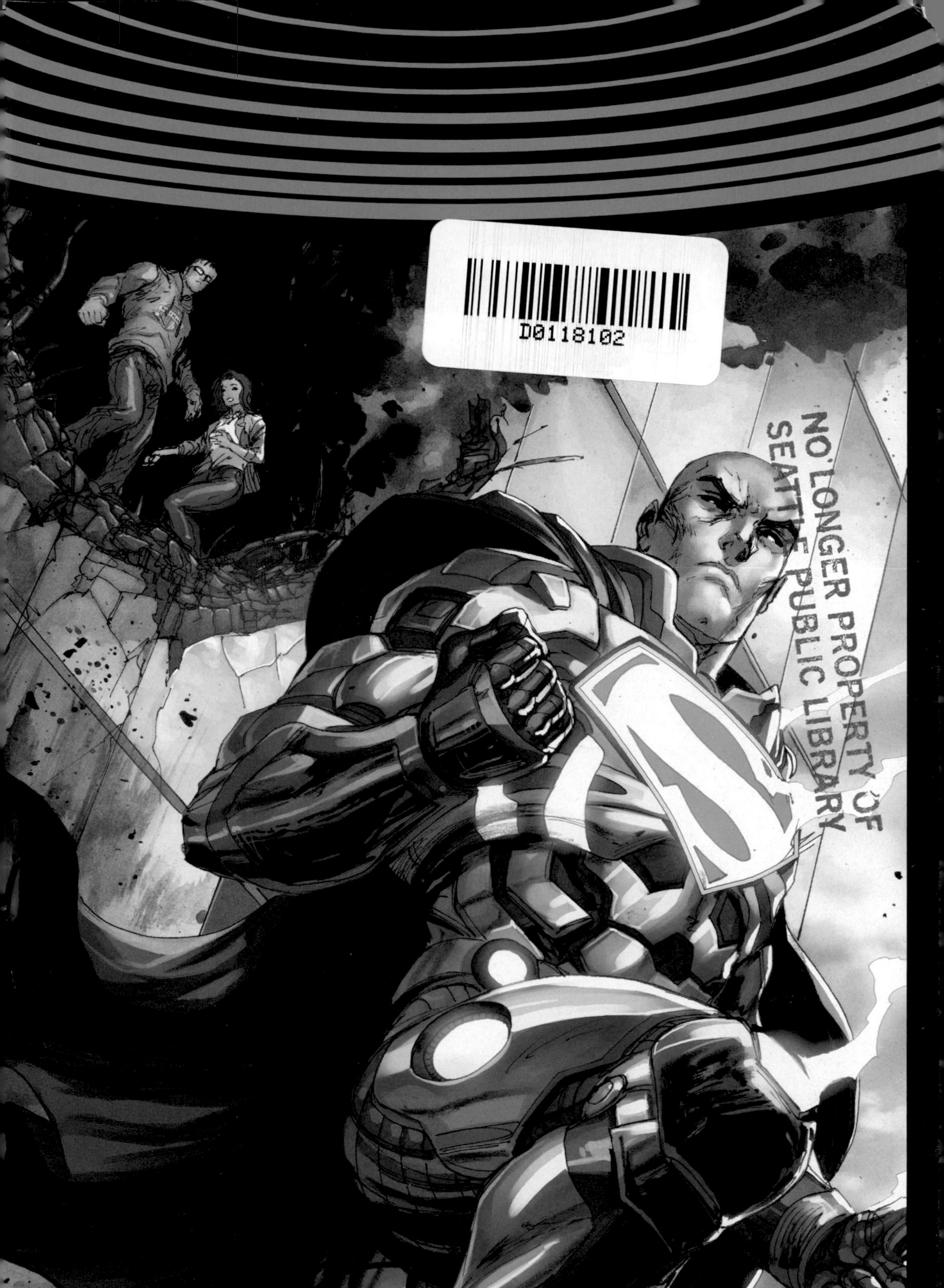

SUPERMAN ACTION COMICS
VOL.3 MEN OF STEEL

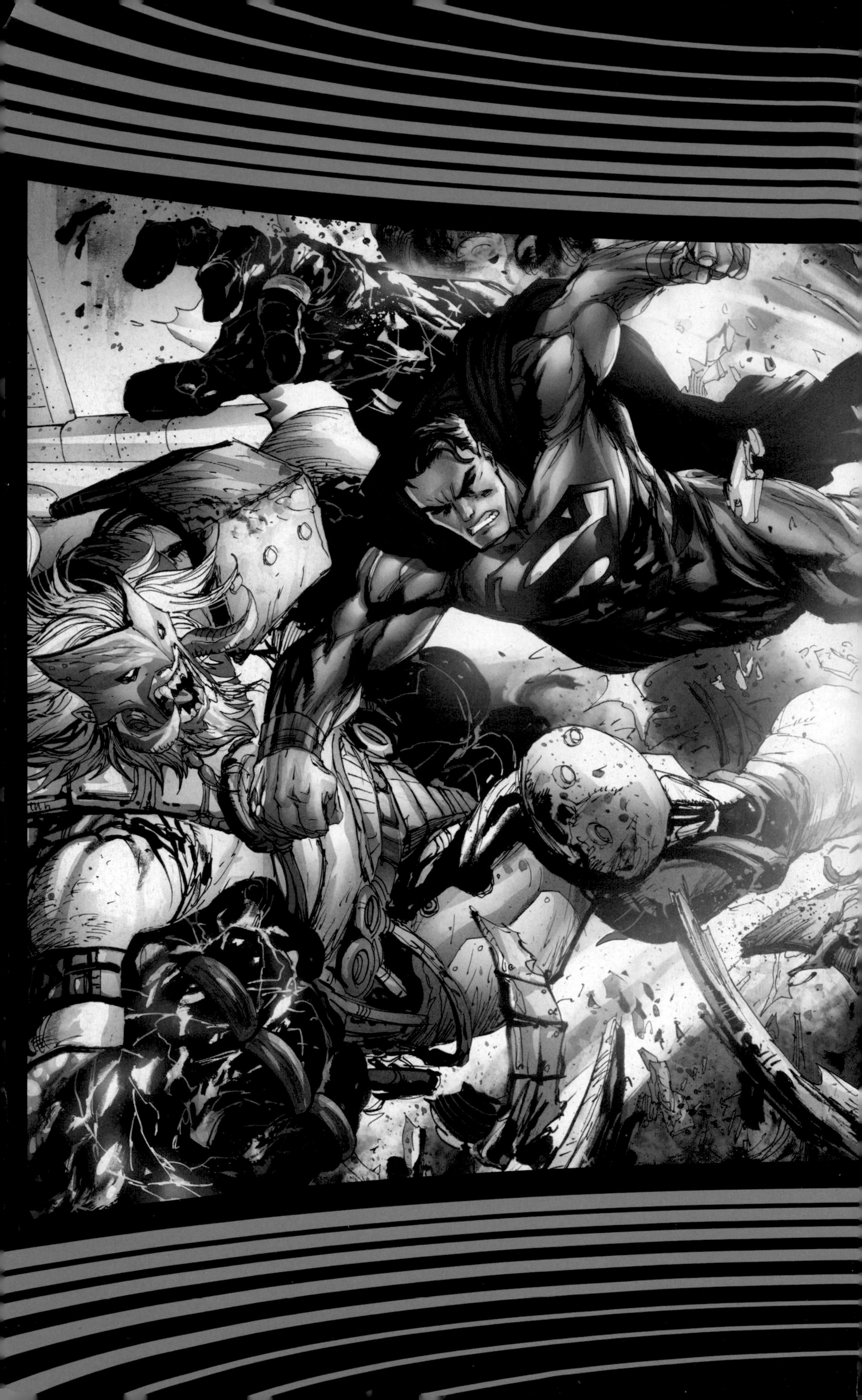

SUPERMAN ACTION COMICS
VOL.3 MEN OF STEEL

DAN JURGENS
writer

PATCH ZIRCHER * **STEPHEN SEGOVIA** * **ART THIBERT**
artists

ARIF PRIANTO * **ULISES ARREOLA**
colorists

ROB LEIGH
letterer

CLAY MANN and BRAD ANDERSON with DAN JURGENS
collection cover artists

SUPERMAN created by **JERRY SIEGEL** and **JOE SHUSTER**
By special arrangement with the Jerry Siegel family

MIKE COTTON Editor - Original Series * PAUL KAMINSKI Associate Editor - Original Series
JEB WOODARD Group Editor - Collected Editions * PAUL SANTOS Editor - Collected Edition
STEVE COOK Design Director - Books * MONIQUE GRUSPE Publication Design

BOB HARRAS Senior VP - Editor-in-Chief, DC Comics

DIANE NELSON President * DAN DiDIO Publisher * JIM LEE Publisher * GEOFF JOHNS President & Chief Creative Officer
AMIT DESAI Executive VP - Business & Marketing Strategy, Direct to Consumer & Global Franchise Management * SAM ADES Senior VP - Direct to Consumer
BOBBIE CHASE VP - Talent Development * MARK CHIARELLO Senior VP - Art, Design & Collected Editions
JOHN CUNNINGHAM Senior VP - Sales & Trade Marketing * ANNE DePIES Senior VP - Business Strategy, Finance & Administration
DON FALLETTI VP - Manufacturing Operations * LAWRENCE GANEM VP - Editorial Administration & Talent Relations
ALISON GILL Senior VP - Manufacturing & Operations * HANK KANALZ Senior VP - Editorial Strategy & Administration
JAY KOGAN VP - Legal Affairs * THOMAS LOFTUS VP - Business Affairs
JACK MAHAN VP - Business Affairs * NICK J. NAPOLITANO VP - Manufacturing Administration
EDDIE SCANNELL VP - Consumer Marketing * COURTNEY SIMMONS Senior VP - Publicity & Communications
JIM (SKI) SOKOLOWSKI VP - Comic Book Specialty Sales & Trade Marketing * NANCY SPEARS VP - Mass, Book, Digital Sales & Trade Marketing

SUPERMAN: ACTION COMICS VOL. 3 – MEN OF STEEL

DC Comics, 2900 West Alameda Ave., Burbank, CA 91505.
Printed by LSC Communications, Salem, VA, USA. 5/26/17. First Printing
ISBN: 978-1-4012-7357-6

Library of Congress Cataloging-in-Publication Data is available.

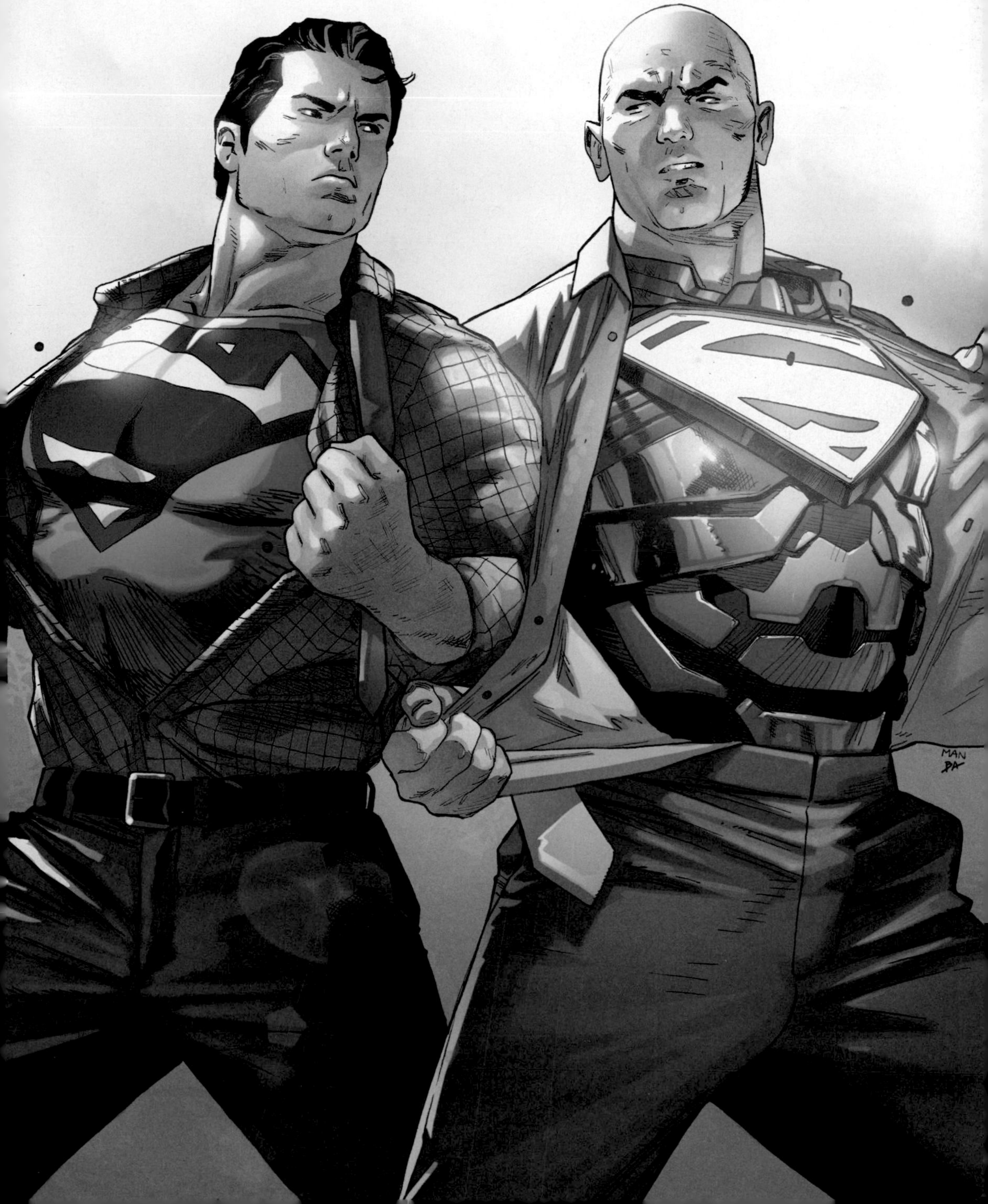
MAN BA

MEN OF STEEL PART 1

TYLER KIRKHAM artist * ARIF PRIANTO colorist
CLAY MANN BRAD ANDERSON DAN JURGENS cover artists

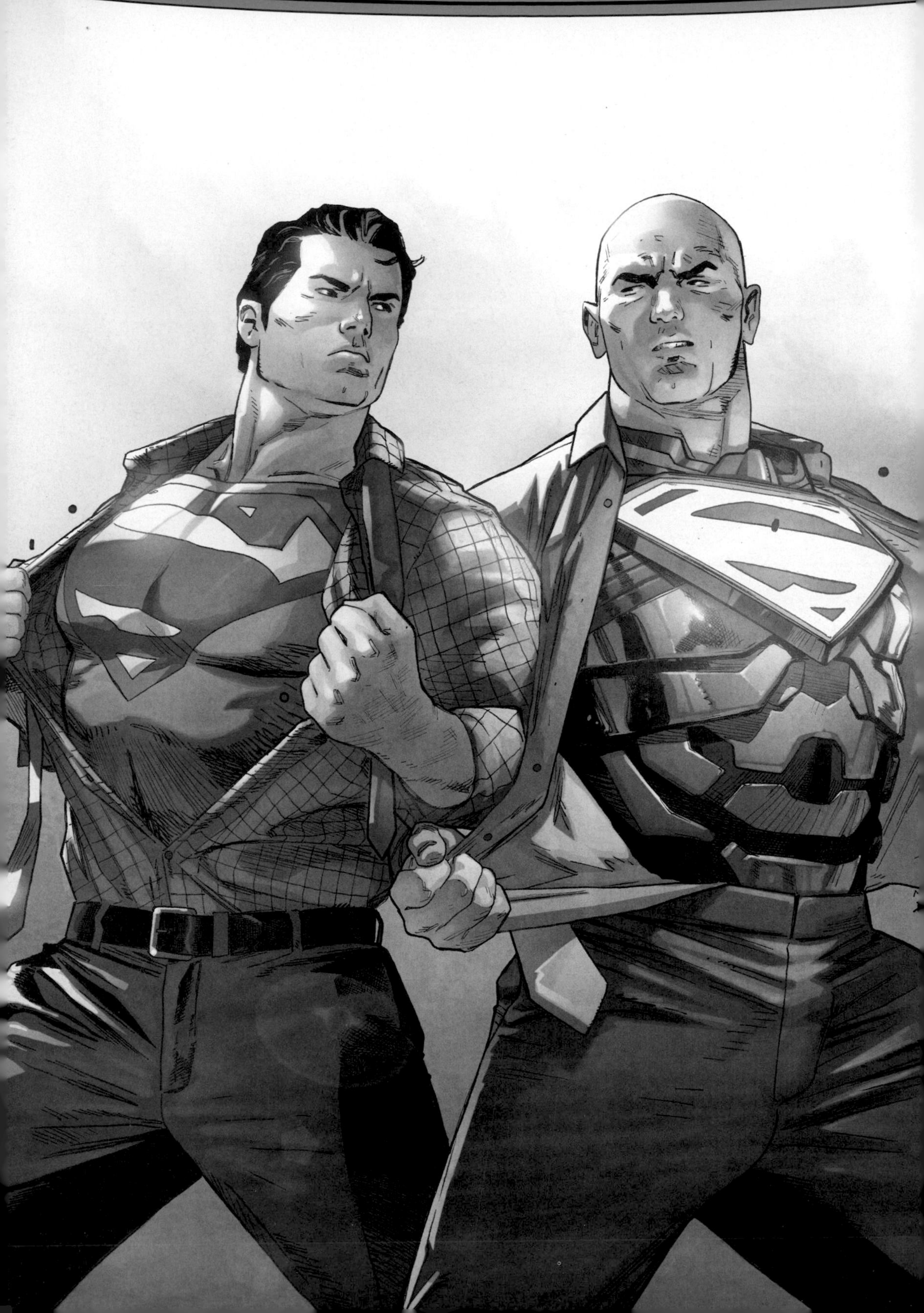

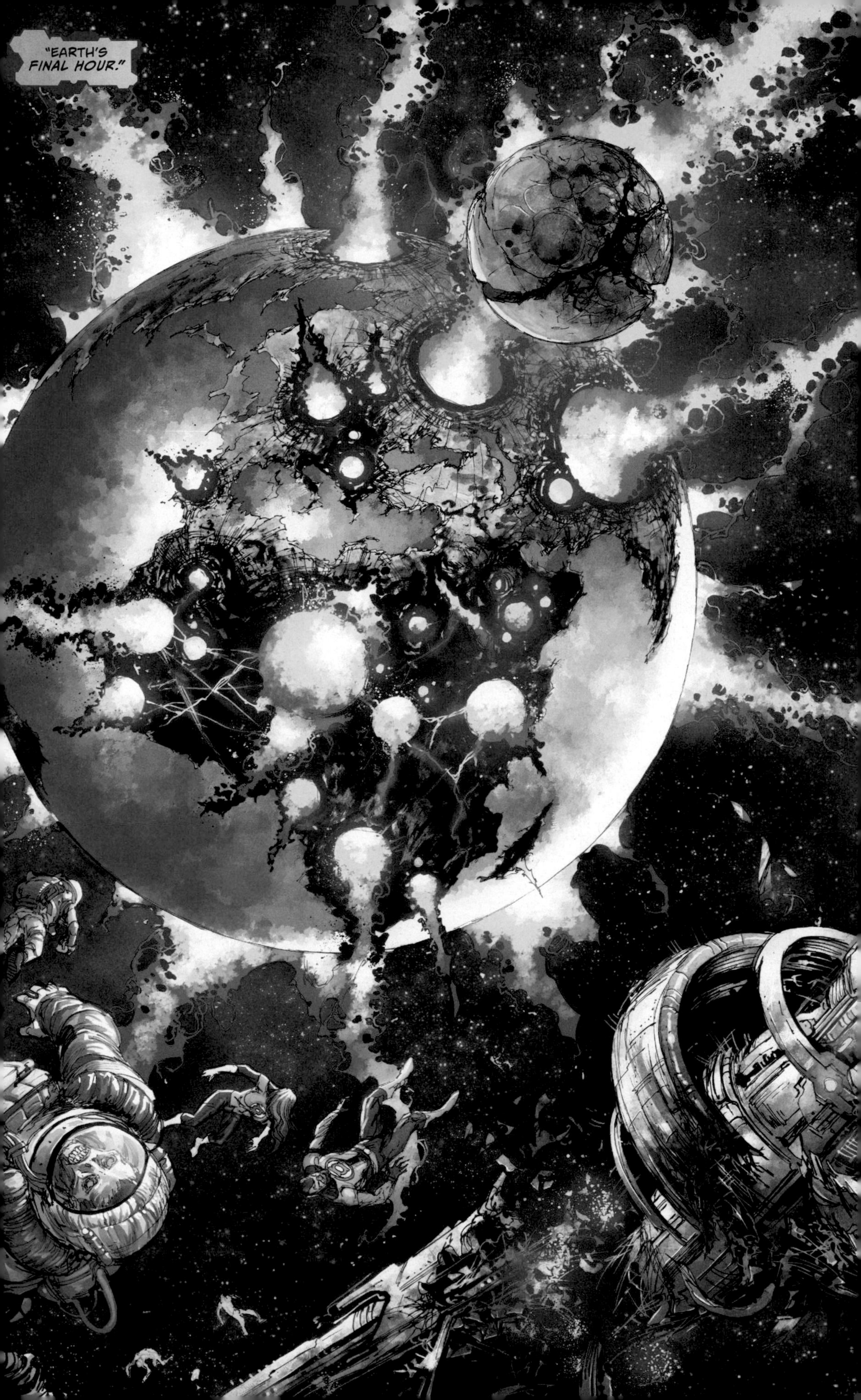
"EARTH'S FINAL HOUR."

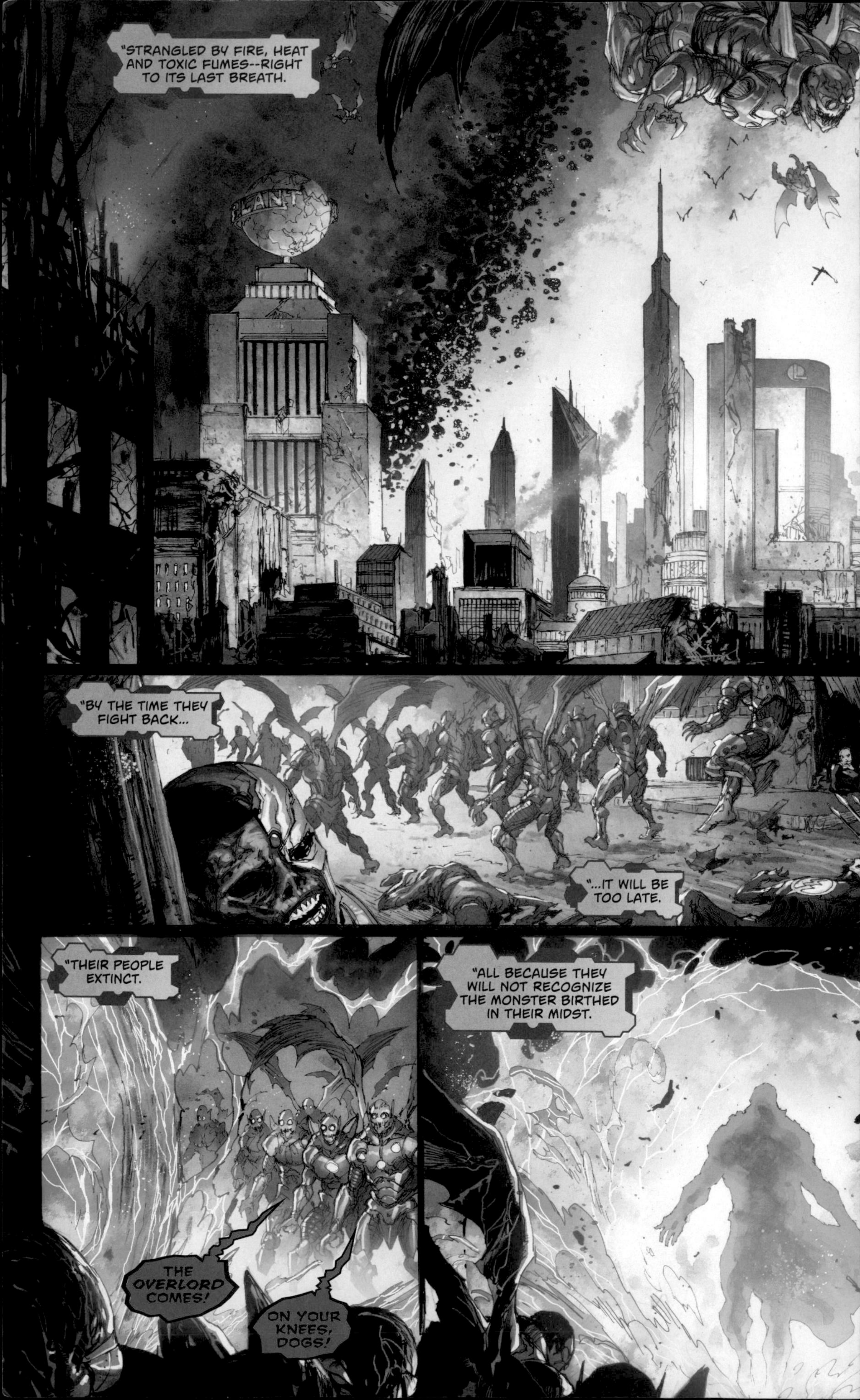
"STRANGLED BY FIRE, HEAT AND TOXIC FUMES--RIGHT TO ITS LAST BREATH.
"BY THE TIME THEY FIGHT BACK...
"...IT WILL BE TOO LATE.
"THEIR PEOPLE EXTINCT.
"ALL BECAUSE THEY WILL NOT RECOGNIZE THE MONSTER BIRTHED IN THEIR MIDST.
THE OVERLORD COMES!
ON YOUR KNEES, DOGS!

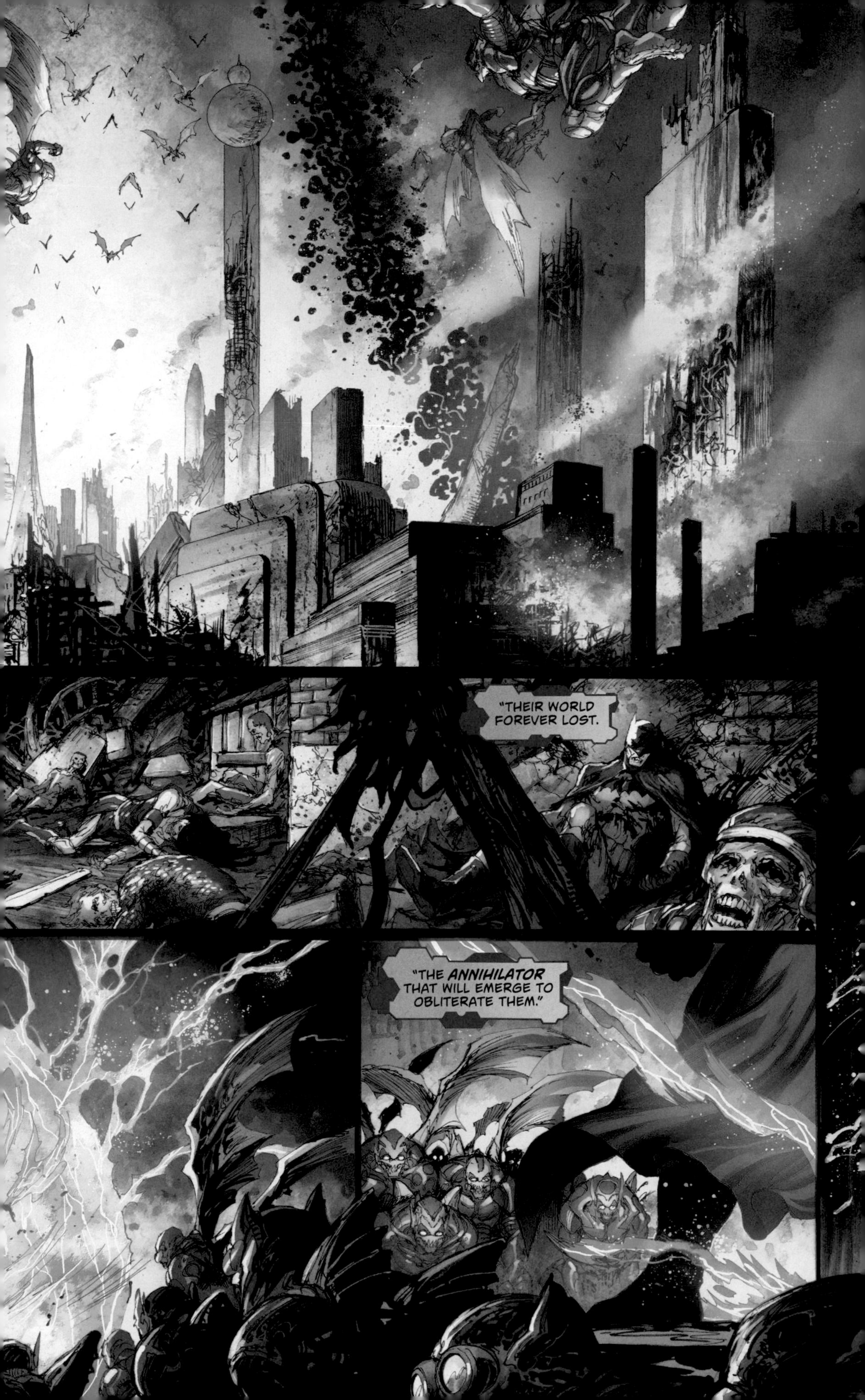
"THEIR WORLD FOREVER LOST.
"THE ANNIHILATOR THAT WILL EMERGE TO OBLITERATE THEM."

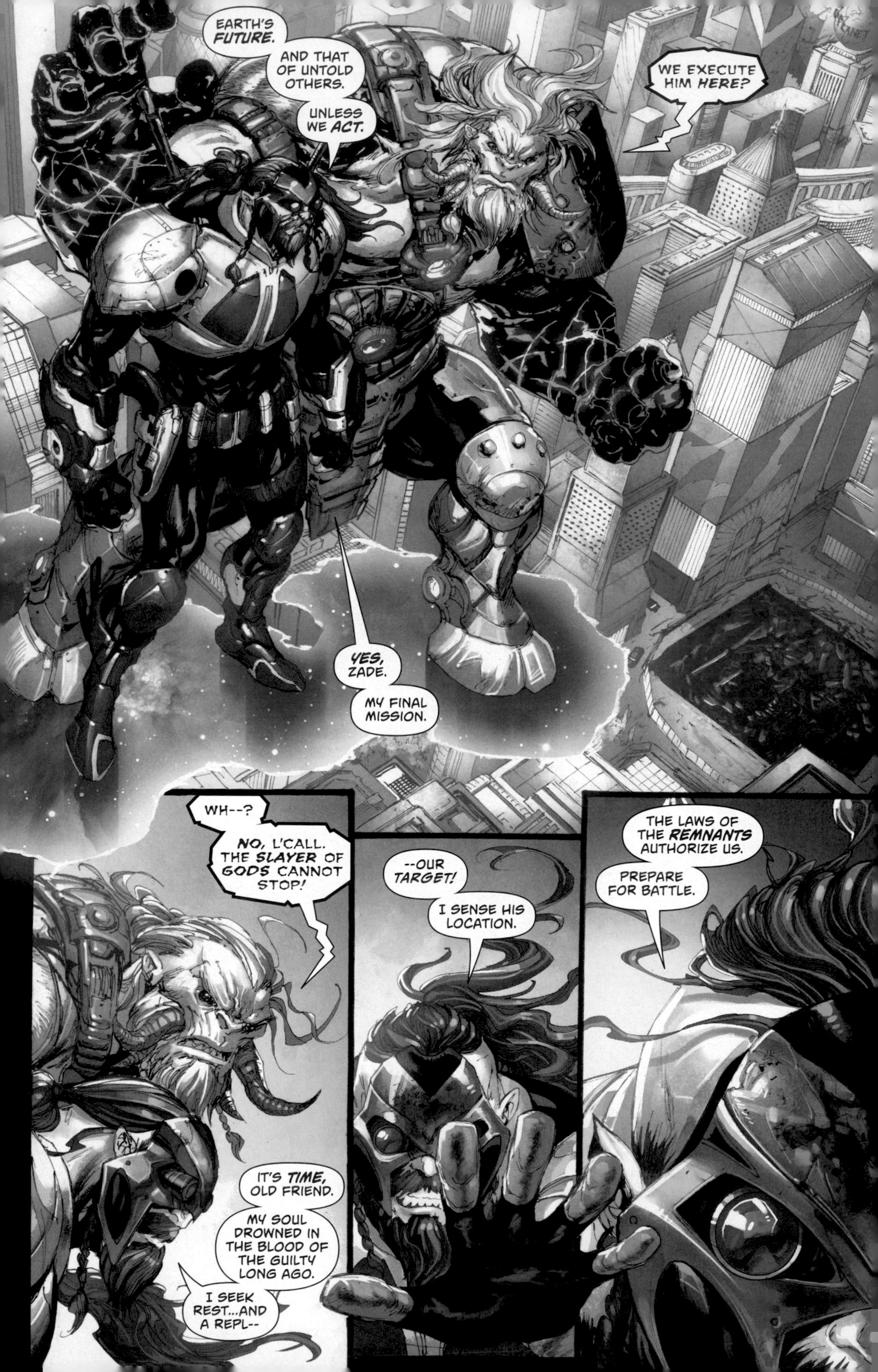
EARTH'S FUTURE.
AND THAT OF UNTOLD OTHERS.
UNLESS WE ACT.
WE EXECUTE HIM HERE?
YES, ZADE.
MY FINAL MISSION.
WH--?
NO, L'CALL. THE SLAYER OF GODS CANNOT STOP!
IT'S TIME, OLD FRIEND.
MY SOUL DROWNED IN THE BLOOD OF THE GUILTY LONG AGO.
I SEEK REST...AND A REPL--
--OUR TARGET!
I SENSE HIS LOCATION.
THE LAWS OF THE REMNANTS AUTHORIZE US.
PREPARE FOR BATTLE.

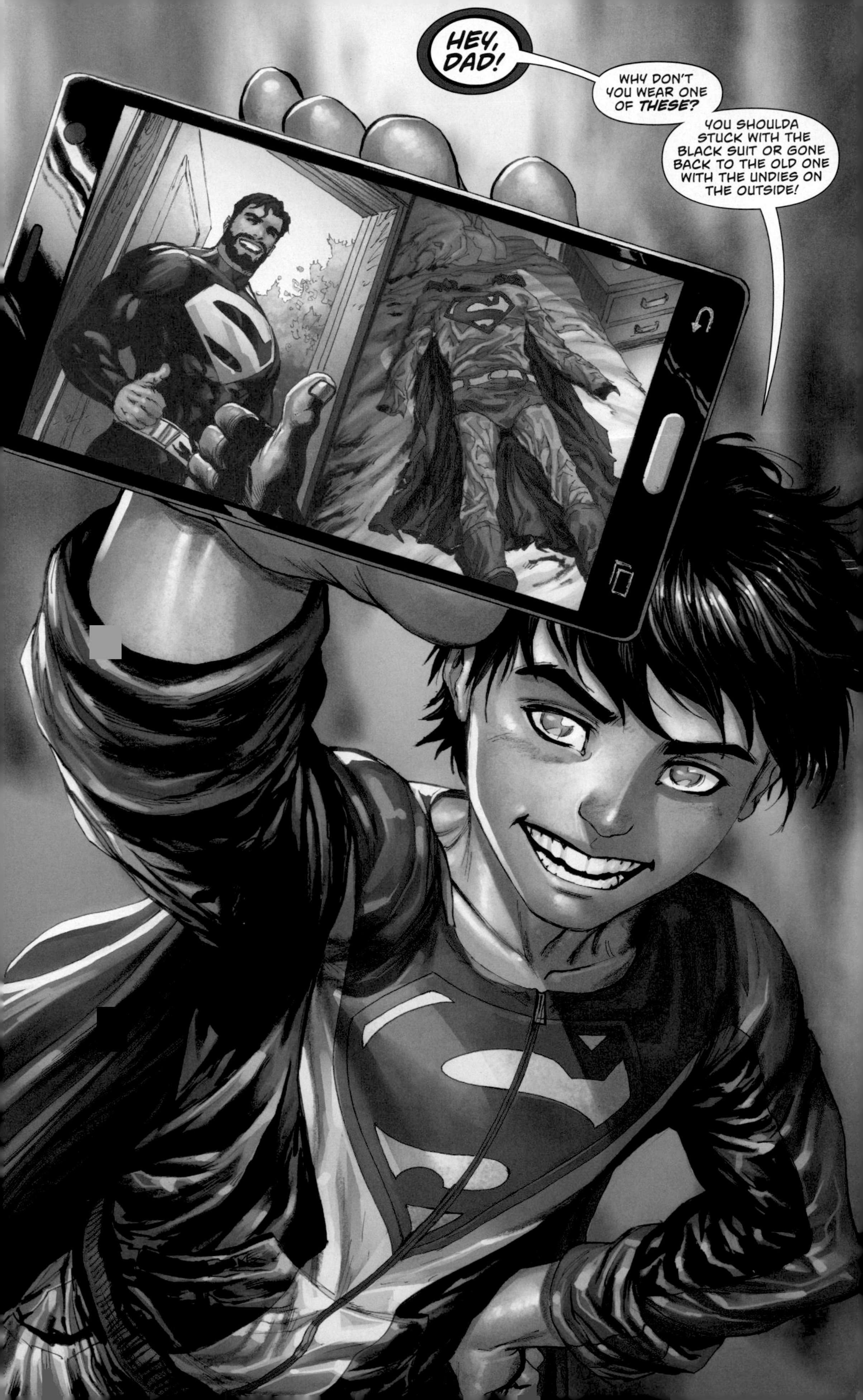
HEY, DAD!
WHY DON'T YOU WEAR ONE OF ***THESE?***
YOU SHOULDA STUCK WITH THE BLACK SUIT OR GONE BACK TO THE OLD ONE WITH THE UNDIES ON THE OUTSIDE!

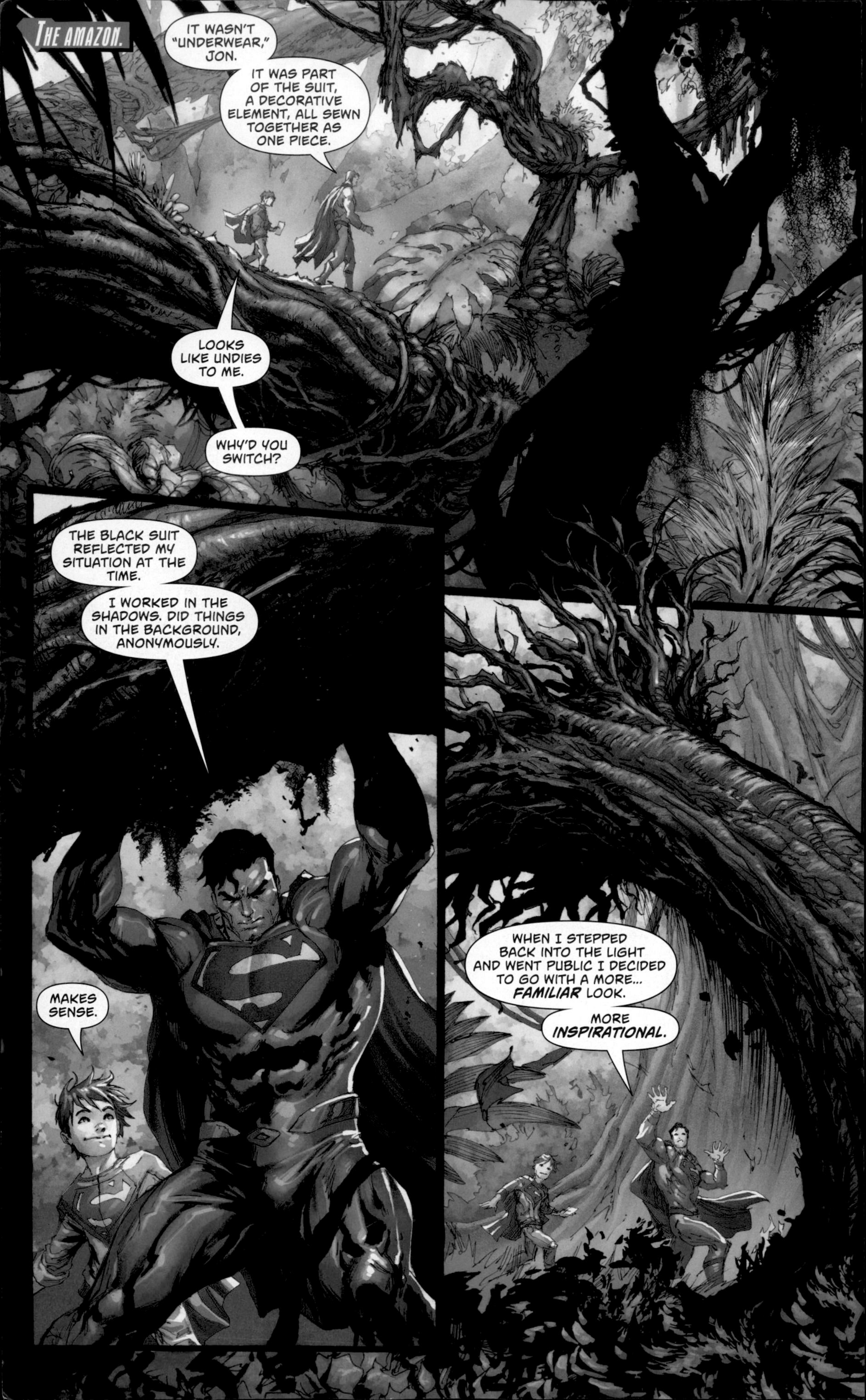
THE AMAZON.
IT WASN'T "UNDERWEAR," JON.
IT WAS PART OF THE SUIT, A DECORATIVE ELEMENT, ALL SEWN TOGETHER AS ONE PIECE.
LOOKS LIKE UNDIES TO ME.
WHY'D YOU SWITCH?
THE BLACK SUIT REFLECTED MY SITUATION AT THE TIME.
I WORKED IN THE SHADOWS. DID THINGS IN THE BACKGROUND, ANONYMOUSLY.
MAKES SENSE.
WHEN I STEPPED BACK INTO THE LIGHT AND WENT PUBLIC I DECIDED TO GO WITH A MORE... FAMILIAR LOOK.
MORE INSPIRATIONAL.

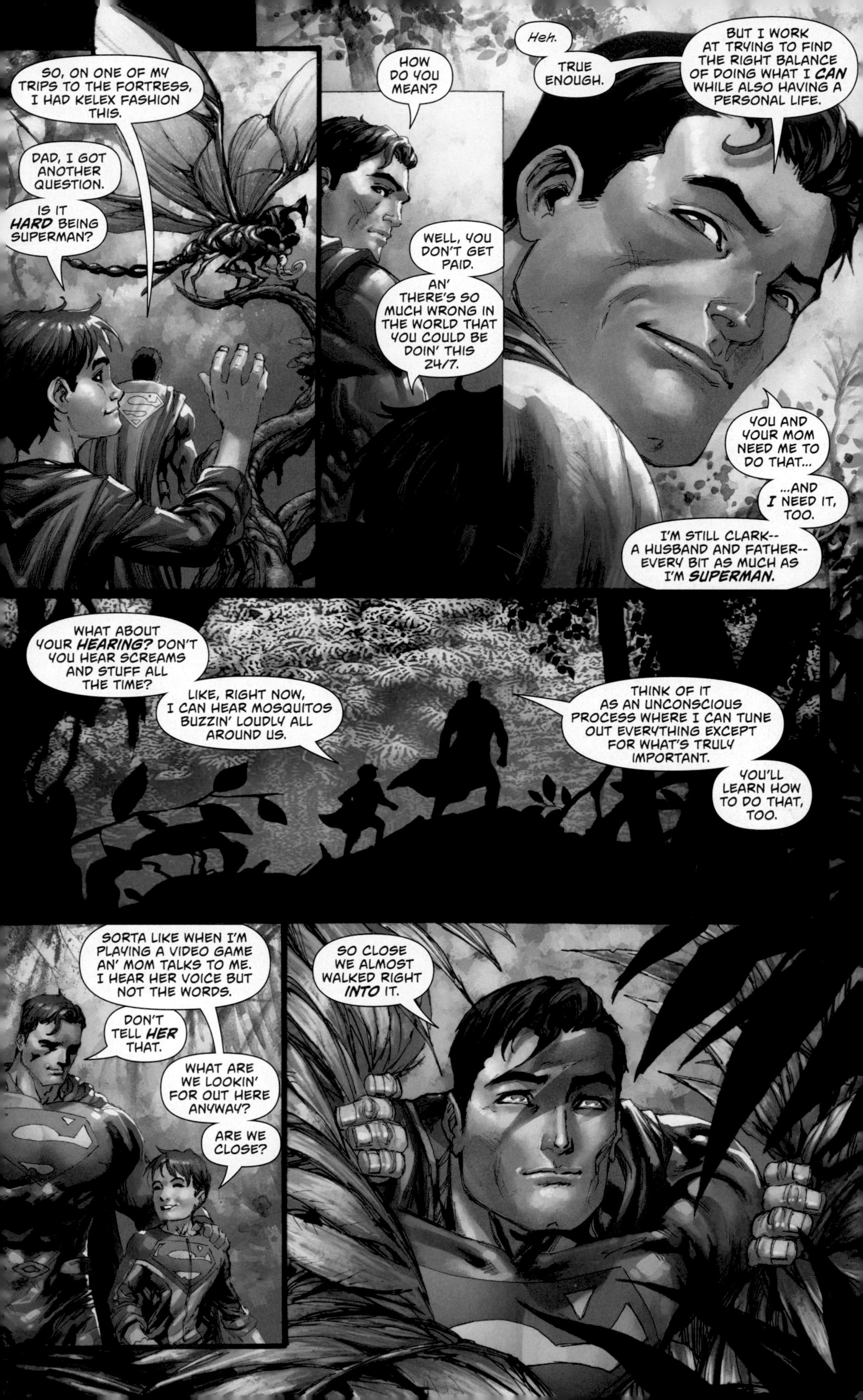
SO, ON ONE OF MY TRIPS TO THE FORTRESS, I HAD KELEX FASHION THIS.
DAD, I GOT ANOTHER QUESTION.
IS IT HARD BEING SUPERMAN?
HOW DO YOU MEAN?
WELL, YOU DON'T GET PAID.
AN' THERE'S SO MUCH WRONG IN THE WORLD THAT YOU COULD BE DOIN' THIS 24/7.
Heh.
TRUE ENOUGH.
BUT I WORK AT TRYING TO FIND THE RIGHT BALANCE OF DOING WHAT I CAN WHILE ALSO HAVING A PERSONAL LIFE.
YOU AND YOUR MOM NEED ME TO DO THAT...
...AND I NEED IT, TOO.
I'M STILL CLARK-- A HUSBAND AND FATHER-- EVERY BIT AS MUCH AS I'M SUPERMAN.
WHAT ABOUT YOUR HEARING? DON'T YOU HEAR SCREAMS AND STUFF ALL THE TIME?
LIKE, RIGHT NOW, I CAN HEAR MOSQUITOS BUZZIN' LOUDLY ALL AROUND US.
THINK OF IT AS AN UNCONSCIOUS PROCESS WHERE I CAN TUNE OUT EVERYTHING EXCEPT FOR WHAT'S TRULY IMPORTANT.
YOU'LL LEARN HOW TO DO THAT, TOO.
SORTA LIKE WHEN I'M PLAYING A VIDEO GAME AN' MOM TALKS TO ME. I HEAR HER VOICE BUT NOT THE WORDS.
DON'T TELL HER THAT.
WHAT ARE WE LOOKIN' FOR OUT HERE ANYWAY?
ARE WE CLOSE?
SO CLOSE WE ALMOST WALKED RIGHT INTO IT.

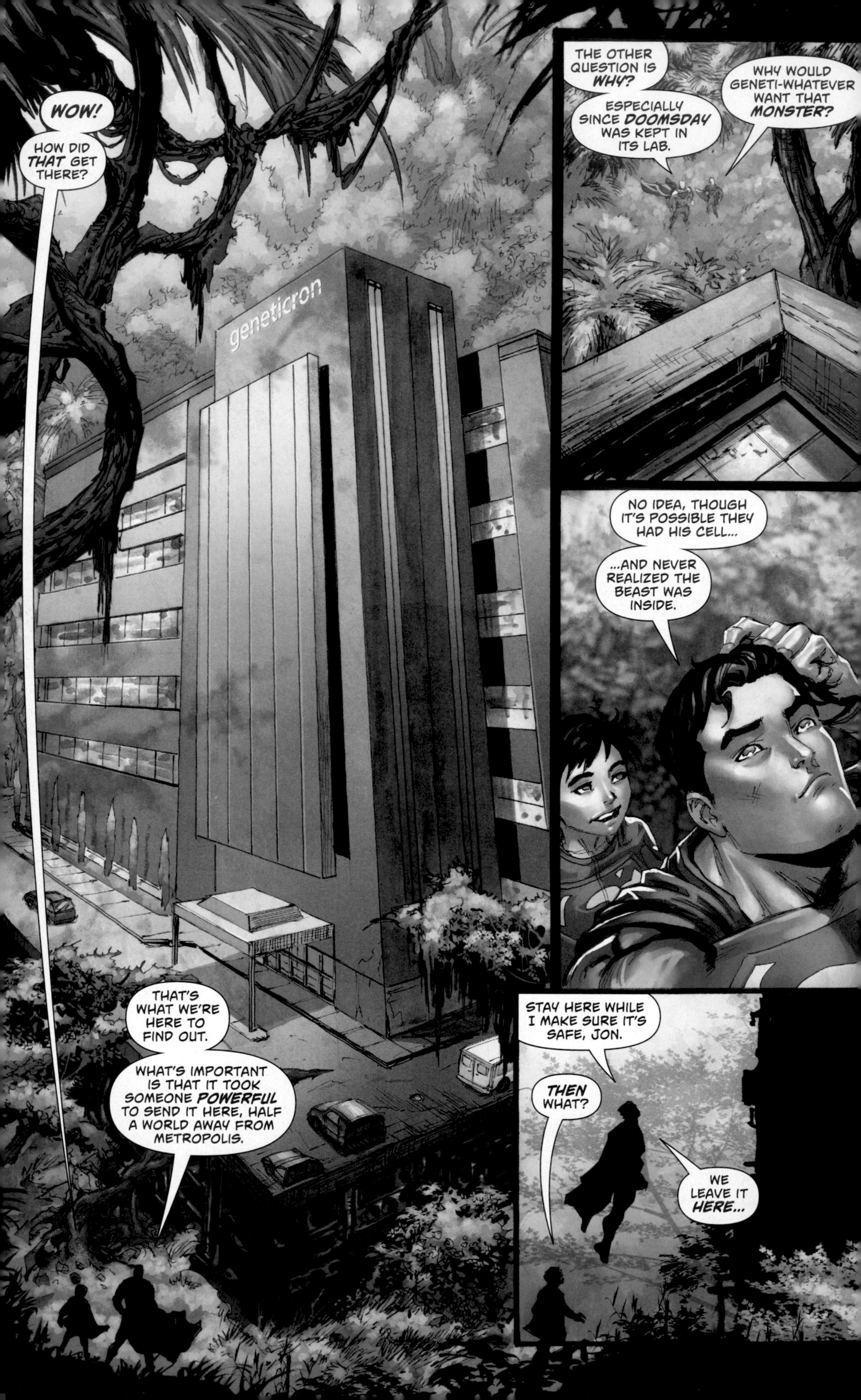
WOW!
HOW DID THAT GET THERE?
geneticron
THE OTHER QUESTION IS WHY?
ESPECIALLY SINCE DOOMSDAY WAS KEPT IN ITS LAB.
WHY WOULD GENETI-WHATEVER WANT THAT MONSTER?
NO IDEA, THOUGH IT'S POSSIBLE THEY HAD HIS CELL...
...AND NEVER REALIZED THE BEAST WAS INSIDE.
THAT'S WHAT WE'RE HERE TO FIND OUT.
WHAT'S IMPORTANT IS THAT IT TOOK SOMEONE POWERFUL TO SEND IT HERE, HALF A WORLD AWAY FROM METROPOLIS.
STAY HERE WHILE I MAKE SURE IT'S SAFE, JON.
THEN WHAT?
WE LEAVE IT HERE...

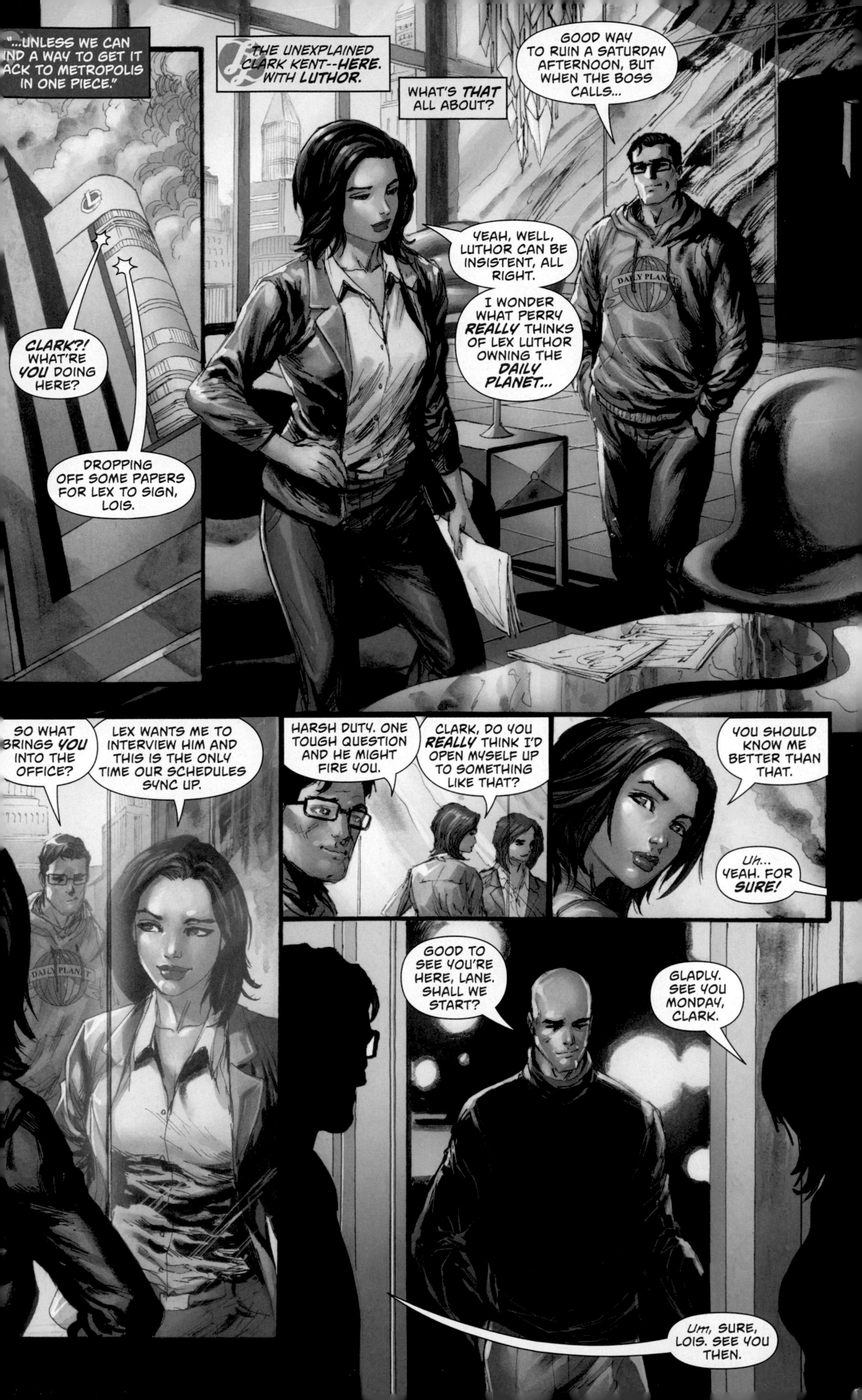
"...UNLESS WE CAN
IND A WAY TO GET IT
ACK TO METROPOLIS
IN ONE PIECE."
THE UNEXPLAINED CLARK KENT--HERE. WITH LUTHOR.
WHAT'S THAT ALL ABOUT?
CLARK?! WHAT'RE YOU DOING HERE?
DROPPING OFF SOME PAPERS FOR LEX TO SIGN, LOIS.
GOOD WAY TO RUIN A SATURDAY AFTERNOON, BUT WHEN THE BOSS CALLS...
YEAH, WELL, LUTHOR CAN BE INSISTENT, ALL RIGHT.
I WONDER WHAT PERRY REALLY THINKS OF LEX LUTHOR OWNING THE DAILY PLANET...
SO WHAT BRINGS YOU INTO THE OFFICE?
LEX WANTS ME TO INTERVIEW HIM AND THIS IS THE ONLY TIME OUR SCHEDULES SYNC UP.
HARSH DUTY. ONE TOUGH QUESTION AND HE MIGHT FIRE YOU.
CLARK, DO YOU REALLY THINK I'D OPEN MYSELF UP TO SOMETHING LIKE THAT?
YOU SHOULD KNOW ME BETTER THAN THAT.
Uh... YEAH. FOR SURE!
GOOD TO SEE YOU'RE HERE, LANE. SHALL WE START?
GLADLY. SEE YOU MONDAY, CLARK.
Um, SURE, LOIS. SEE YOU THEN.

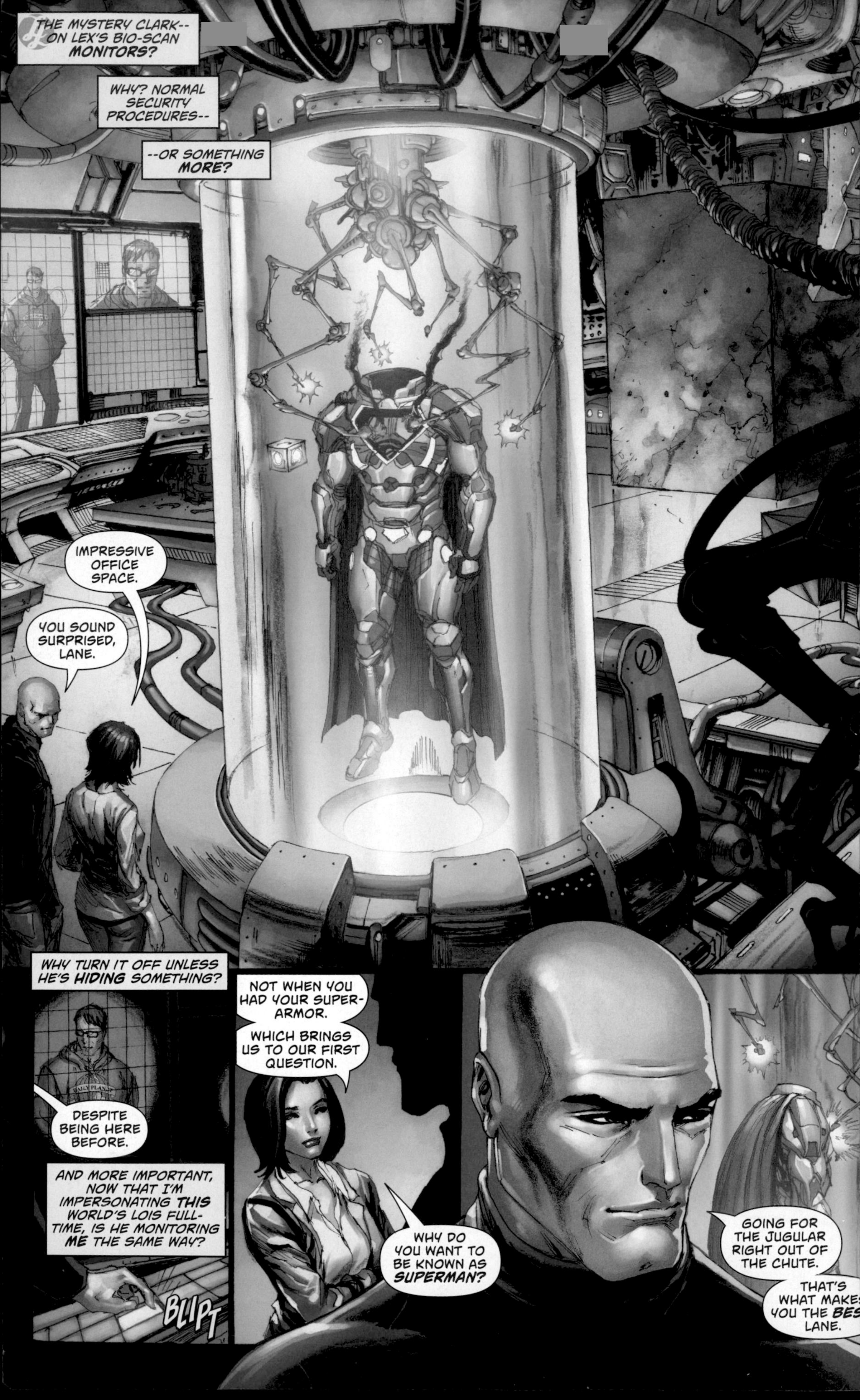
THE MYSTERY CLARK-- ON LEX'S BIO-SCAN MONITORS?
WHY? NORMAL SECURITY PROCEDURES--
--OR SOMETHING MORE?
IMPRESSIVE OFFICE SPACE.
YOU SOUND SURPRISED, LANE.
WHY TURN IT OFF UNLESS HE'S HIDING SOMETHING?
DESPITE BEING HERE BEFORE.
AND MORE IMPORTANT, NOW THAT I'M IMPERSONATING THIS WORLD'S LOIS FULL-TIME, IS HE MONITORING ME THE SAME WAY?
BLIPT
NOT WHEN YOU HAD YOUR SUPER-ARMOR.
WHICH BRINGS US TO OUR FIRST QUESTION.
WHY DO YOU WANT TO BE KNOWN AS SUPERMAN?
GOING FOR THE JUGULAR RIGHT OUT OF THE CHUTE.
THAT'S WHAT MAKES YOU THE BES LANE.

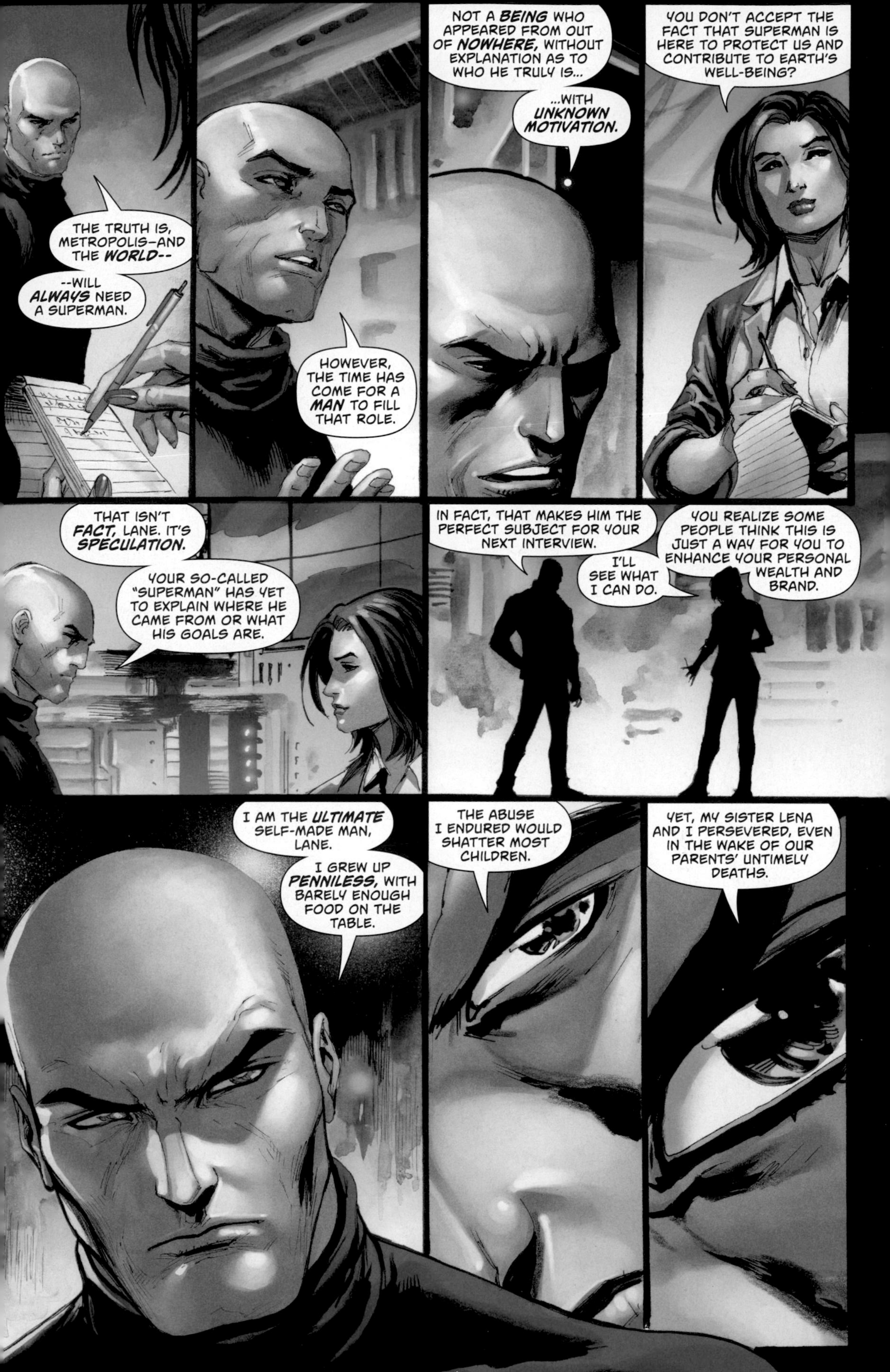
THE TRUTH IS, METROPOLIS--AND THE WORLD--
--WILL ALWAYS NEED A SUPERMAN.
HOWEVER, THE TIME HAS COME FOR A MAN TO FILL THAT ROLE.
NOT A BEING WHO APPEARED FROM OUT OF NOWHERE, WITHOUT EXPLANATION AS TO WHO HE TRULY IS...
...WITH UNKNOWN MOTIVATION.
YOU DON'T ACCEPT THE FACT THAT SUPERMAN IS HERE TO PROTECT US AND CONTRIBUTE TO EARTH'S WELL-BEING?
THAT ISN'T FACT, LANE. IT'S SPECULATION.
YOUR SO-CALLED "SUPERMAN" HAS YET TO EXPLAIN WHERE HE CAME FROM OR WHAT HIS GOALS ARE.
IN FACT, THAT MAKES HIM THE PERFECT SUBJECT FOR YOUR NEXT INTERVIEW.
I'LL SEE WHAT I CAN DO.
YOU REALIZE SOME PEOPLE THINK THIS IS JUST A WAY FOR YOU TO ENHANCE YOUR PERSONAL WEALTH AND BRAND.
I AM THE ULTIMATE SELF-MADE MAN, LANE.
I GREW UP PENNILESS, WITH BARELY ENOUGH FOOD ON THE TABLE.
THE ABUSE I ENDURED WOULD SHATTER MOST CHILDREN.
YET, MY SISTER LENA AND I PERSEVERED, EVEN IN THE WAKE OF OUR PARENTS' UNTIMELY DEATHS.

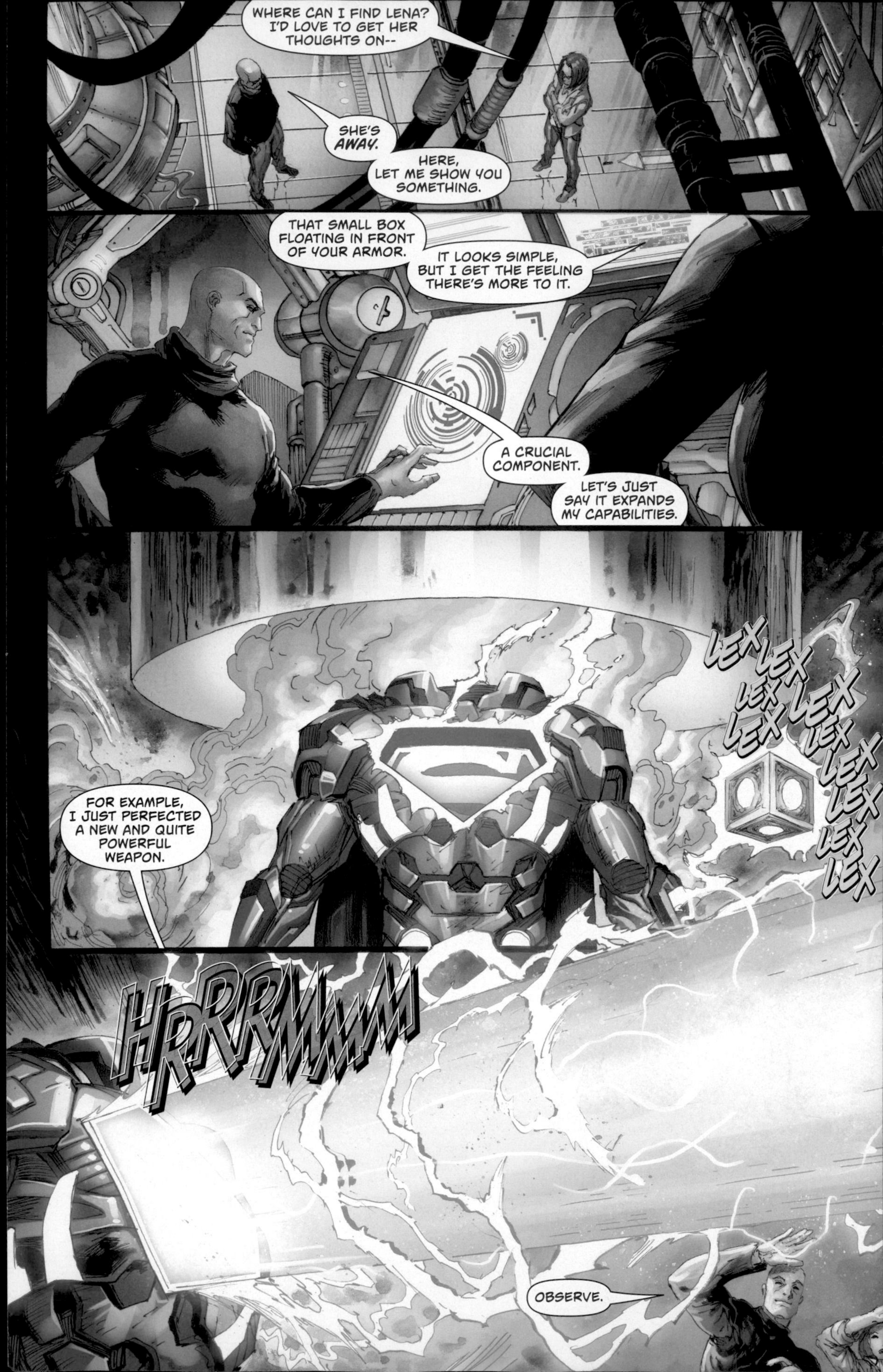
WHERE CAN I FIND LENA? I'D LOVE TO GET HER THOUGHTS ON--
SHE'S *AWAY.*
HERE, LET ME SHOW YOU SOMETHING.
THAT SMALL BOX FLOATING IN FRONT OF YOUR ARMOR.
IT LOOKS SIMPLE, BUT I GET THE FEELING THERE'S MORE TO IT.
A CRUCIAL COMPONENT.
LET'S JUST SAY IT EXPANDS MY CAPABILITIES.
LEX LEX LEX LEX LEX LEX LEX LEX LEX LEX LEX LEX
FOR EXAMPLE, I JUST PERFECTED A NEW AND QUITE POWERFUL WEAPON.
HRRRMMMM
OBSERVE.

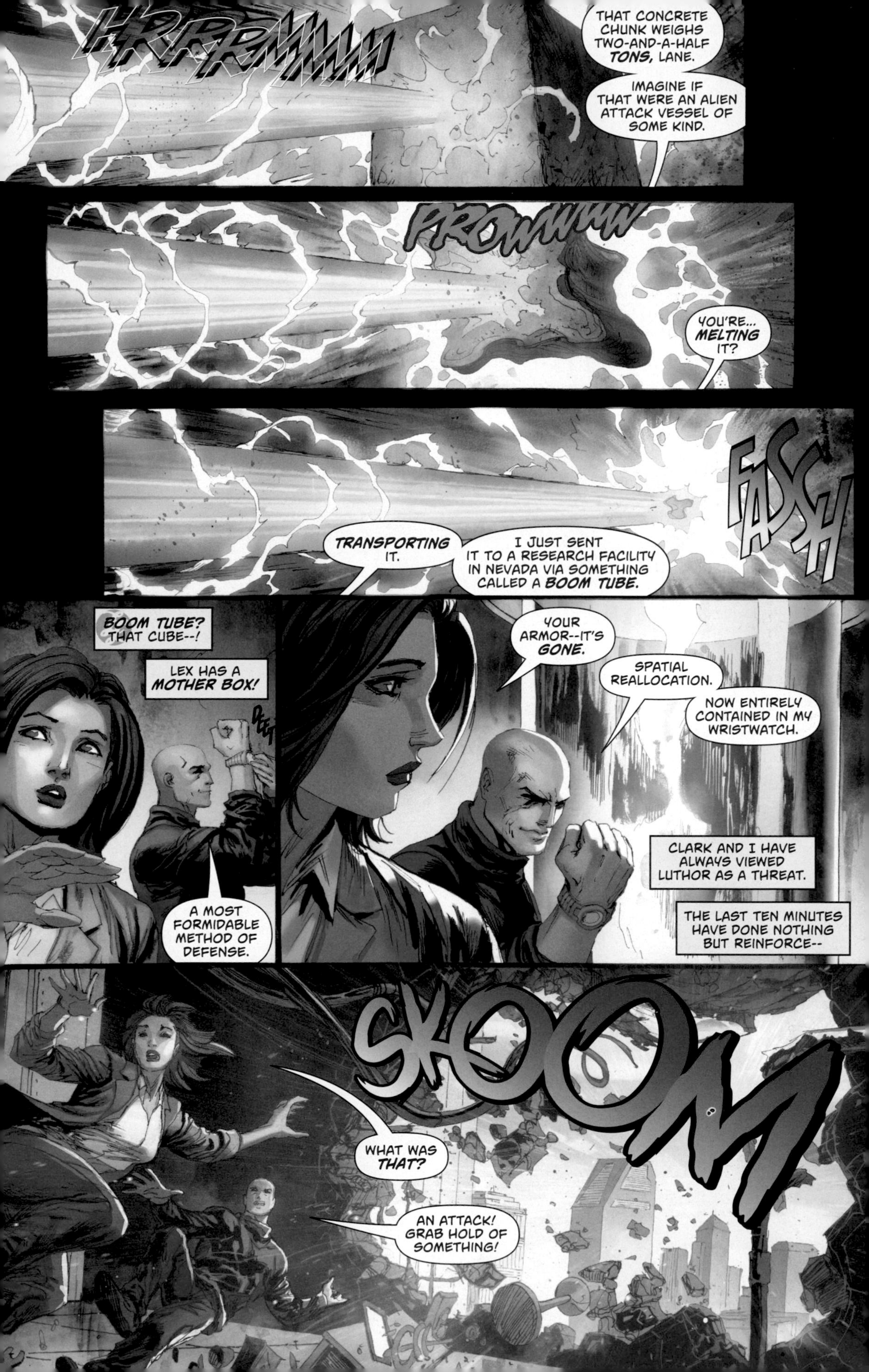
HRRRMMMM
THAT CONCRETE CHUNK WEIGHS TWO-AND-A-HALF TONS, LANE.
IMAGINE IF THAT WERE AN ALIEN ATTACK VESSEL OF SOME KIND.
PROWWWW
YOU'RE... MELTING IT?
FASSH
TRANSPORTING IT.
I JUST SENT IT TO A RESEARCH FACILITY IN NEVADA VIA SOMETHING CALLED A BOOM TUBE.
BOOM TUBE? THAT CUBE--!
LEX HAS A MOTHER BOX!
A MOST FORMIDABLE METHOD OF DEFENSE.
YOUR ARMOR--IT'S GONE.
SPATIAL REALLOCATION.
NOW ENTIRELY CONTAINED IN MY WRISTWATCH.
CLARK AND I HAVE ALWAYS VIEWED LUTHOR AS A THREAT.
THE LAST TEN MINUTES HAVE DONE NOTHING BUT REINFORCE--
SKOOOM
WHAT WAS THAT?
AN ATTACK! GRAB HOLD OF SOMETHING!

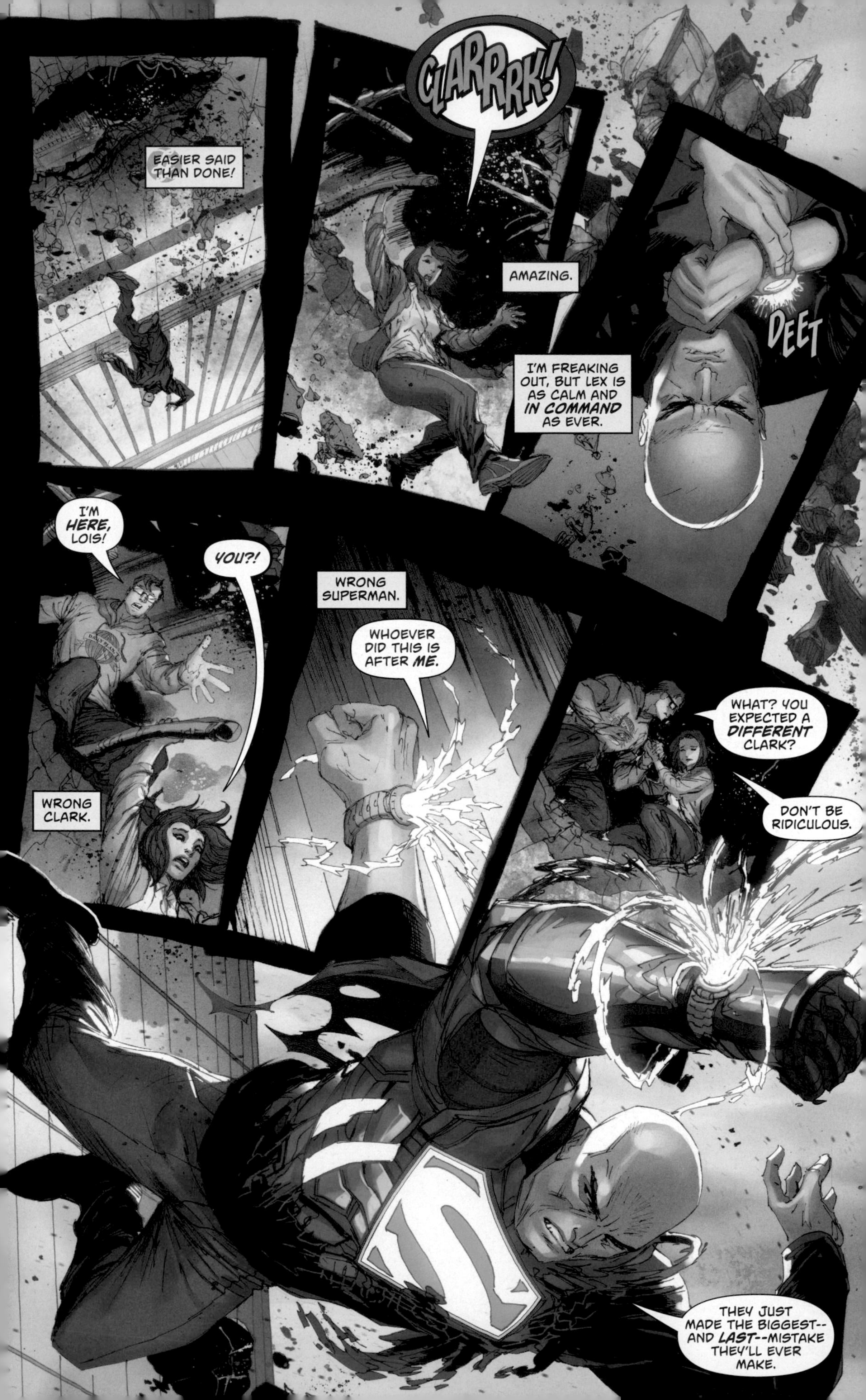

EASIER SAID THAN DONE!
CLARRRK!
AMAZING.
DEET
I'M FREAKING OUT, BUT LEX IS AS CALM AND IN COMMAND AS EVER.
I'M HERE, LOIS!
YOU?!
WRONG CLARK.
WRONG SUPERMAN.
WHOEVER DID THIS IS AFTER ME.
WHAT? YOU EXPECTED A DIFFERENT CLARK?
DON'T BE RIDICULOUS.
THEY JUST MADE THE BIGGEST--AND LAST--MISTAKE THEY'LL EVER MAKE.

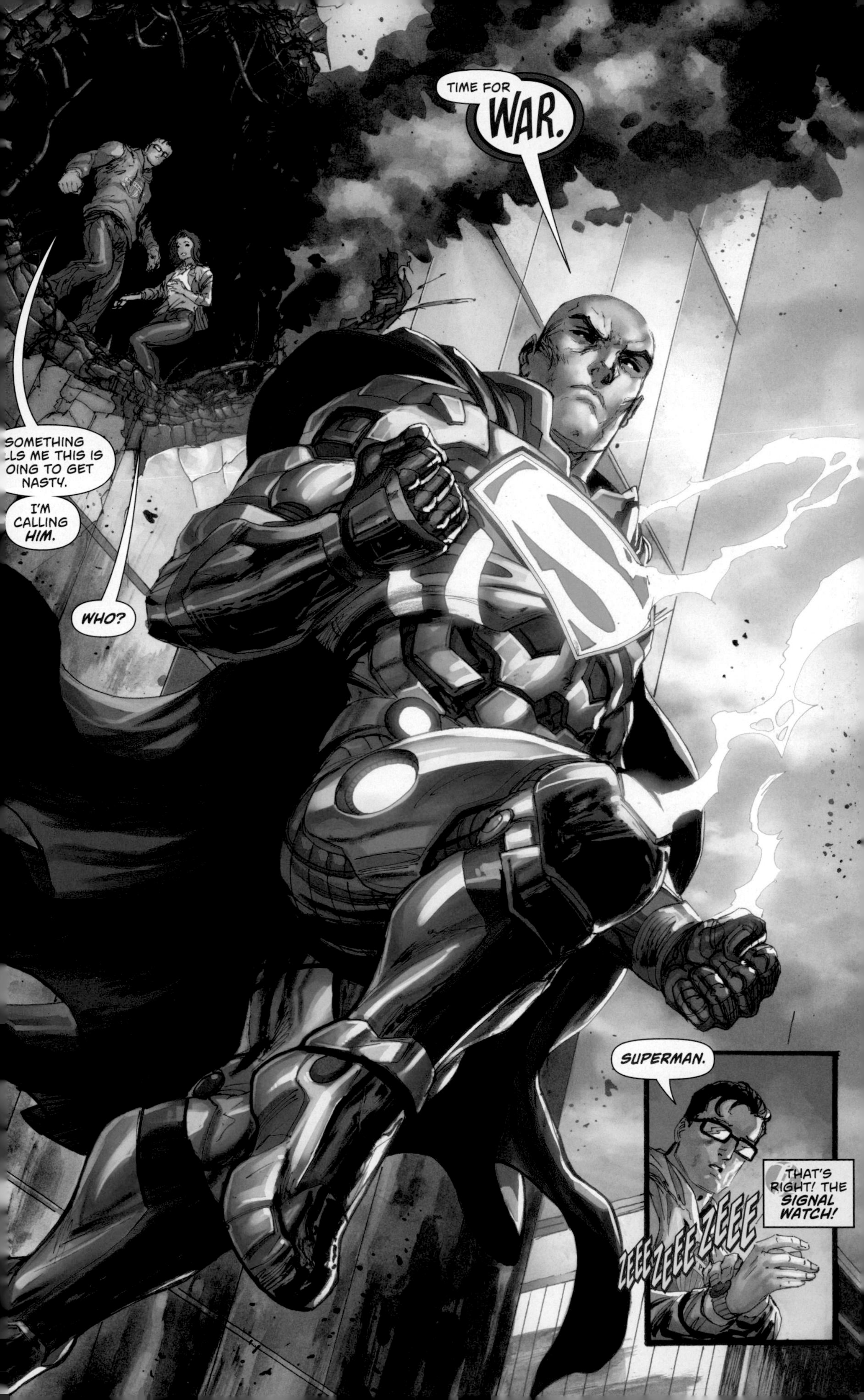
TIME FOR WAR.
SOMETHING
LLS ME THIS IS
OING TO GET
NASTY.
I'M CALLING HIM.
WHO?
SUPERMAN.
THAT'S RIGHT! THE SIGNAL WATCH!
ZEEE ZEEE ZEEE

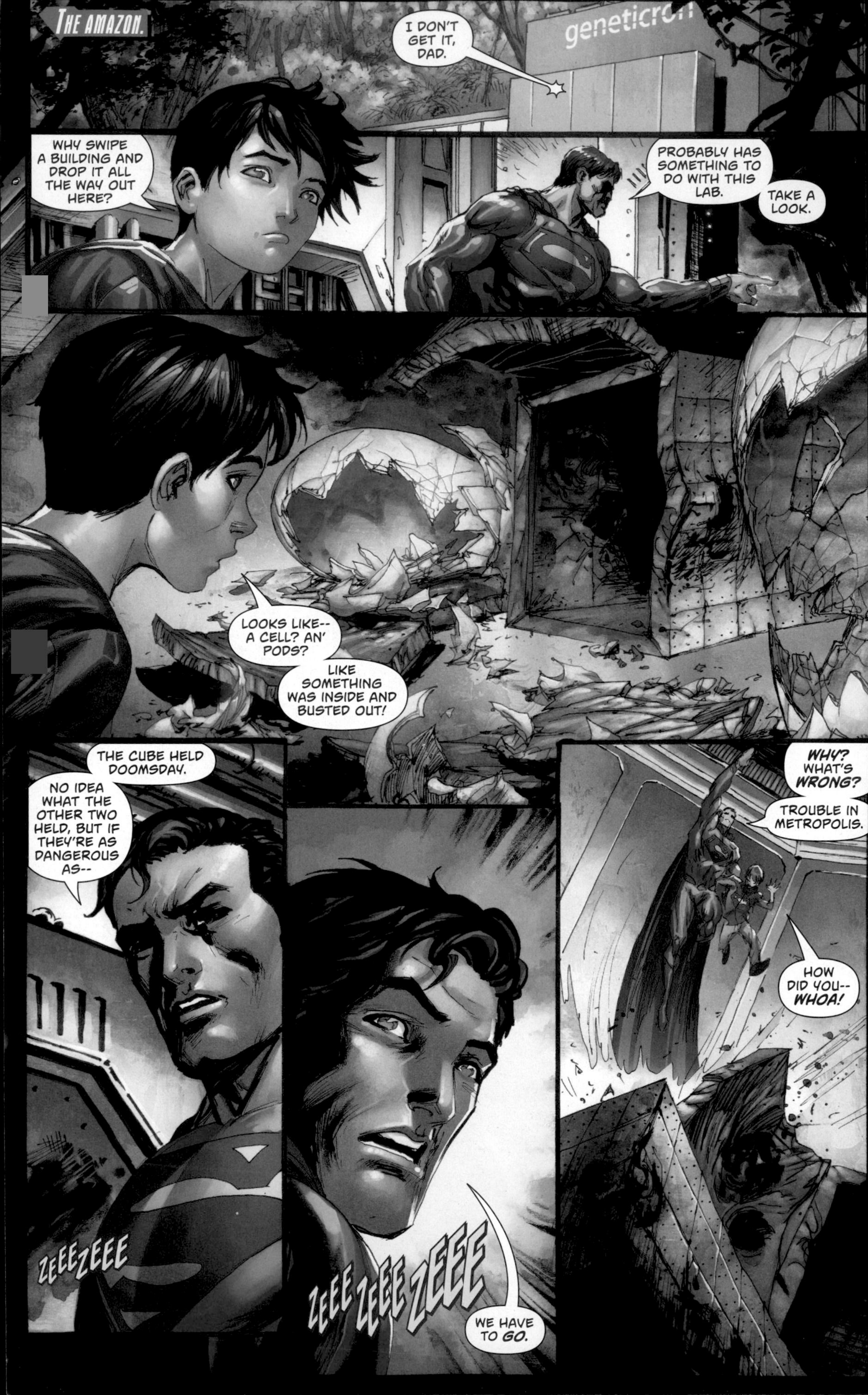
THE AMAZON.
I DON'T GET IT, DAD.
geneticron
WHY SWIPE A BUILDING AND DROP IT ALL THE WAY OUT HERE?
PROBABLY HAS SOMETHING TO DO WITH THIS LAB.
TAKE A LOOK.
LOOKS LIKE-- A CELL? AN' PODS?
LIKE SOMETHING WAS INSIDE AND BUSTED OUT!
THE CUBE HELD DOOMSDAY.
NO IDEA WHAT THE OTHER TWO HELD, BUT IF THEY'RE AS DANGEROUS AS--
ZEEEZEEE
ZEEE ZEEE ZEEE
WE HAVE TO GO.
WHY? WHAT'S WRONG?
TROUBLE IN METROPOLIS.
HOW DID YOU-- WHOA!

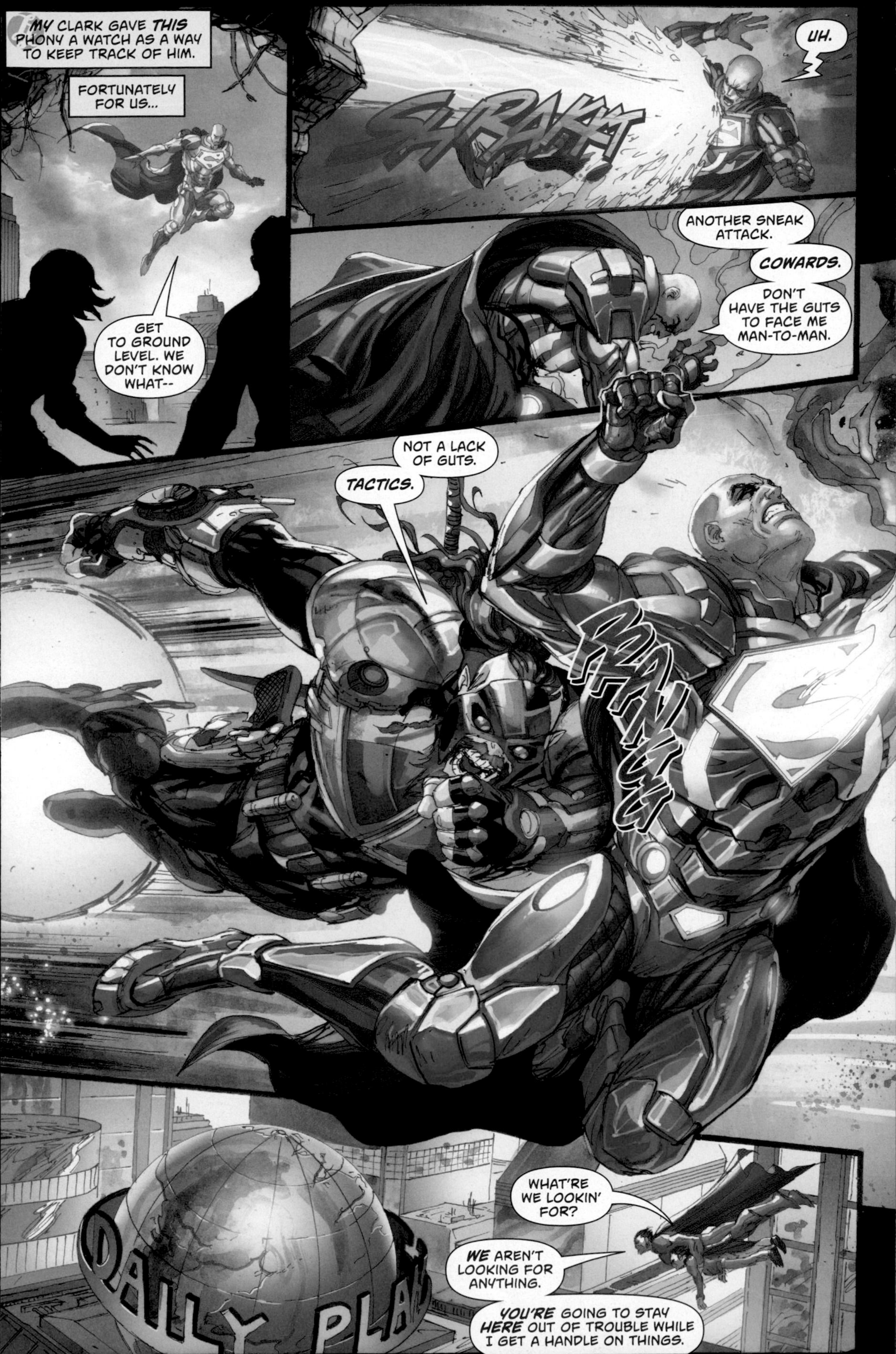
MY CLARK GAVE THIS PHONY A WATCH AS A WAY TO KEEP TRACK OF HIM.
FORTUNATELY FOR US...
SHRAKK!
UH.
GET TO GROUND LEVEL. WE DON'T KNOW WHAT--
ANOTHER SNEAK ATTACK.
COWARDS.
DON'T HAVE THE GUTS TO FACE ME MAN-TO-MAN.
NOT A LACK OF GUTS.
TACTICS.
WHAT'RE WE LOOKIN' FOR?
WE AREN'T LOOKING FOR ANYTHING.
YOU'RE GOING TO STAY HERE OUT OF TROUBLE WHILE I GET A HANDLE ON THINGS.
DAILY PLA

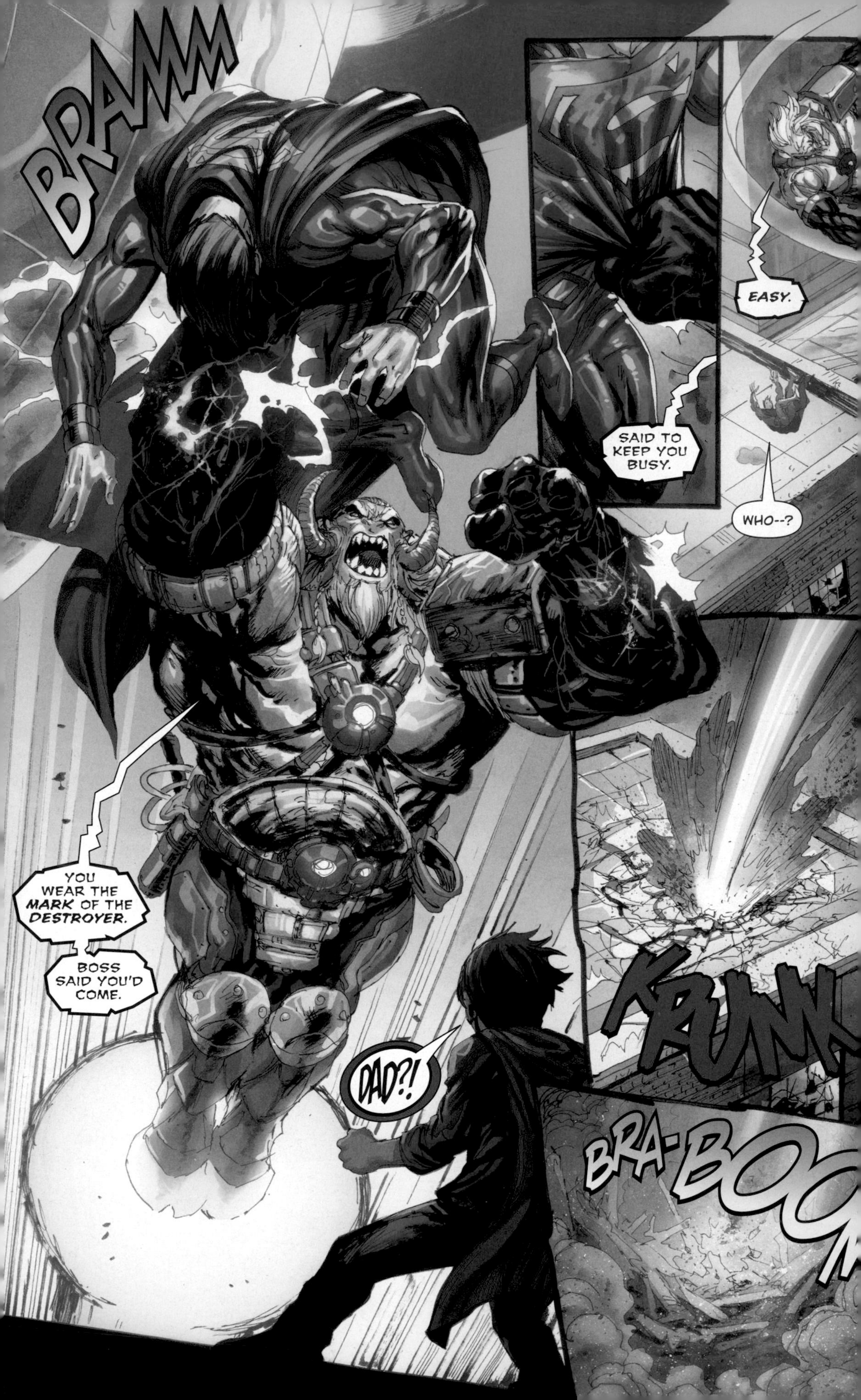
BRAMM
EASY.
SAID TO KEEP YOU BUSY.
WHO--?
YOU WEAR THE MARK OF THE DESTROYER.
BOSS SAID YOU'D COME.
KRUNK
DAD?!
BRA-BOOM

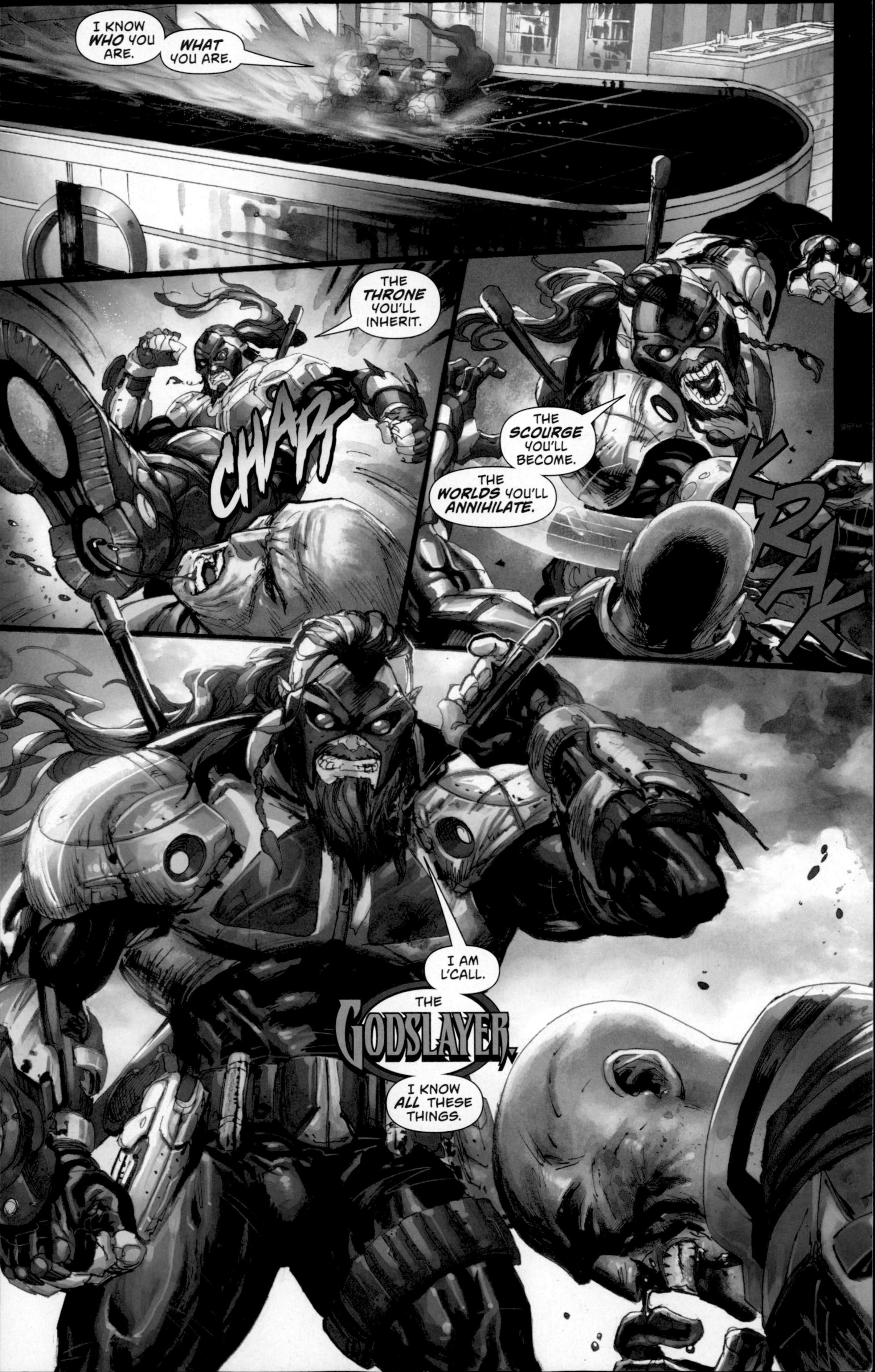

I KNOW WHO YOU ARE.
WHAT YOU ARE.
THE THRONE YOU'LL INHERIT.
CHAP
THE SCOURGE YOU'LL BECOME.
THE WORLDS YOU'LL ANNIHILATE.
KRAK
I AM L'CALL.
THE GODSLAYER.
I KNOW ALL THESE THINGS.

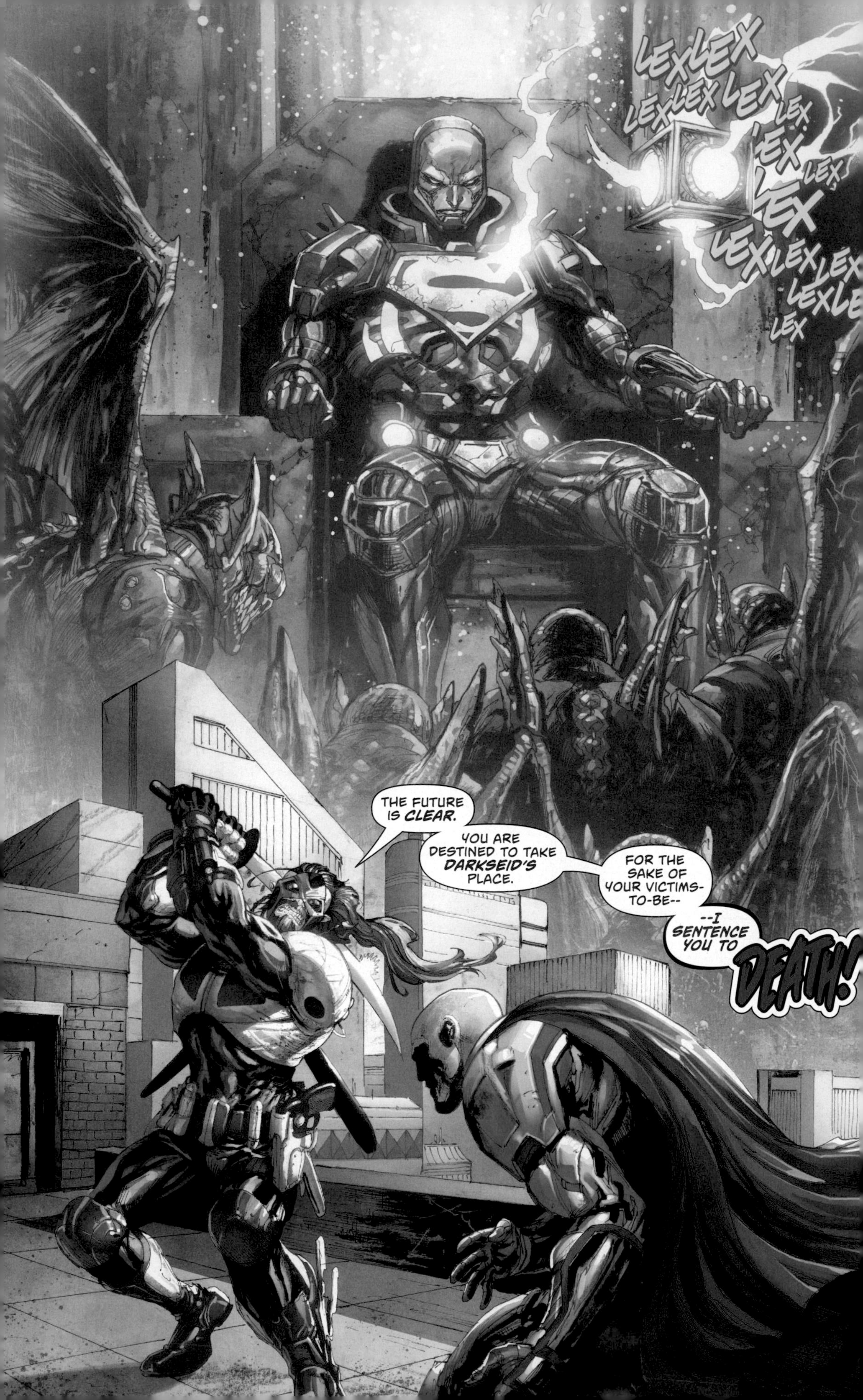
LEX LEX LEX LEX LEX LEX LEX LEX LEX LEX LEX LEX LEX LEX LEX LEX LEX
THE FUTURE IS CLEAR.
YOU ARE DESTINED TO TAKE DARKSEID'S PLACE.
FOR THE SAKE OF YOUR VICTIMS-TO-BE--
--I SENTENCE YOU TO DEATH!

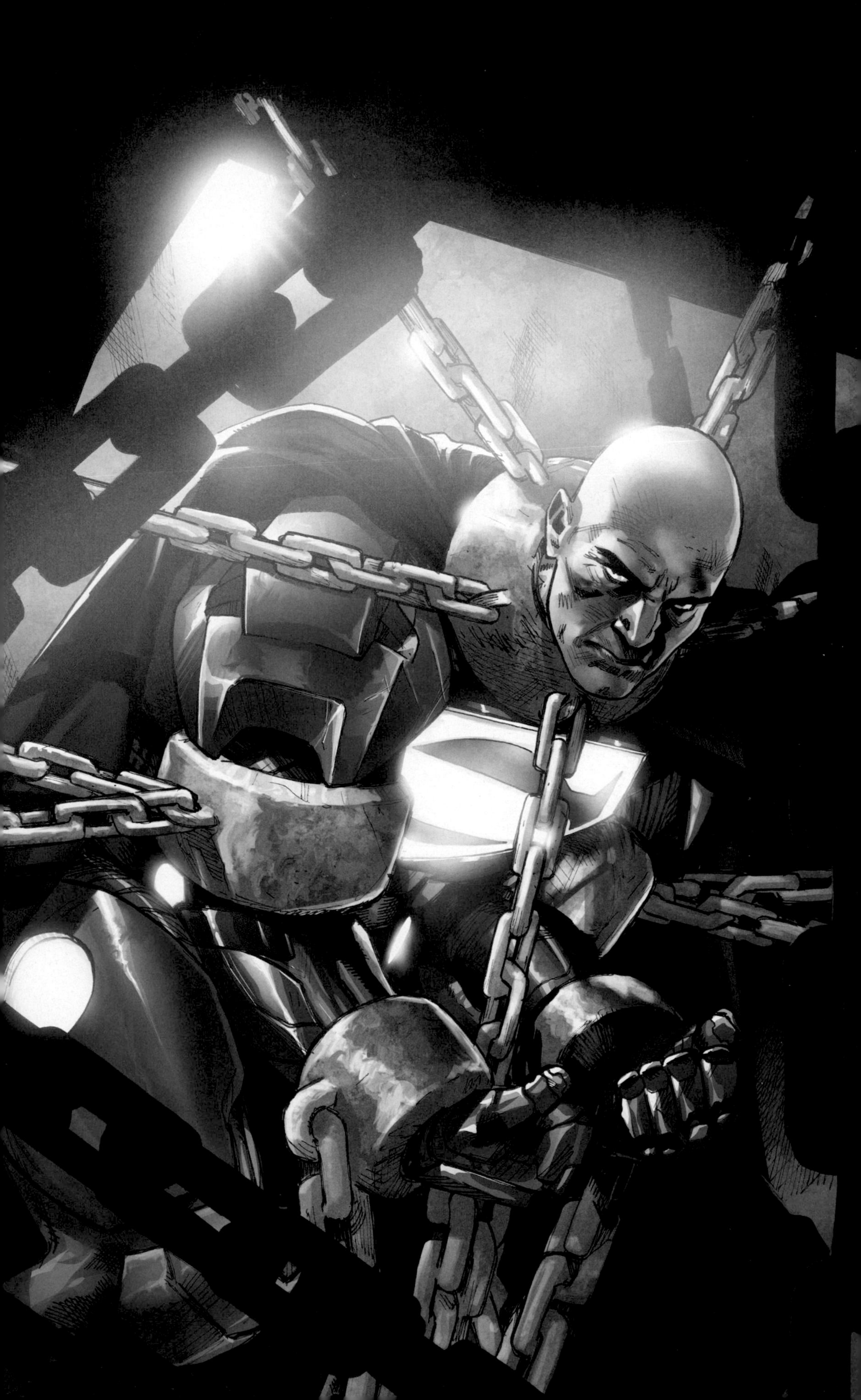

MEN OF STEEL PART 2

TYLER KIRKHAM artist * ULISES ARREOLA colorist

CLAY MANN ULISES ARREOLA DAN JURGENS cover artists

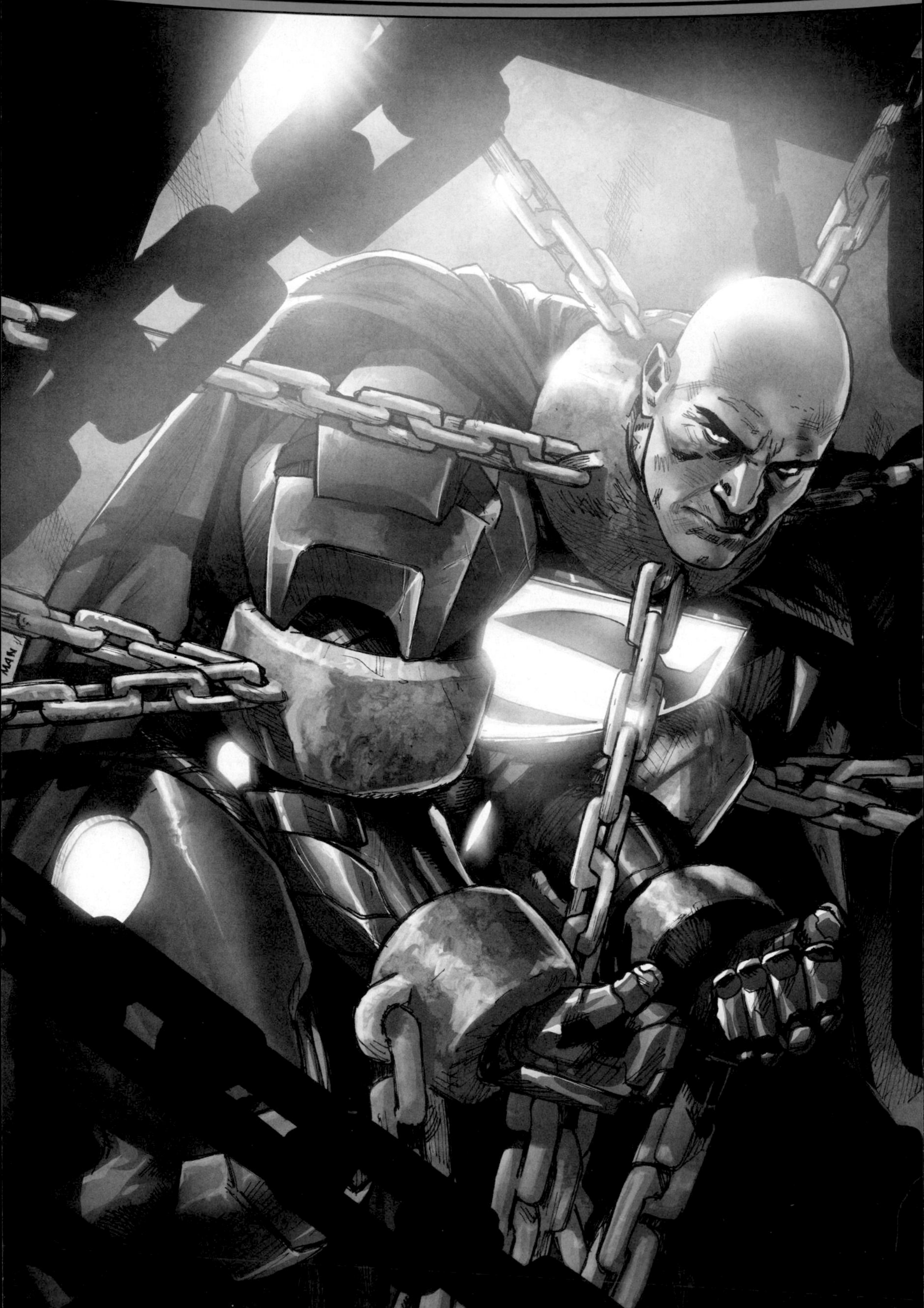

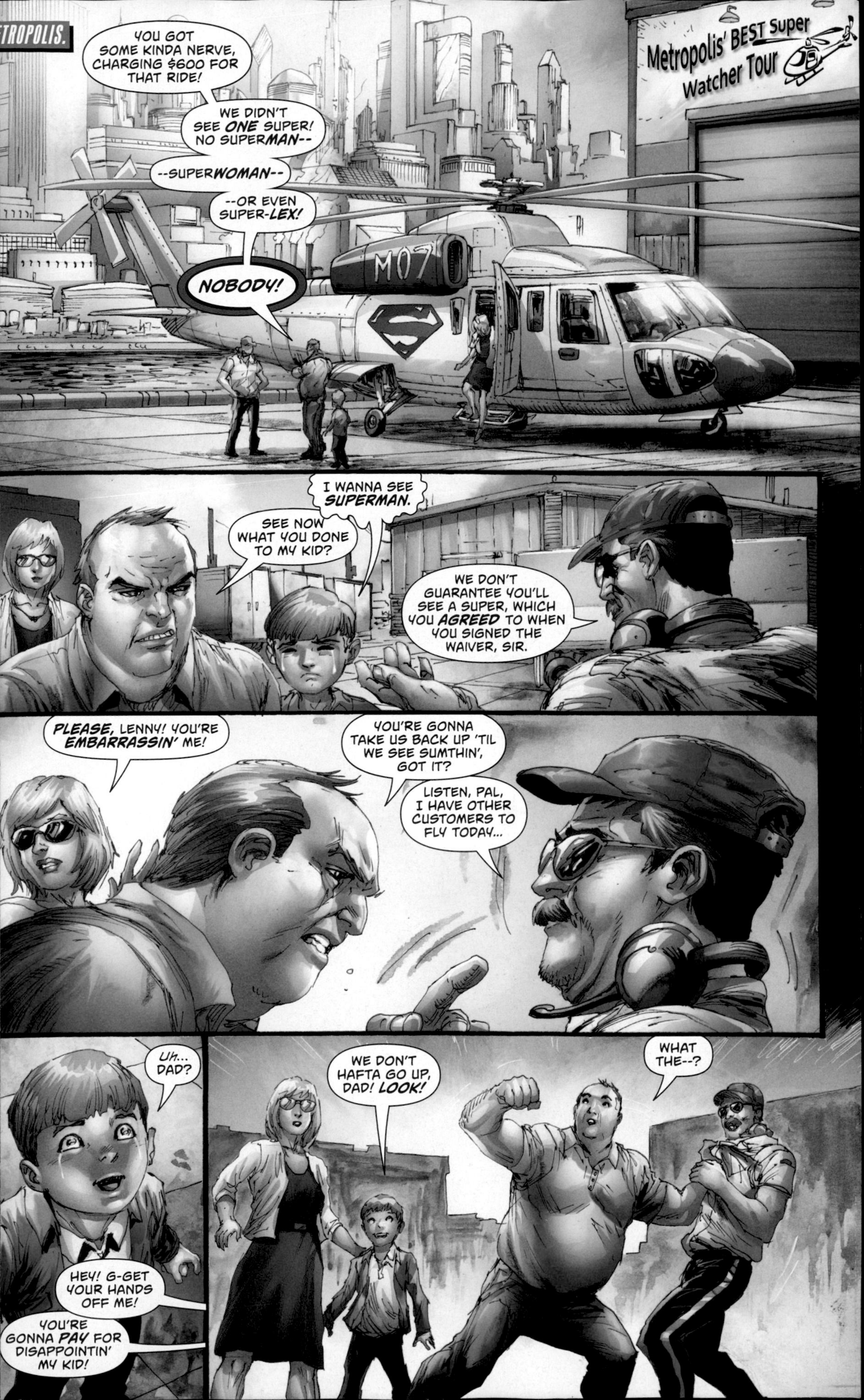
METROPOLIS.
YOU GOT SOME KINDA NERVE, CHARGING $600 FOR THAT RIDE!
WE DIDN'T SEE ONE SUPER! NO SUPERMAN--
--SUPERWOMAN--
--OR EVEN SUPER-LEX!
NOBODY!
Metropolis' BEST Super Watcher Tour
M07
SEE NOW WHAT YOU DONE TO MY KID?
I WANNA SEE SUPERMAN.
WE DON'T GUARANTEE YOU'LL SEE A SUPER, WHICH YOU AGREED TO WHEN YOU SIGNED THE WAIVER, SIR.
PLEASE, LENNY! YOU'RE EMBARRASSIN' ME!
YOU'RE GONNA TAKE US BACK UP 'TIL WE SEE SUMTHIN', GOT IT?
LISTEN, PAL, I HAVE OTHER CUSTOMERS TO FLY TODAY...
UH... DAD?
HEY! G-GET YOUR HANDS OFF ME!
YOU'RE GONNA PAY FOR DISAPPOINTIN' MY KID!
WE DON'T HAFTA GO UP, DAD! LOOK!
WHAT THE--?

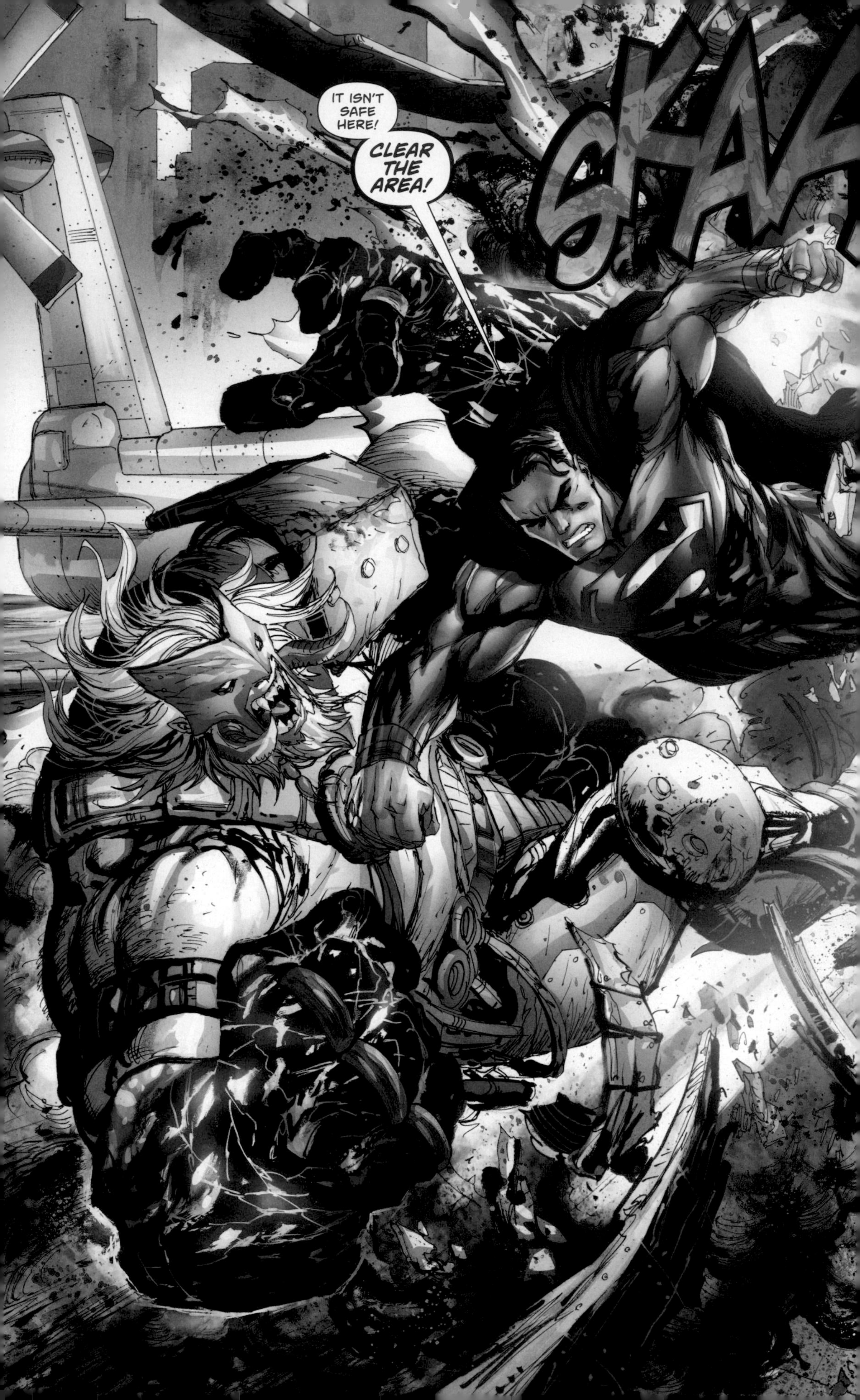
IT ISN'T SAFE HERE!
CLEAR THE AREA!

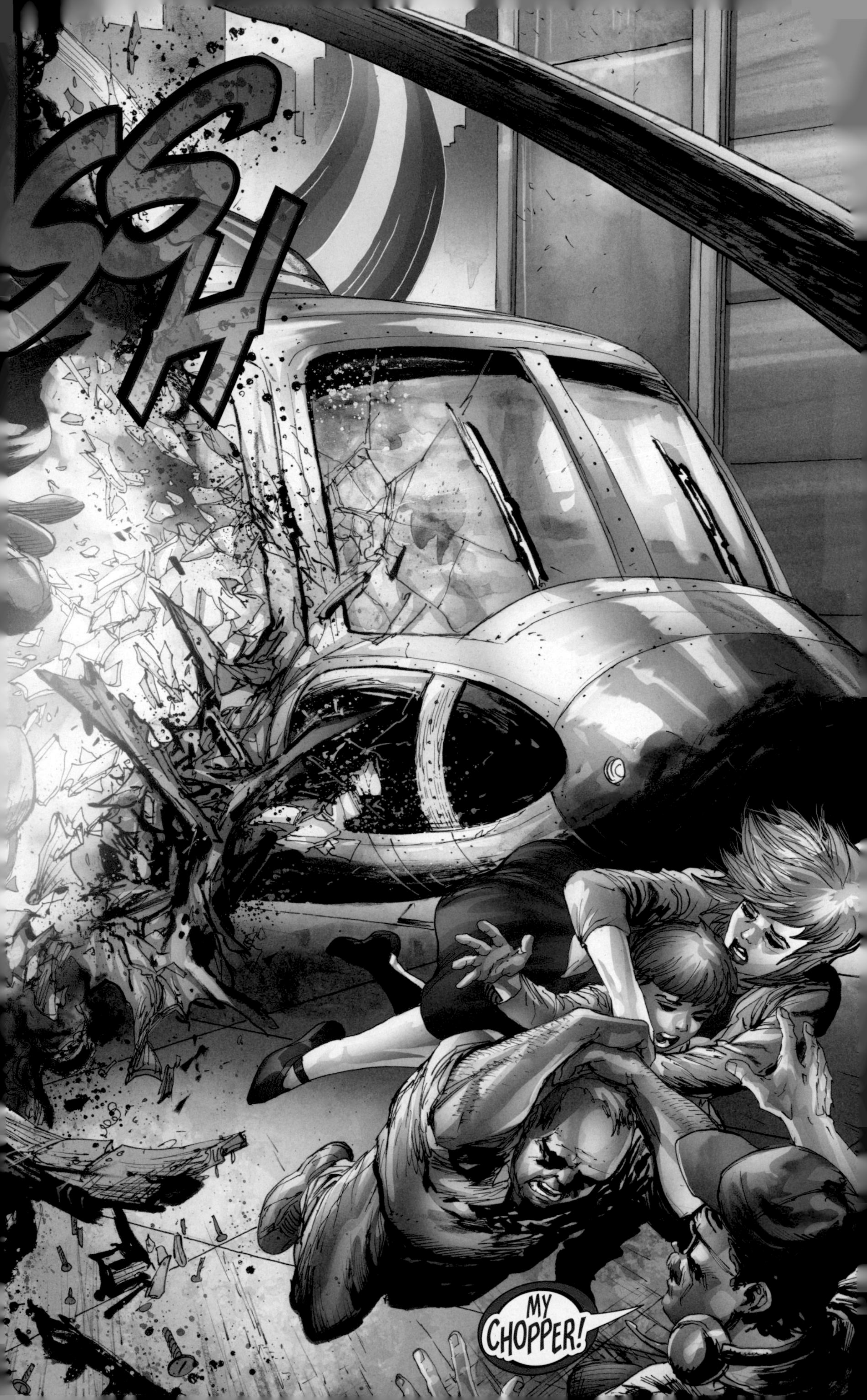

SSH
MY CHOPPER!

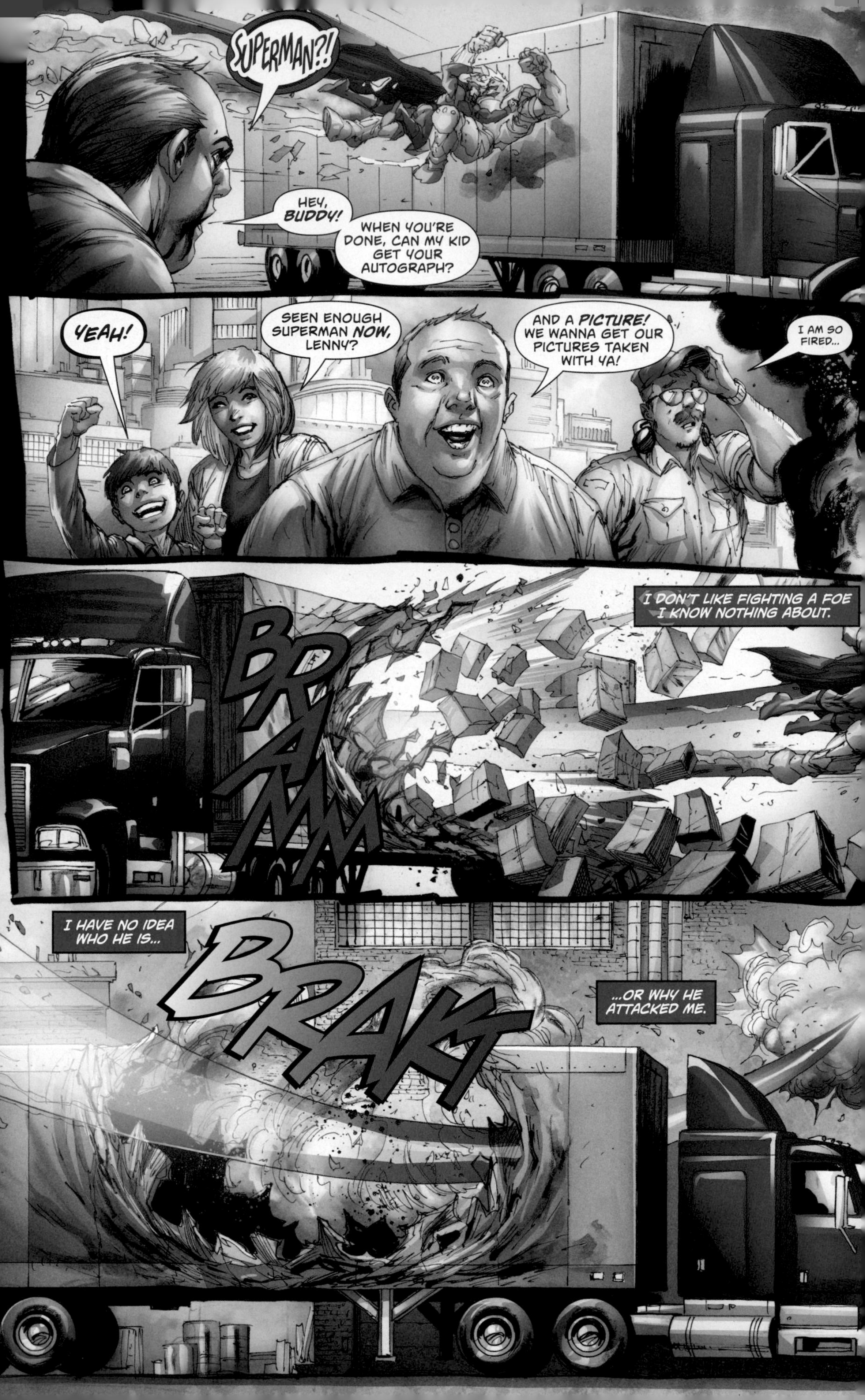
SUPERMAN?!
HEY, BUDDY!
WHEN YOU'RE DONE, CAN MY KID GET YOUR AUTOGRAPH?
YEAH!
SEEN ENOUGH SUPERMAN NOW, LENNY?
AND A PICTURE! WE WANNA GET OUR PICTURES TAKEN WITH YA!
I AM SO FIRED...
I DON'T LIKE FIGHTING A FOE I KNOW NOTHING ABOUT.
BRAMM
I HAVE NO IDEA WHO HE IS...
BRAKT
...OR WHY HE ATTACKED ME.

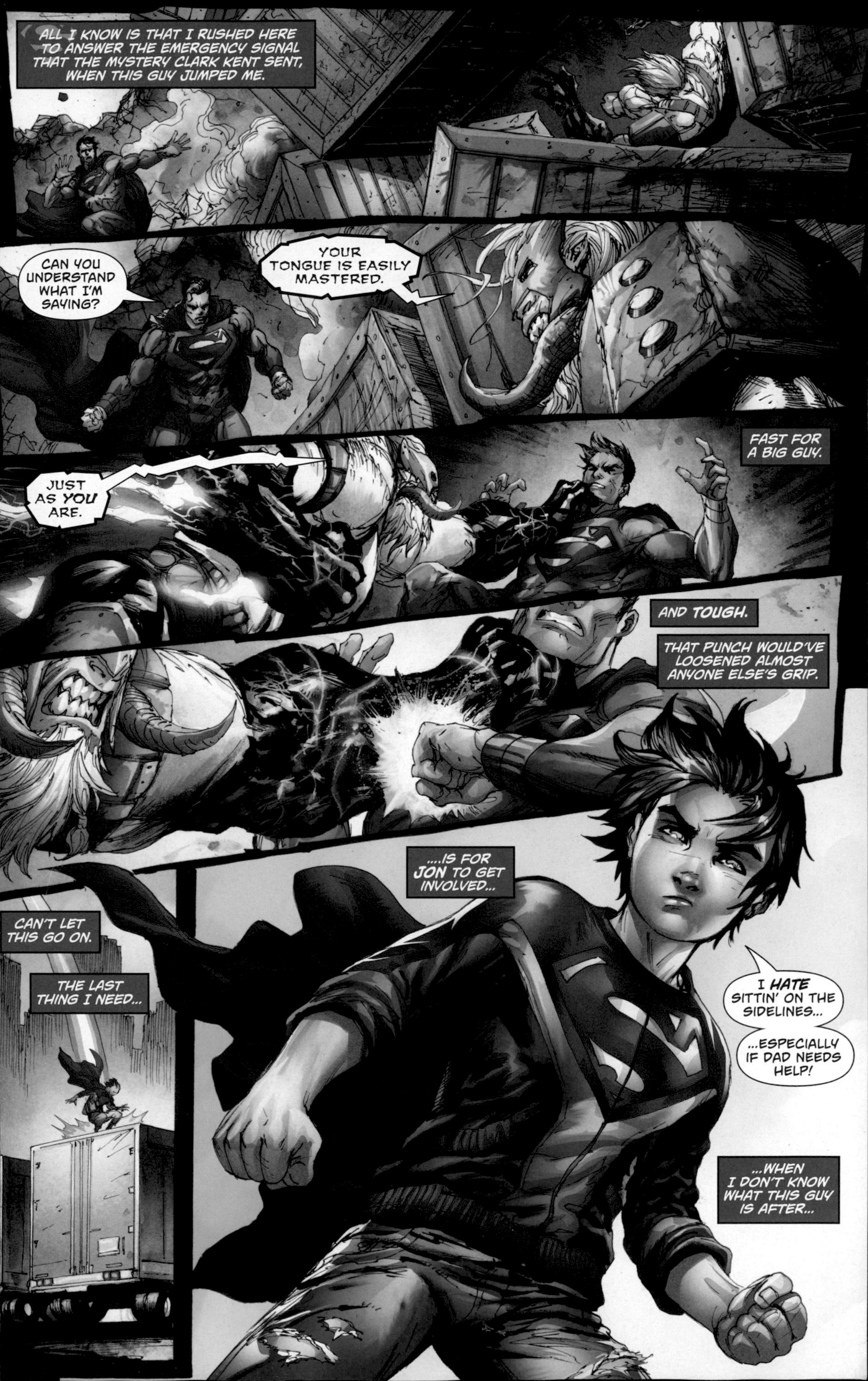
ALL I KNOW IS THAT I RUSHED HERE TO ANSWER THE EMERGENCY SIGNAL THAT THE MYSTERY CLARK KENT SENT, WHEN THIS GUY JUMPED ME.
CAN YOU UNDERSTAND WHAT I'M SAYING?
YOUR TONGUE IS EASILY MASTERED.
JUST AS YOU ARE.
FAST FOR A BIG GUY.
AND TOUGH.
THAT PUNCH WOULD'VE LOOSENED ALMOST ANYONE ELSE'S GRIP.
CAN'T LET THIS GO ON.
THE LAST THING I NEED...
...IS FOR JON TO GET INVOLVED...
...WHEN I DON'T KNOW WHAT THIS GUY IS AFTER...
I HATE SITTIN' ON THE SIDELINES...
...ESPECIALLY IF DAD NEEDS HELP!

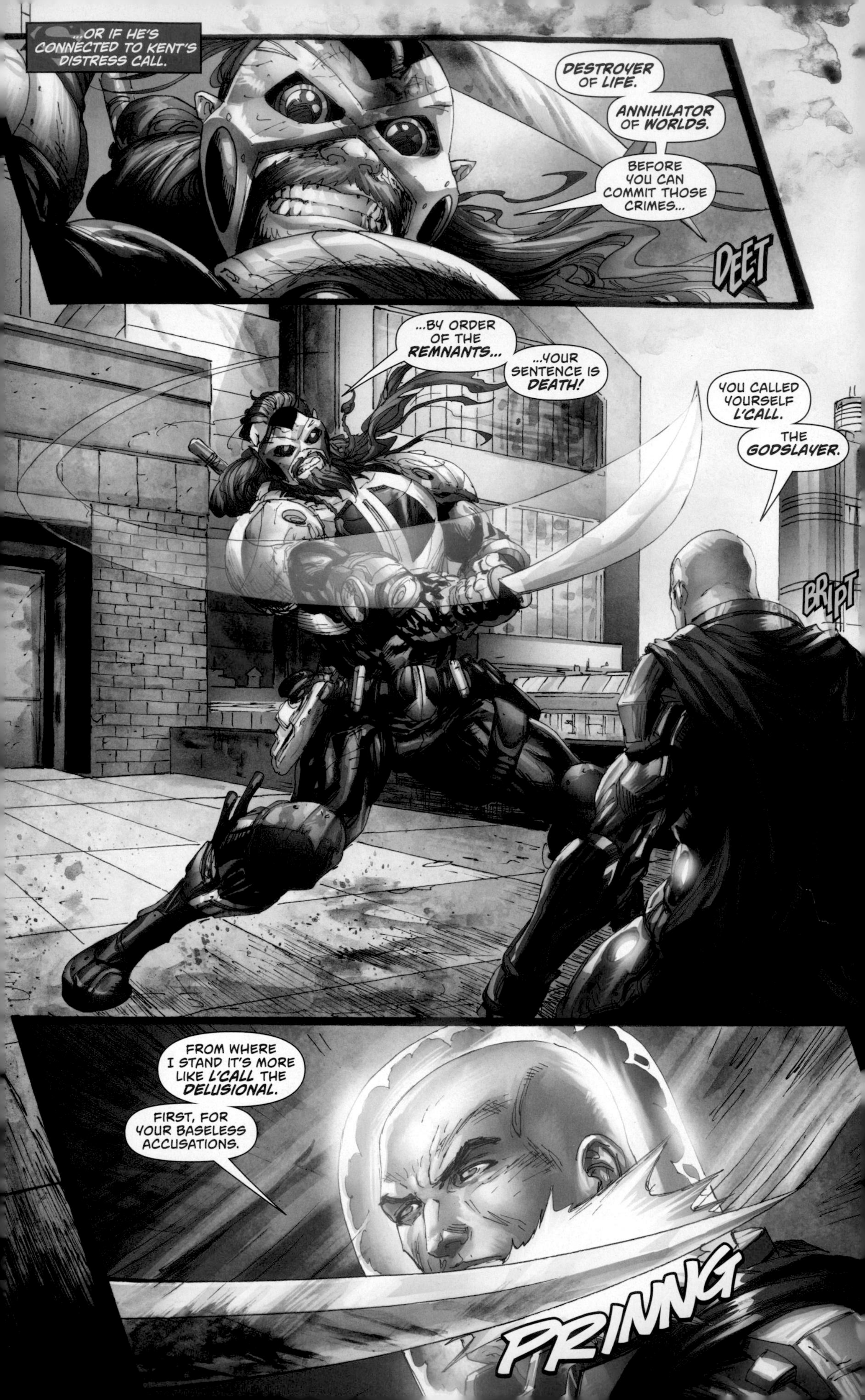
...OR IF HE'S CONNECTED TO KENT'S DISTRESS CALL.
DESTROYER OF LIFE.
ANNIHILATOR OF WORLDS.
BEFORE YOU CAN COMMIT THOSE CRIMES...
DEET
...BY ORDER OF THE REMNANTS...
...YOUR SENTENCE IS DEATH!
YOU CALLED YOURSELF L'CALL.
THE GODSLAYER.
BRIPT
FROM WHERE I STAND IT'S MORE LIKE L'CALL THE DELUSIONAL.
FIRST, FOR YOUR BASELESS ACCUSATIONS.
PRINNG

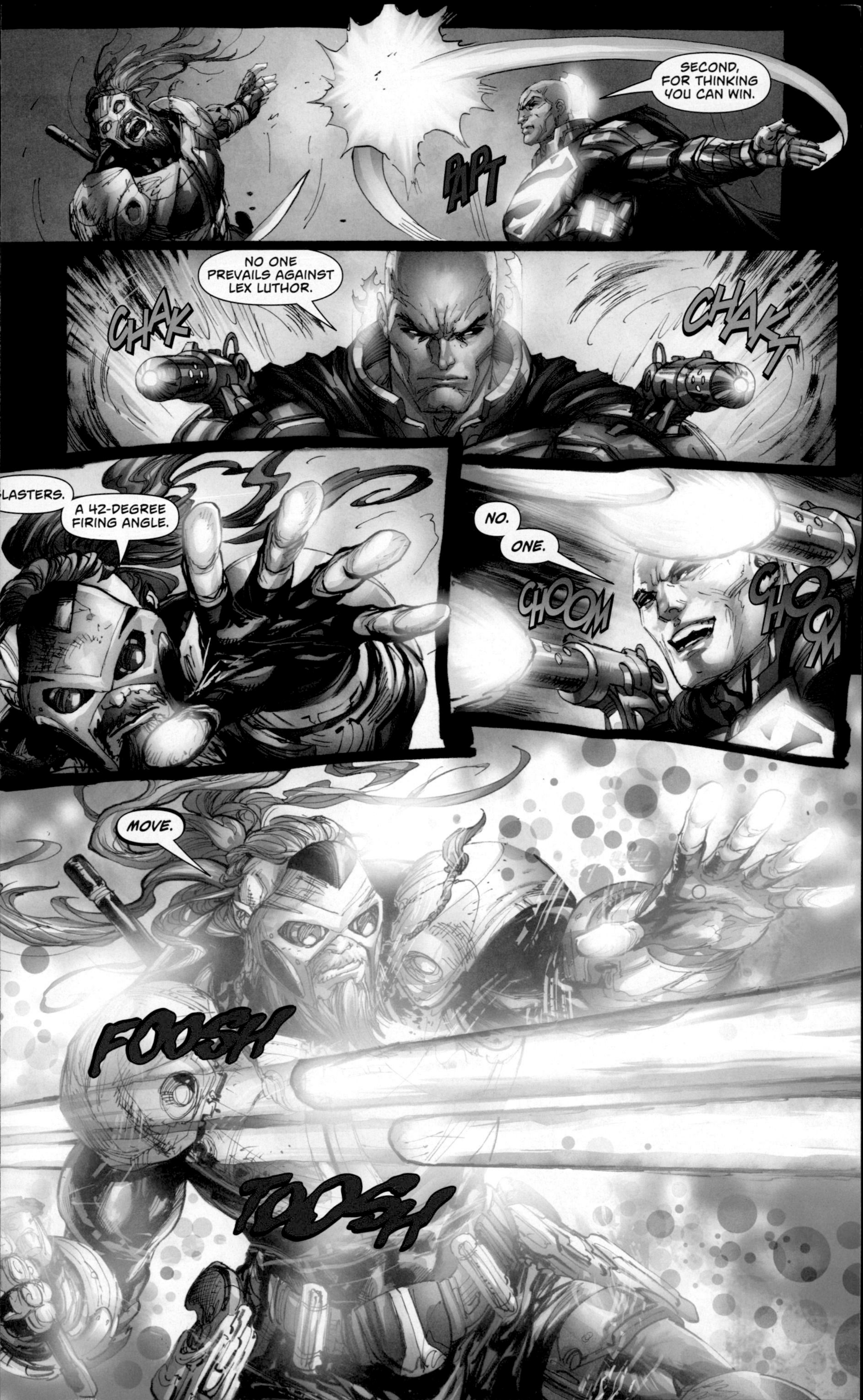
SECOND, FOR THINKING YOU CAN WIN.
PAPT
NO ONE PREVAILS AGAINST LEX LUTHOR.
CHAK
CHAKT
BLASTERS.
A 42-DEGREE FIRING ANGLE.
NO.
ONE.
CHOOM
CHOOM
MOVE.
FOOSH
TOOSH

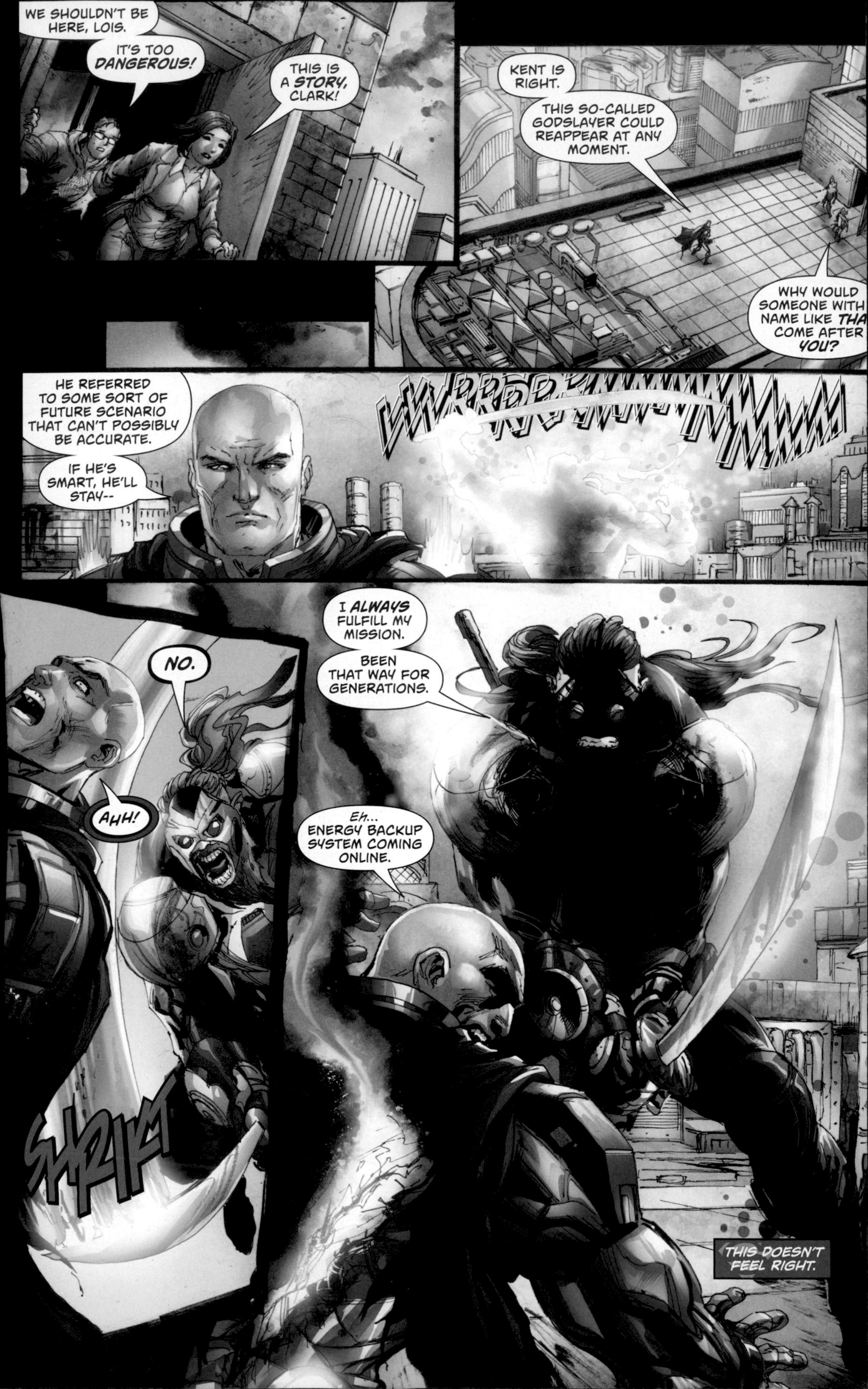
WE SHOULDN'T BE HERE, LOIS.
IT'S TOO DANGEROUS!
THIS IS A STORY, CLARK!
KENT IS RIGHT.
THIS SO-CALLED GODSLAYER COULD REAPPEAR AT ANY MOMENT.
WHY WOULD SOMEONE WITH NAME LIKE THA COME AFTER YOU?
HE REFERRED TO SOME SORT OF FUTURE SCENARIO THAT CAN'T POSSIBLY BE ACCURATE.
IF HE'S SMART, HE'LL STAY--
I ALWAYS FULFILL MY MISSION.
BEEN THAT WAY FOR GENERATIONS.
NO.
AHH!
Eh... ENERGY BACKUP SYSTEM COMING ONLINE.
SHRIKT
THIS DOESN'T FEEL RIGHT.

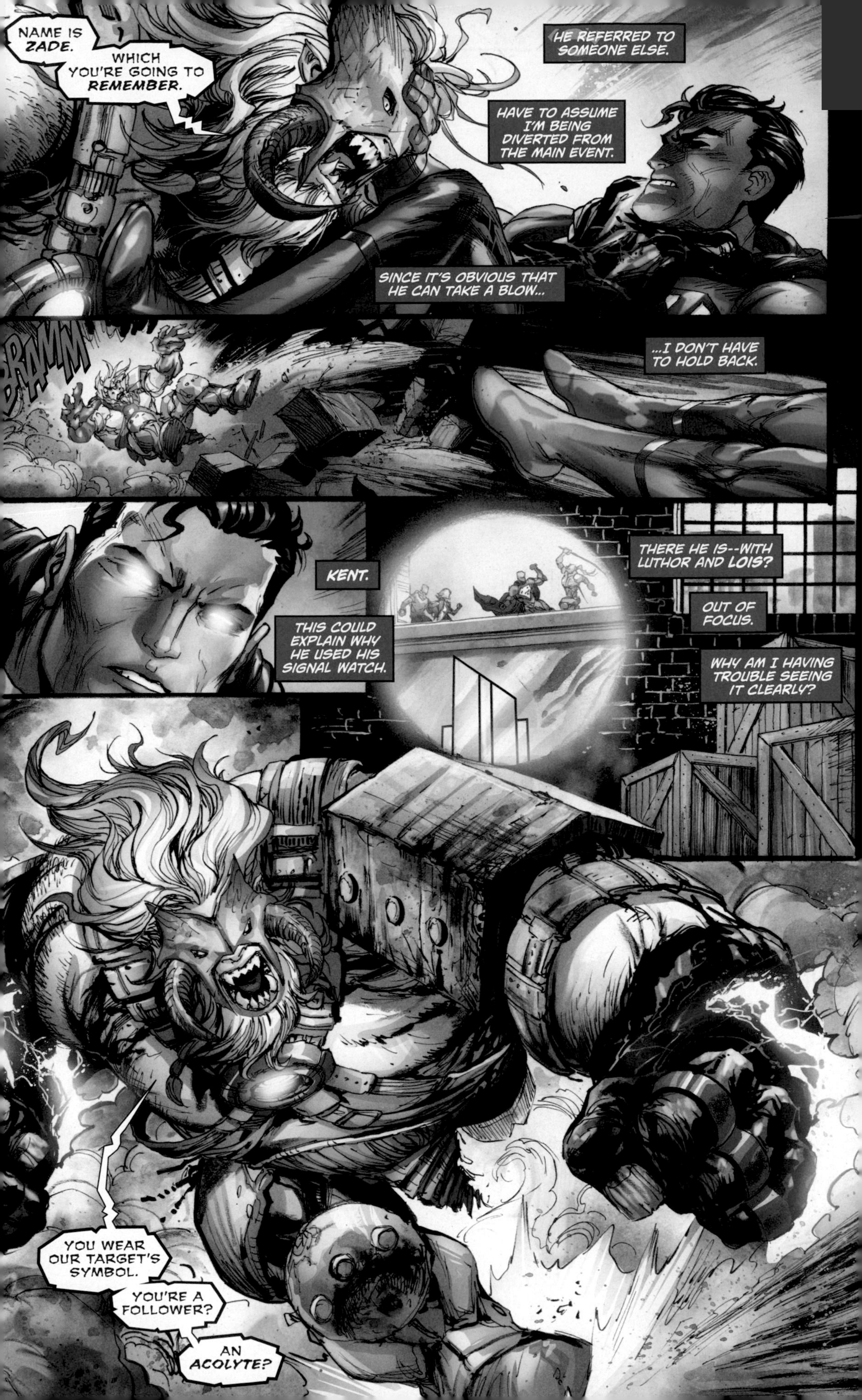
NAME IS ZADE.
WHICH YOU'RE GOING TO REMEMBER.
HE REFERRED TO SOMEONE ELSE.
HAVE TO ASSUME I'M BEING DIVERTED FROM THE MAIN EVENT.
SINCE IT'S OBVIOUS THAT HE CAN TAKE A BLOW...
BRAMM
...I DON'T HAVE TO HOLD BACK.
KENT.
THIS COULD EXPLAIN WHY HE USED HIS SIGNAL WATCH.
THERE HE IS--WITH LUTHOR AND LOIS?
OUT OF FOCUS.
WHY AM I HAVING TROUBLE SEEING IT CLEARLY?
YOU WEAR OUR TARGET'S SYMBOL.
YOU'RE A FOLLOWER?
AN ACOLYTE?

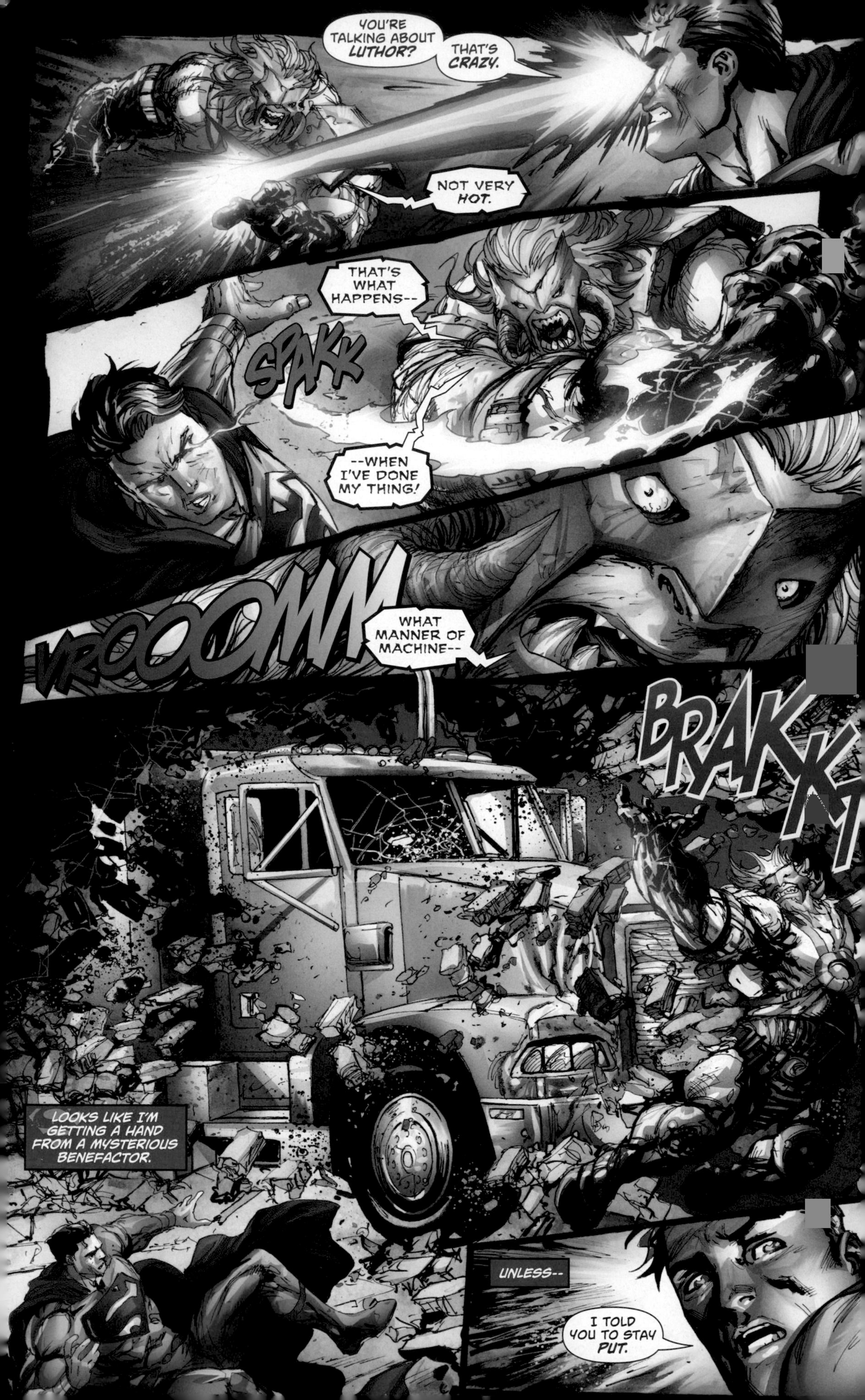
YOU'RE TALKING ABOUT LUTHOR?
THAT'S CRAZY.
NOT VERY HOT.
THAT'S WHAT HAPPENS--
SPAKK
--WHEN I'VE DONE MY THING!
VROOOOMM
WHAT MANNER OF MACHINE--
BRAKKT
LOOKS LIKE I'M GETTING A HAND FROM A MYSTERIOUS BENEFACTOR.
UNLESS--
I TOLD YOU TO STAY PUT.

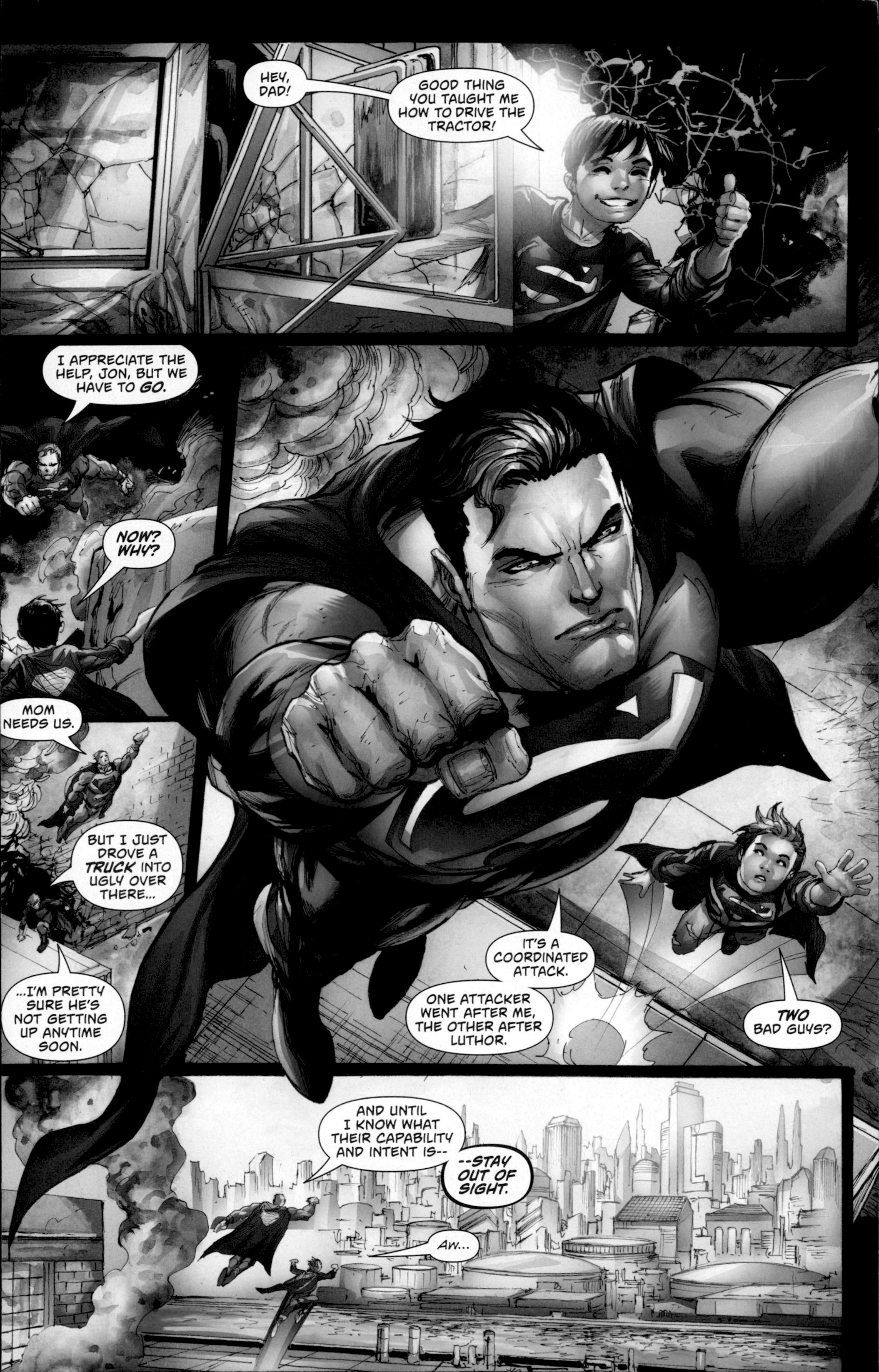

HEY, DAD!
GOOD THING YOU TAUGHT ME HOW TO DRIVE THE TRACTOR!
I APPRECIATE THE HELP, JON, BUT WE HAVE TO GO.
NOW? WHY?
MOM NEEDS US.
BUT I JUST DROVE A TRUCK INTO UGLY OVER THERE...
...I'M PRETTY SURE HE'S NOT GETTING UP ANYTIME SOON.
IT'S A COORDINATED ATTACK.
ONE ATTACKER WENT AFTER ME, THE OTHER AFTER LUTHOR.
TWO BAD GUYS?
AND UNTIL I KNOW WHAT THEIR CAPABILITY AND INTENT IS--
--STAY OUT OF SIGHT.
AW...

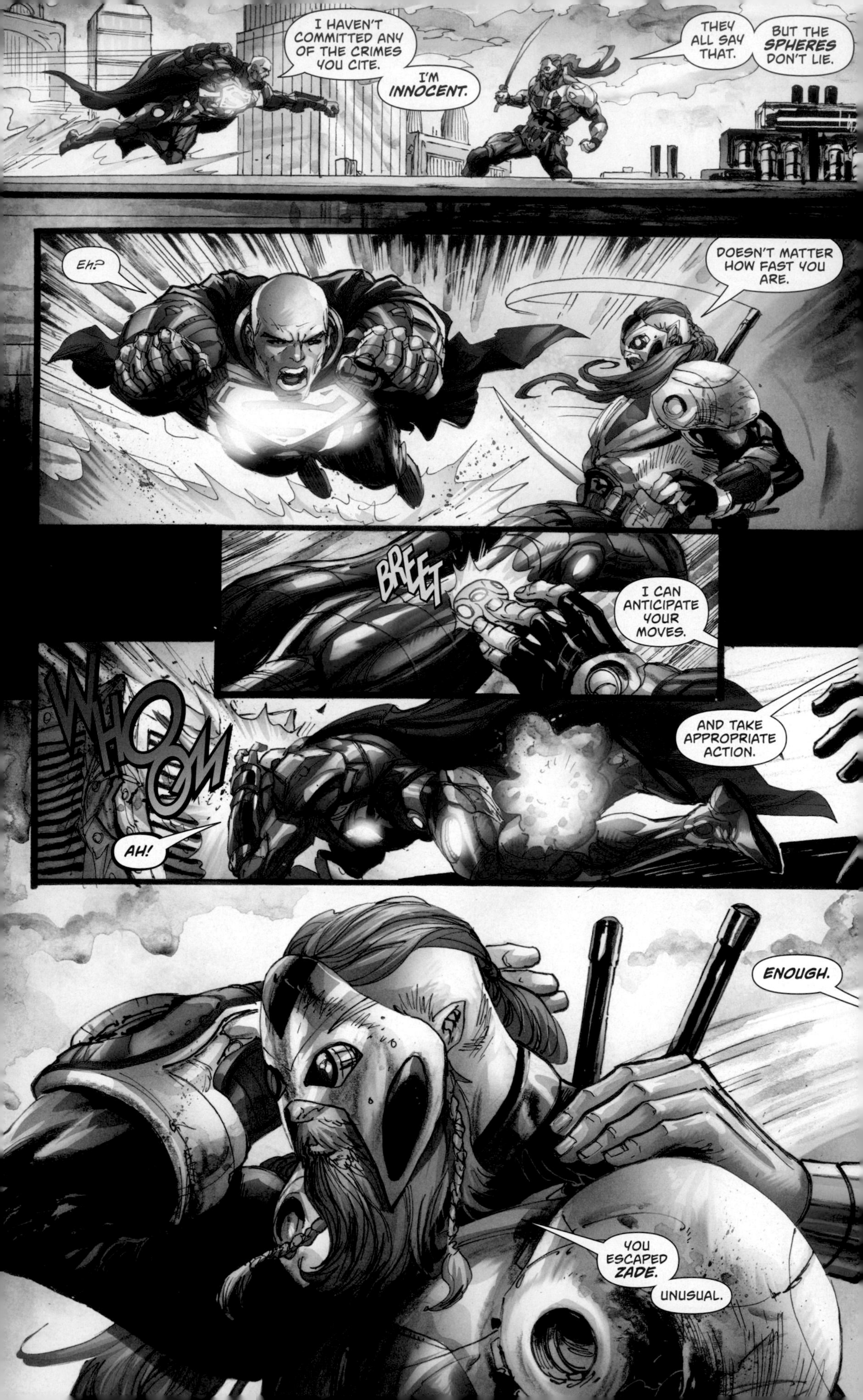
I HAVEN'T COMMITTED ANY OF THE CRIMES YOU CITE.
I'M INNOCENT.
THEY ALL SAY THAT.
BUT THE SPHERES DON'T LIE.
Eh?
DOESN'T MATTER HOW FAST YOU ARE.
BREEET
I CAN ANTICIPATE YOUR MOVES.
WHOOM
AND TAKE APPROPRIATE ACTION.
AH!
ENOUGH.
YOU ESCAPED ZADE.
UNUSUAL.

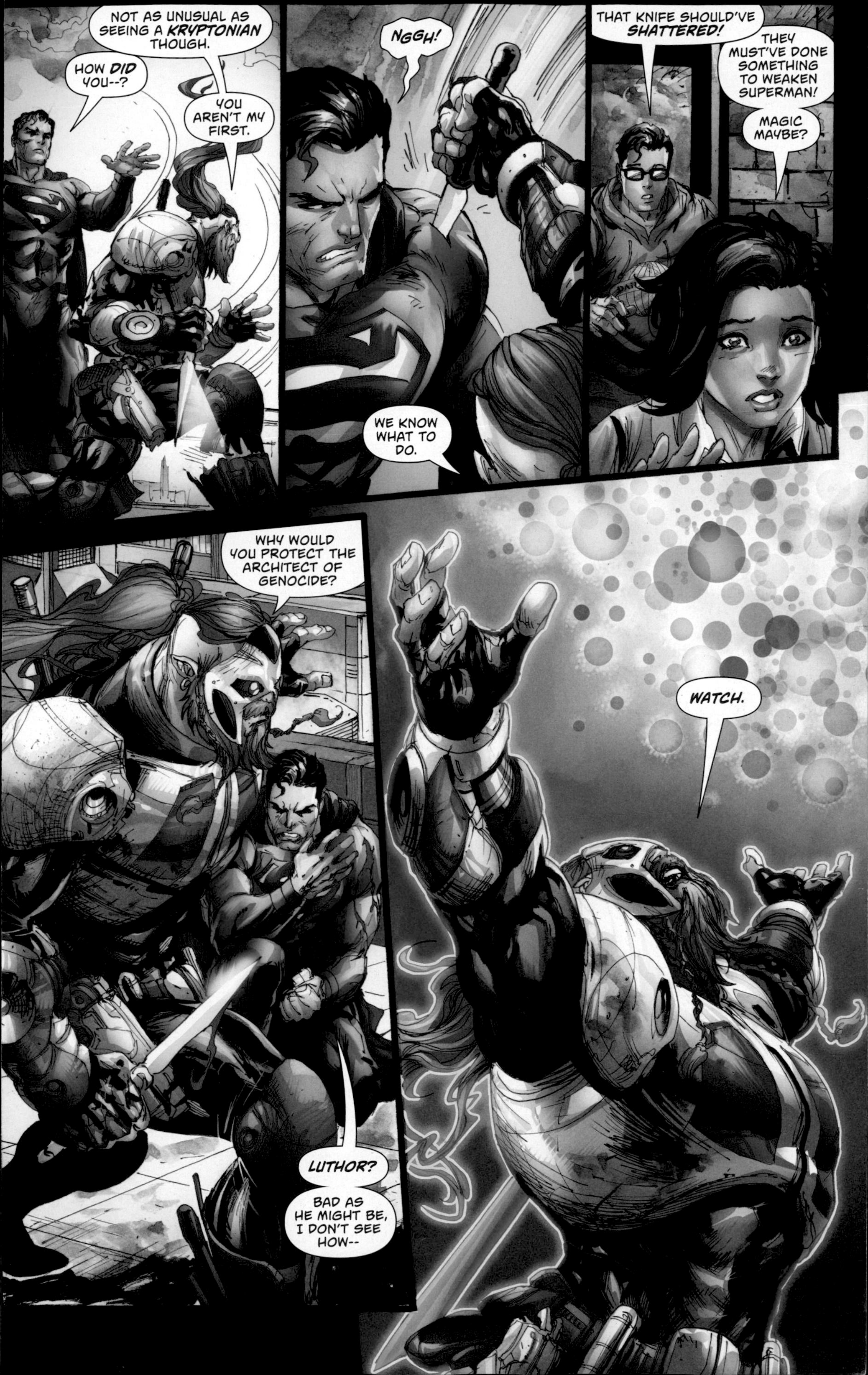
HOW DID YOU--?
NOT AS UNUSUAL AS SEEING A KRYPTONIAN THOUGH.
YOU AREN'T MY FIRST.
NGGH!
WE KNOW WHAT TO DO.
THAT KNIFE SHOULD'VE SHATTERED!
THEY MUST'VE DONE SOMETHING TO WEAKEN SUPERMAN!
MAGIC MAYBE?
WHY WOULD YOU PROTECT THE ARCHITECT OF GENOCIDE?
LUTHOR?
BAD AS HE MIGHT BE, I DON'T SEE HOW--
WATCH.

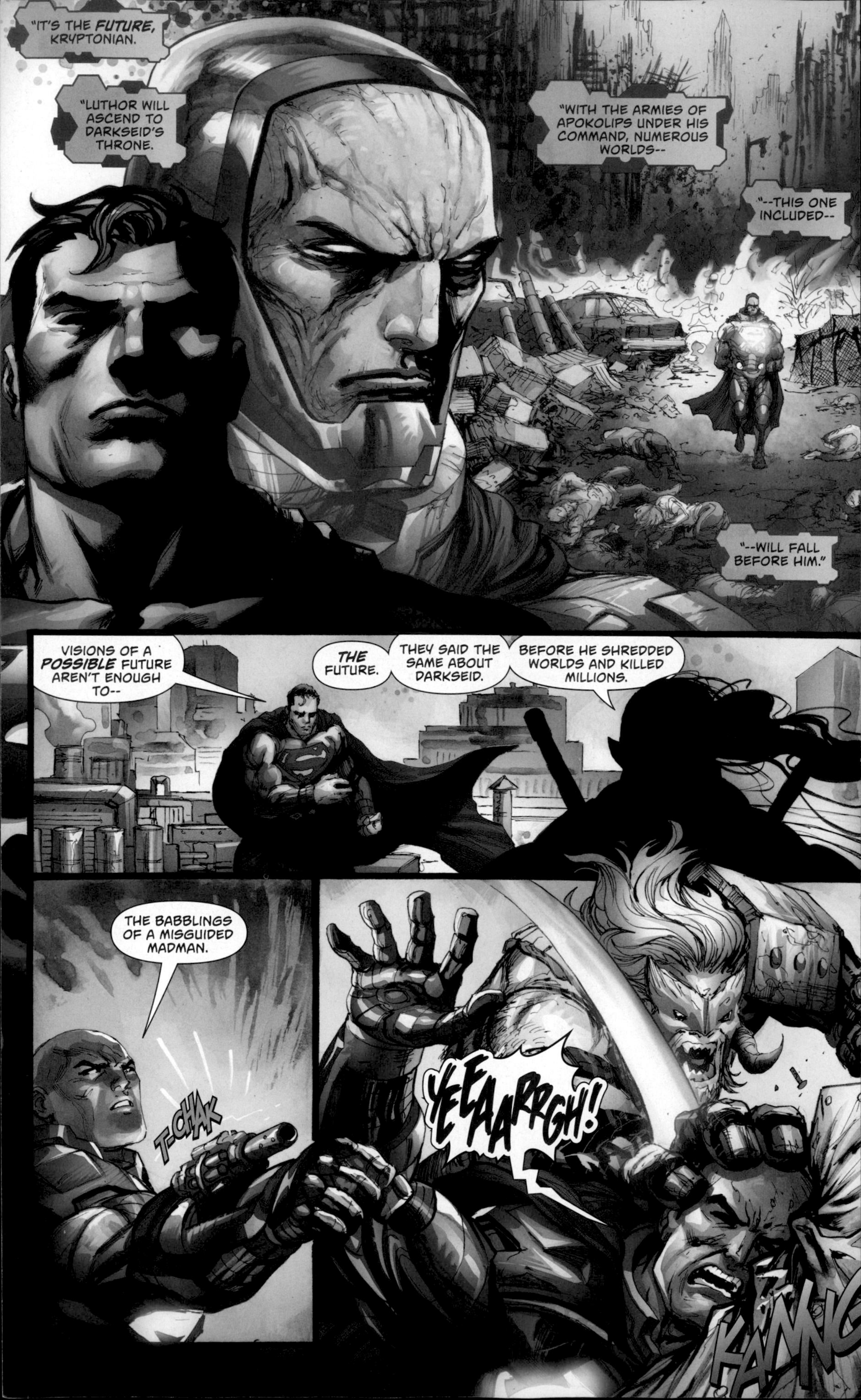
"IT'S THE *FUTURE*, KRYPTONIAN.
"LUTHOR WILL ASCEND TO DARKSEID'S THRONE.
"WITH THE ARMIES OF APOKOLIPS UNDER HIS COMMAND, NUMEROUS WORLDS--
"--THIS ONE INCLUDED--
"--WILL FALL BEFORE HIM."
VISIONS OF A *POSSIBLE* FUTURE AREN'T ENOUGH TO--
THE FUTURE.
THEY SAID THE SAME ABOUT DARKSEID.
BEFORE HE SHREDDED WORLDS AND KILLED MILLIONS.
THE BABBLINGS OF A MISGUIDED MADMAN.
T-CHAK
YEEAARRGH!

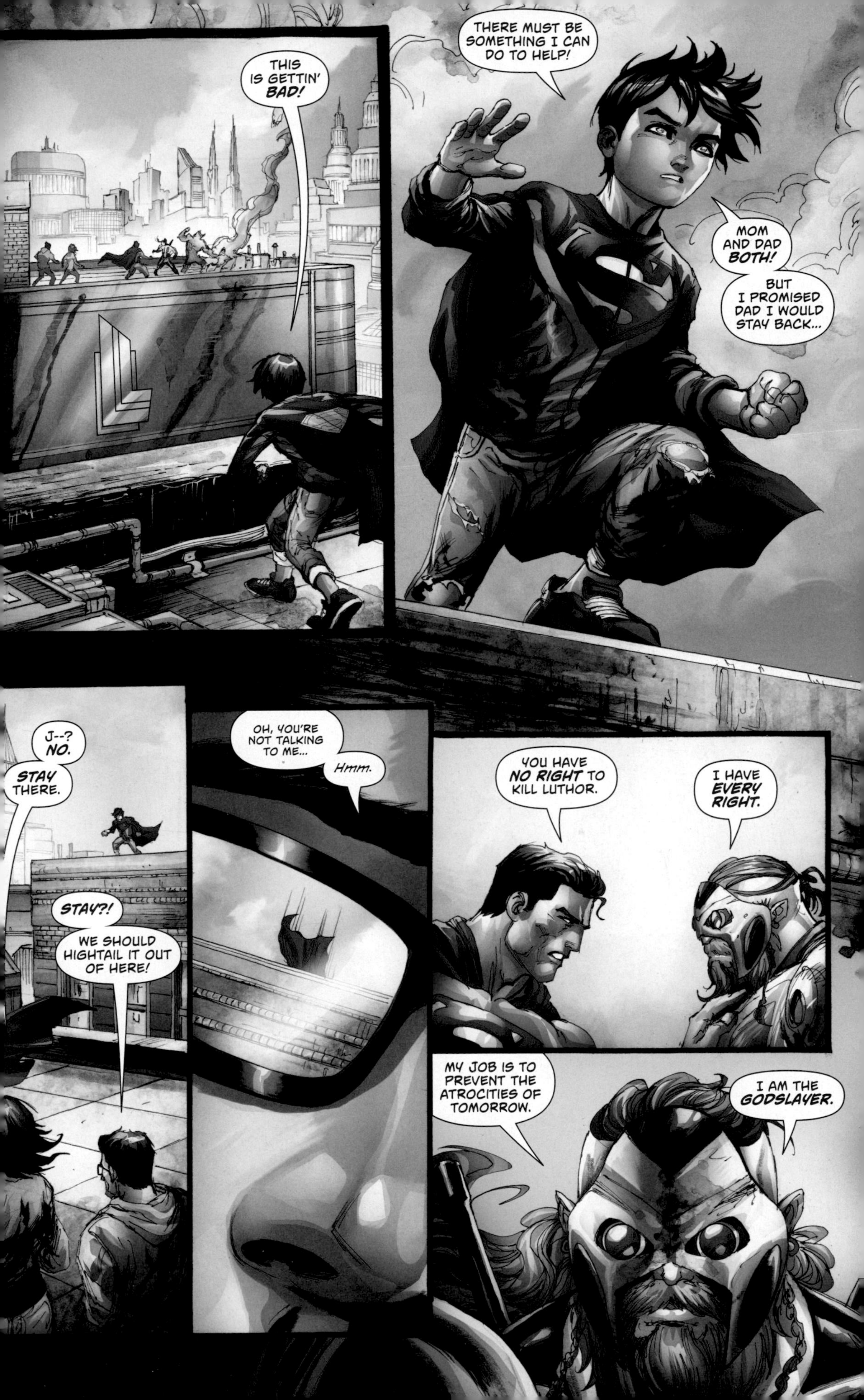
THIS IS GETTIN' BAD!
THERE MUST BE SOMETHING I CAN DO TO HELP!
MOM AND DAD BOTH!
BUT I PROMISED DAD I WOULD STAY BACK...
J--? NO.
STAY THERE.
STAY?!
WE SHOULD HIGHTAIL IT OUT OF HERE!
OH, YOU'RE NOT TALKING TO ME...
Hmm.
YOU HAVE NO RIGHT TO KILL LUTHOR.
I HAVE EVERY RIGHT.
MY JOB IS TO PREVENT THE ATROCITIES OF TOMORROW.
I AM THE GODSLAYER.

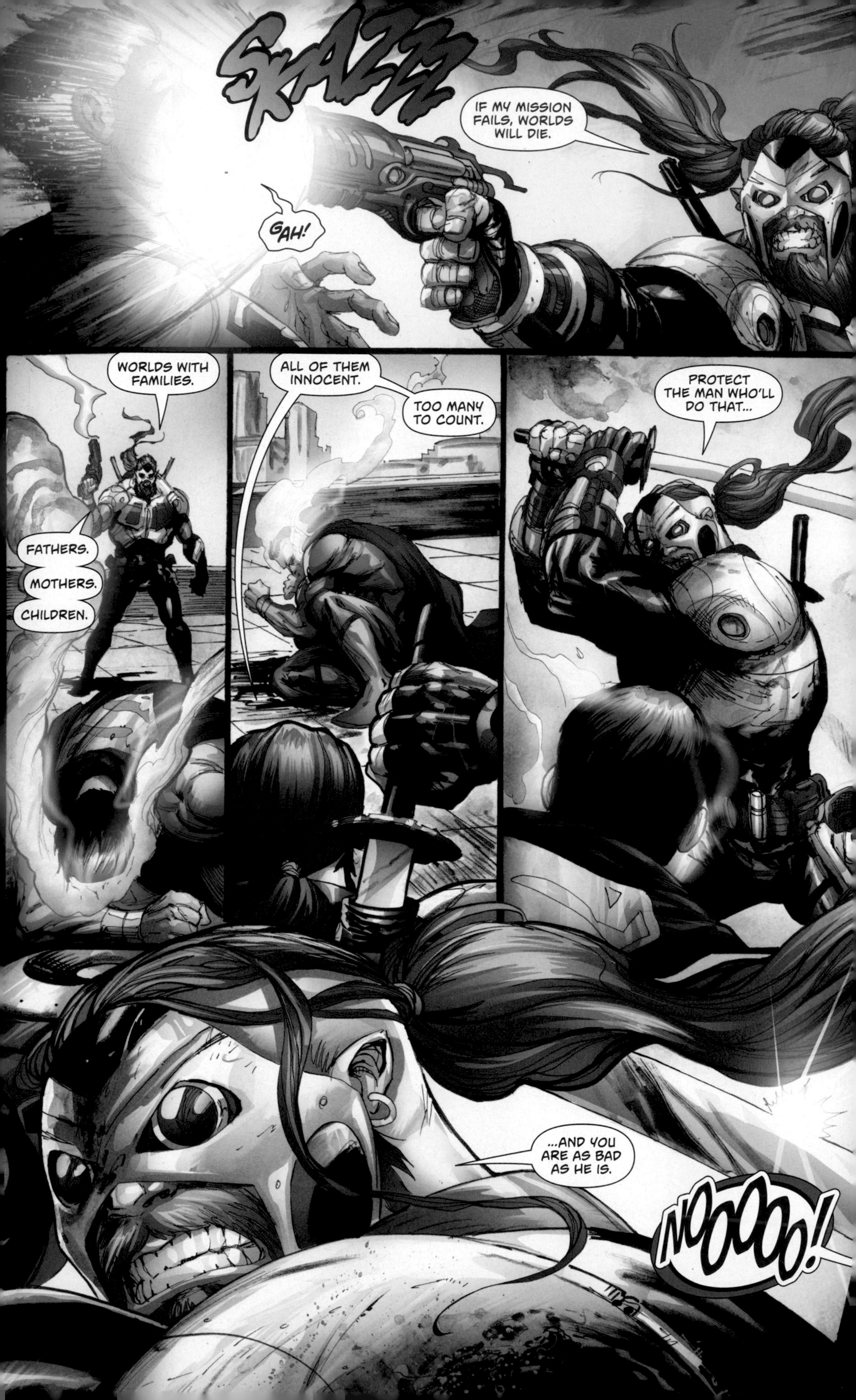
SKAZZZ
IF MY MISSION FAILS, WORLDS WILL DIE.
GAH!
WORLDS WITH FAMILIES.
FATHERS.
MOTHERS.
CHILDREN.
ALL OF THEM INNOCENT.
TOO MANY TO COUNT.
PROTECT THE MAN WHO'LL DO THAT...
...AND YOU ARE AS BAD AS HE IS.
NOOOOO!

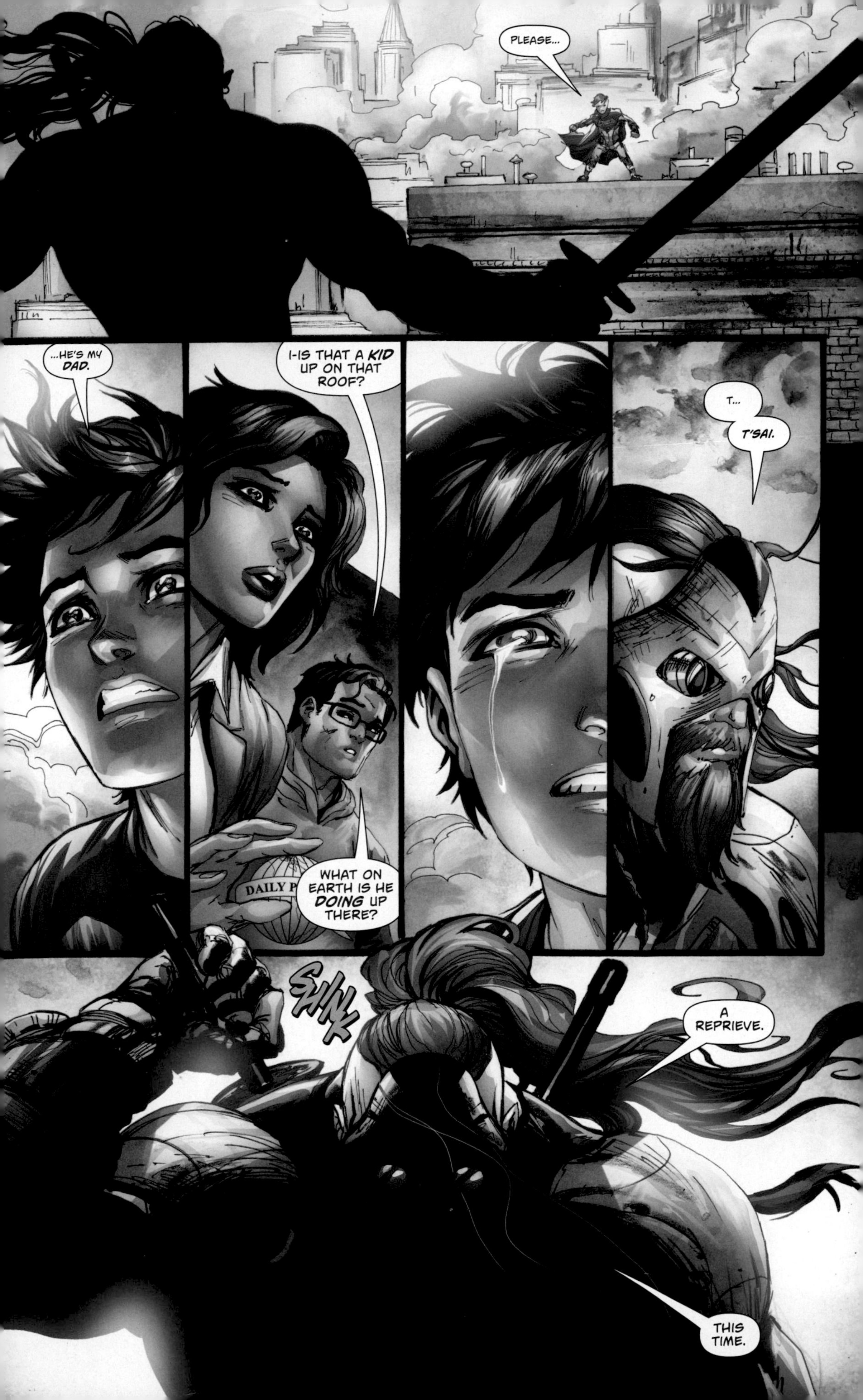
PLEASE...
...HE'S MY DAD.
I-IS THAT A KID UP ON THAT ROOF?
WHAT ON EARTH IS HE DOING UP THERE?
DAILY P
T...
T'SAI.
SHUNK
A REPRIEVE.
THIS TIME.

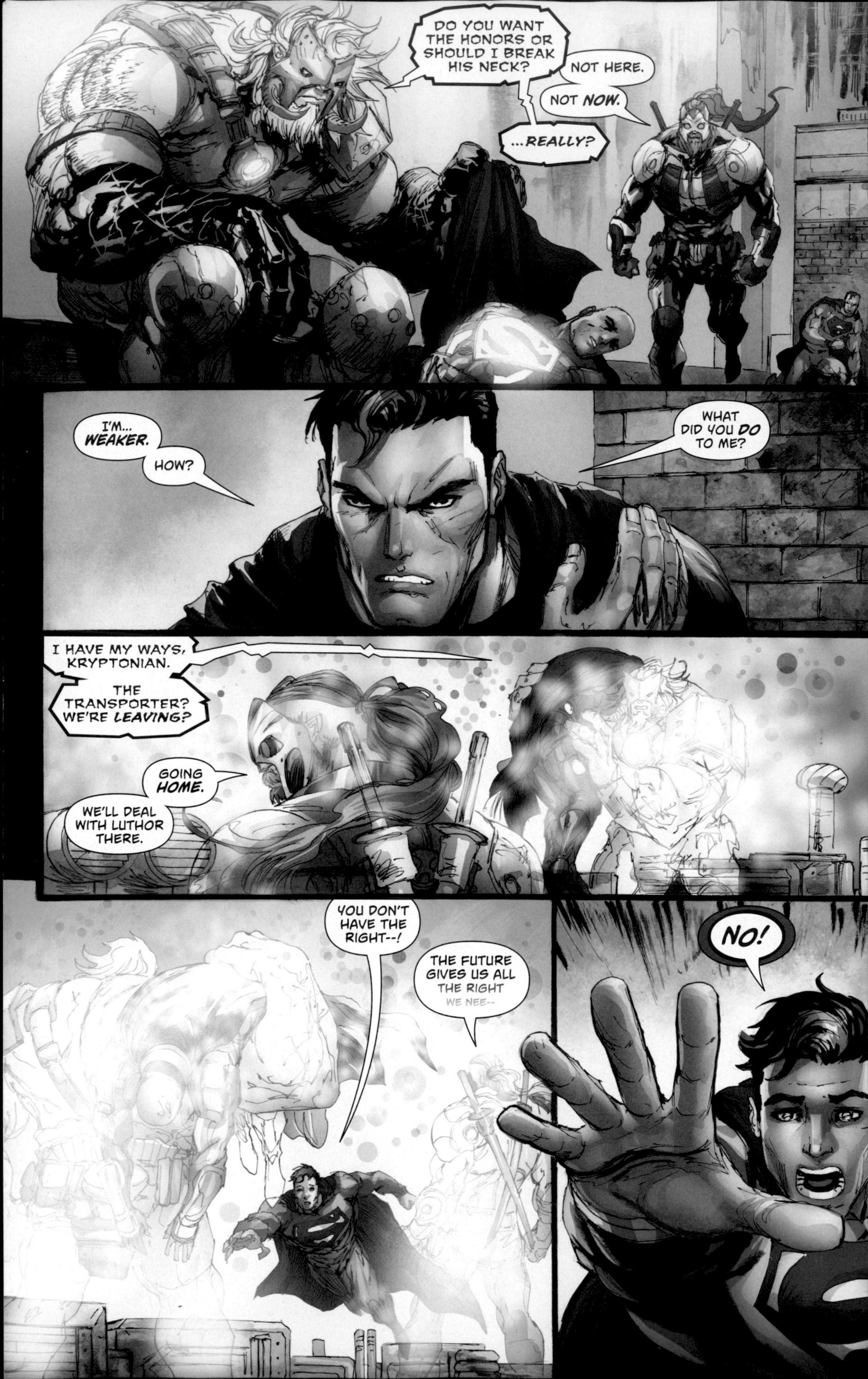
DO YOU WANT THE HONORS OR SHOULD I BREAK HIS NECK?
NOT HERE.
NOT NOW.
...REALLY?
I'M... WEAKER.
HOW?
WHAT DID YOU DO TO ME?
I HAVE MY WAYS, KRYPTONIAN.
THE TRANSPORTER? WE'RE LEAVING?
GOING HOME.
WE'LL DEAL WITH LUTHOR THERE.
YOU DON'T HAVE THE RIGHT--!
THE FUTURE GIVES US ALL THE RIGHT WE NEE--
NO!

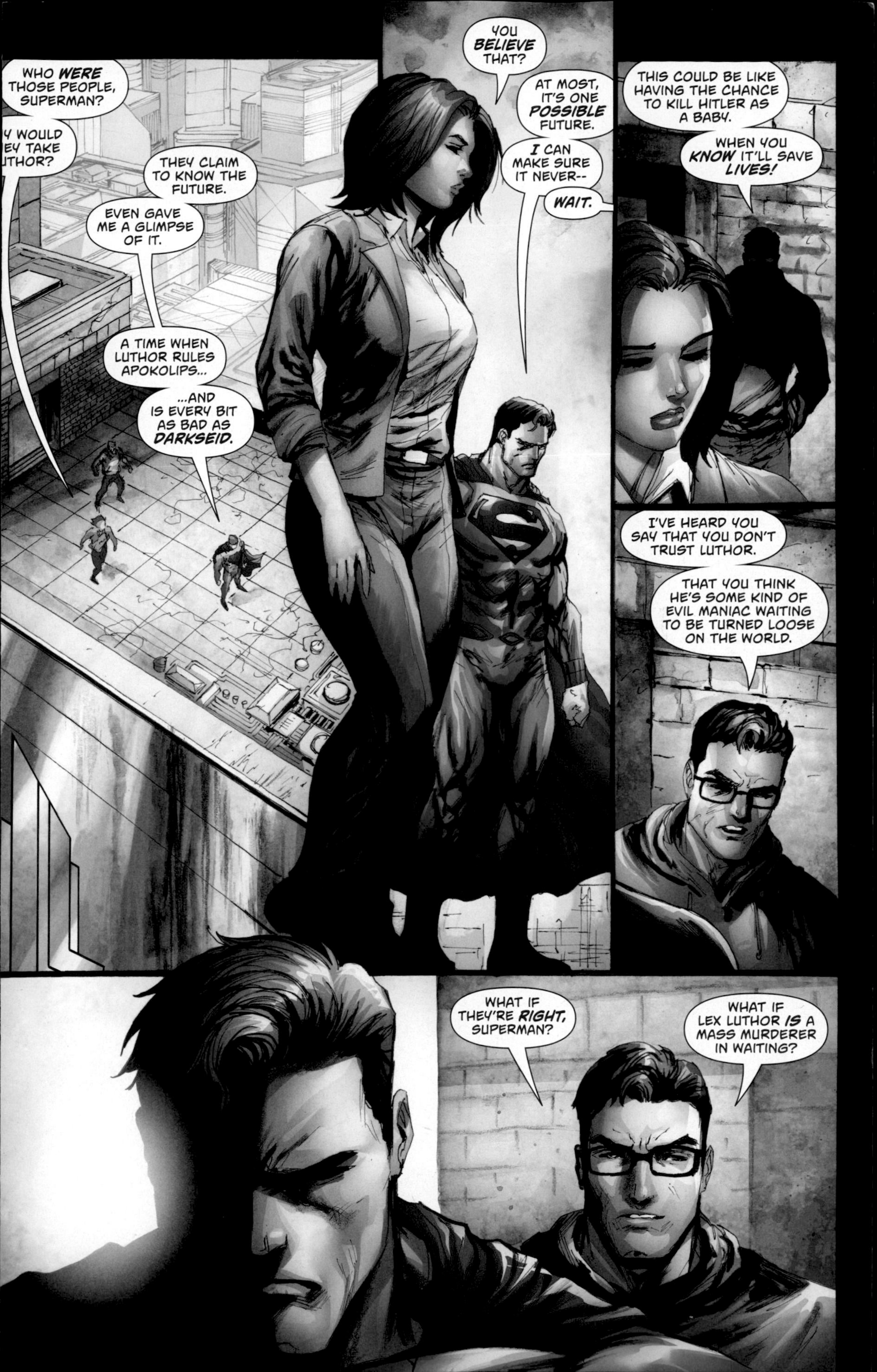
WHO WERE THOSE PEOPLE, SUPERMAN?
Y WOULD EY TAKE UTHOR?
THEY CLAIM TO KNOW THE FUTURE.
EVEN GAVE ME A GLIMPSE OF IT.
A TIME WHEN LUTHOR RULES APOKOLIPS...
...AND IS EVERY BIT AS BAD AS DARKSEID.
YOU BELIEVE THAT?
AT MOST, IT'S ONE POSSIBLE FUTURE.
I CAN MAKE SURE IT NEVER--
WAIT.
THIS COULD BE LIKE HAVING THE CHANCE TO KILL HITLER AS A BABY.
WHEN YOU KNOW IT'LL SAVE LIVES!
I'VE HEARD YOU SAY THAT YOU DON'T TRUST LUTHOR.
THAT YOU THINK HE'S SOME KIND OF EVIL MANIAC WAITING TO BE TURNED LOOSE ON THE WORLD.
WHAT IF THEY'RE RIGHT, SUPERMAN?
WHAT IF LEX LUTHOR IS A MASS MURDERER IN WAITING?

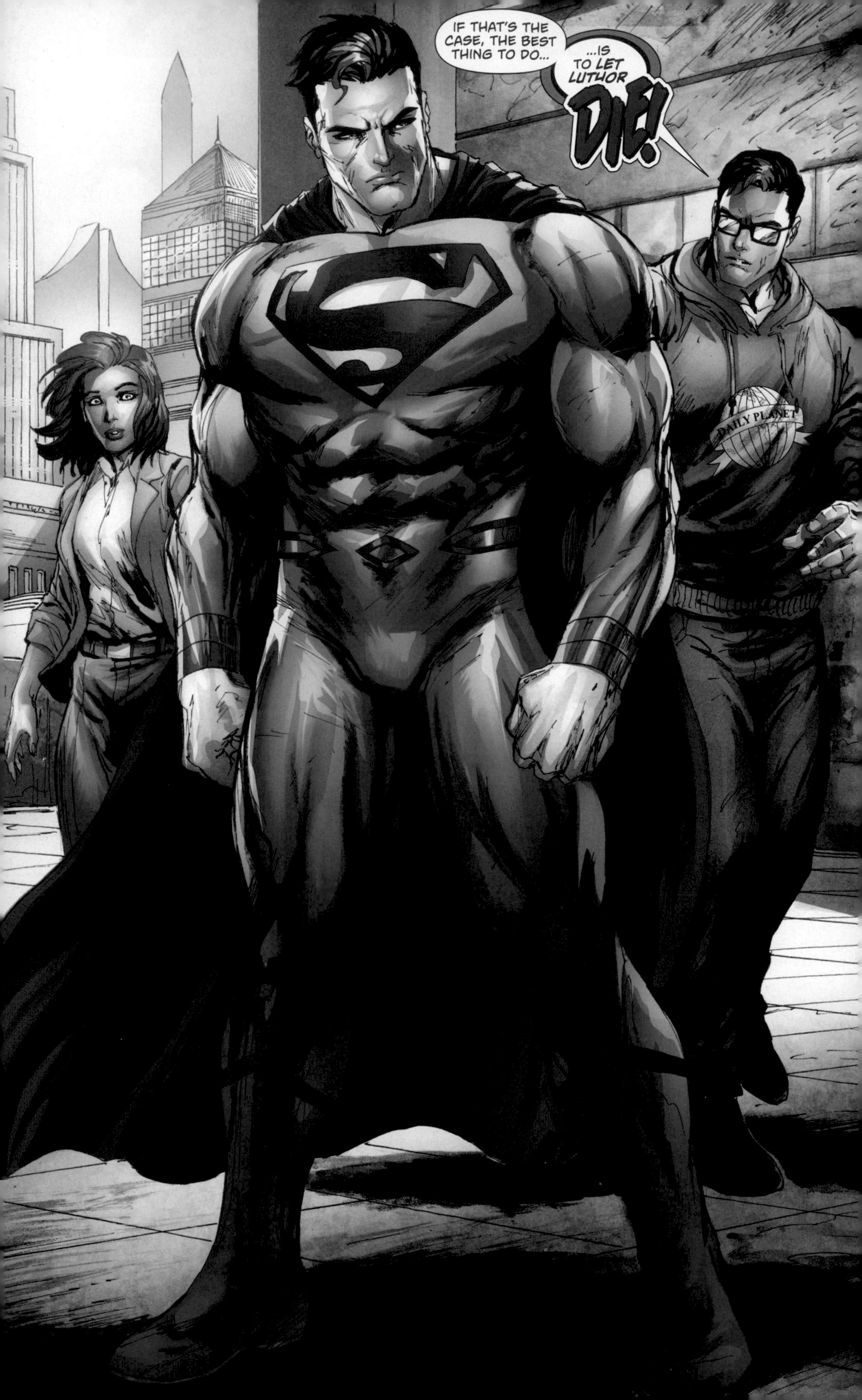
IF THAT'S THE CASE, THE BEST THING TO DO...
...IS TO LET LUTHOR DIE!

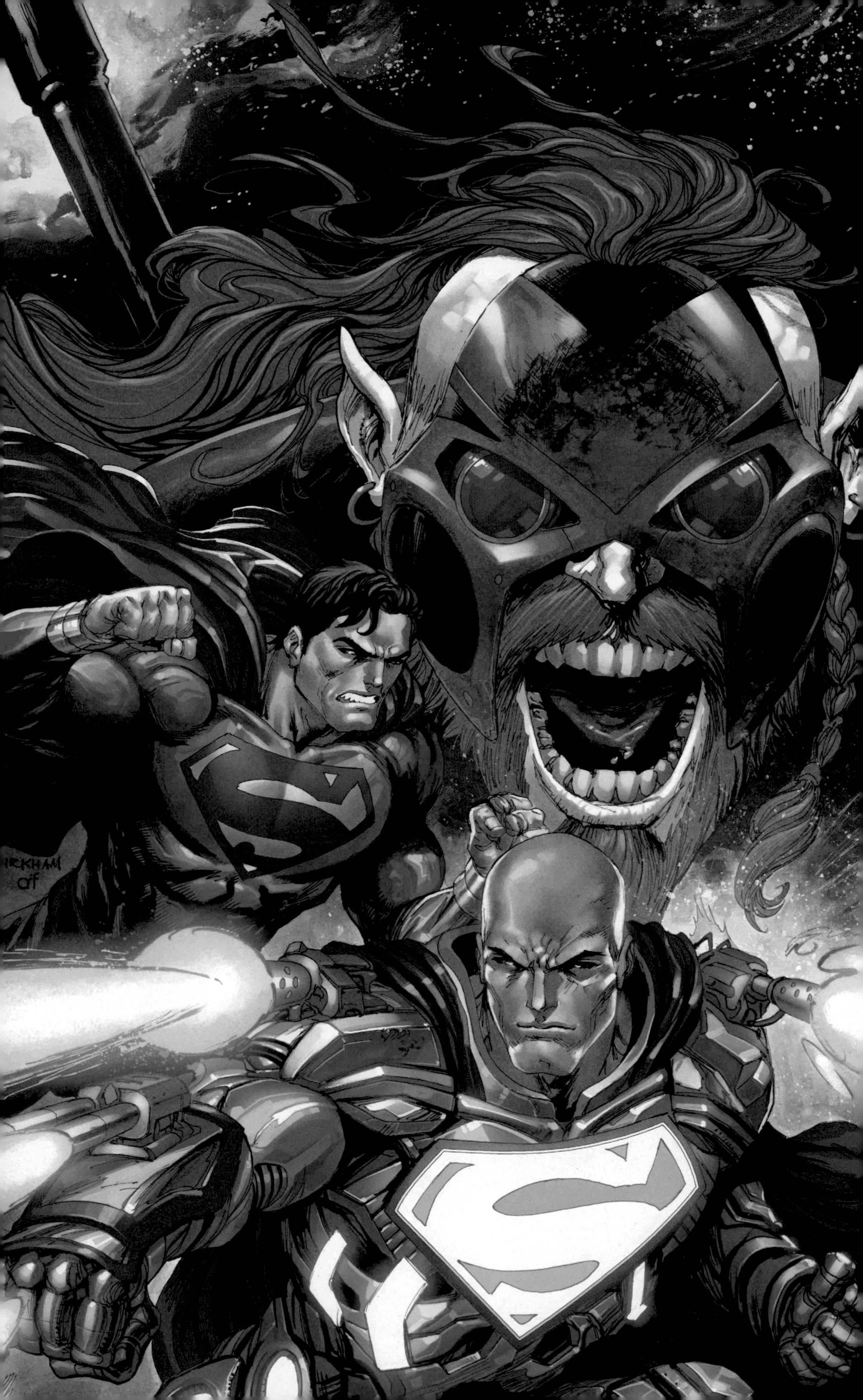

MEN OF STEEL PART 3

PATCH ZIRCHER artist * ARIF PRIANTO colorist
TYLER KIRKHAM ARIF PRIANTO cover artists

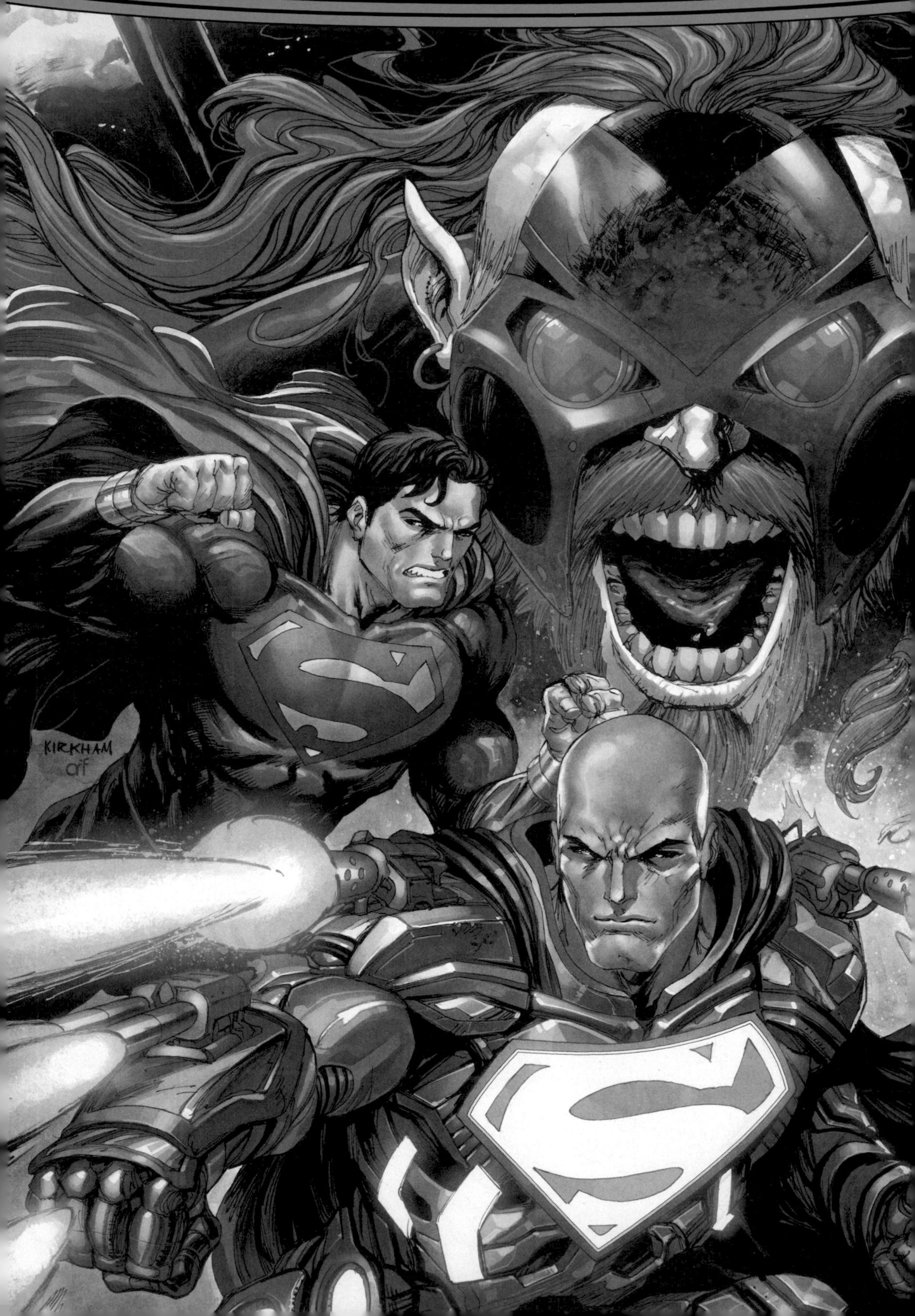
KIRKHAM
arif

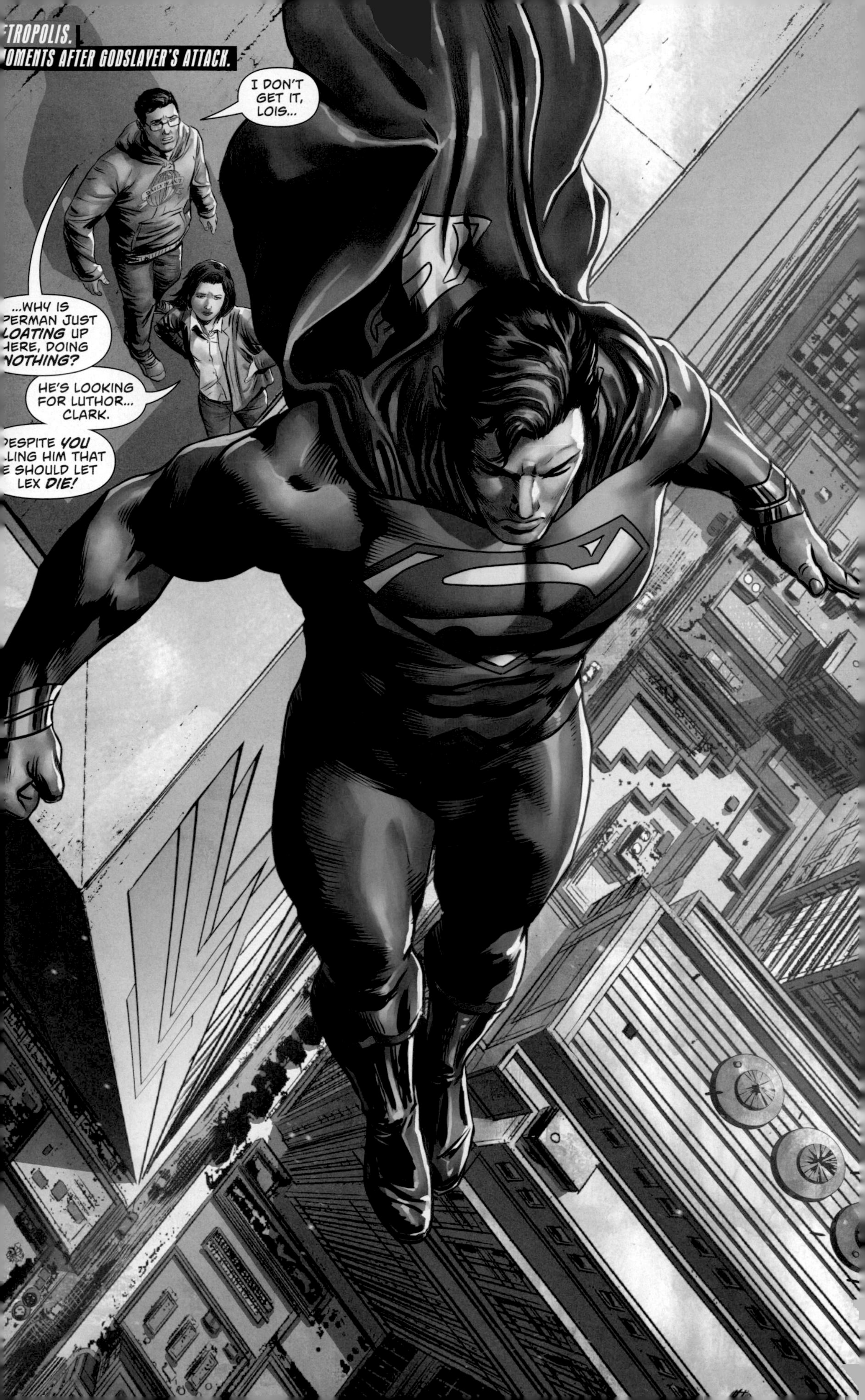

TROPOLIS.
OMENTS AFTER GODSLAYER'S ATTACK.
I DON'T GET IT, LOIS...
...WHY IS PERMAN JUST LOATING UP HERE, DOING NOTHING?
HE'S LOOKING FOR LUTHOR... CLARK.
ESPITE YOU LING HIM THAT E SHOULD LET LEX DIE!

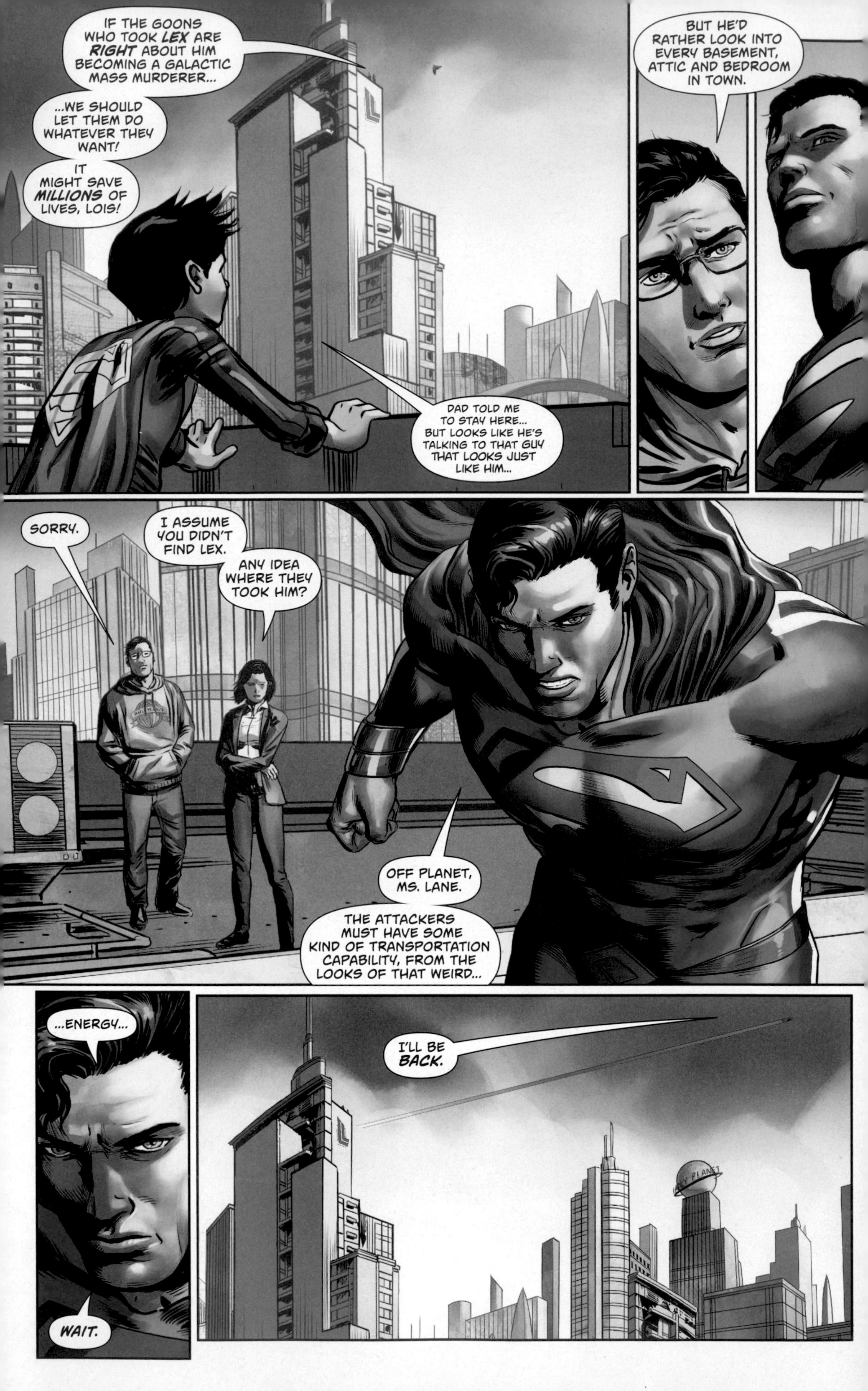
IF THE GOONS WHO TOOK LEX ARE RIGHT ABOUT HIM BECOMING A GALACTIC MASS MURDERER...
...WE SHOULD LET THEM DO WHATEVER THEY WANT!
IT MIGHT SAVE MILLIONS OF LIVES, LOIS!
DAD TOLD ME TO STAY HERE... BUT LOOKS LIKE HE'S TALKING TO THAT GUY THAT LOOKS JUST LIKE HIM...
BUT HE'D RATHER LOOK INTO EVERY BASEMENT, ATTIC AND BEDROOM IN TOWN.
SORRY.
I ASSUME YOU DIDN'T FIND LEX.
ANY IDEA WHERE THEY TOOK HIM?
OFF PLANET, MS. LANE.
THE ATTACKERS MUST HAVE SOME KIND OF TRANSPORTATION CAPABILITY, FROM THE LOOKS OF THAT WEIRD...
...ENERGY...
WAIT.
I'LL BE BACK.

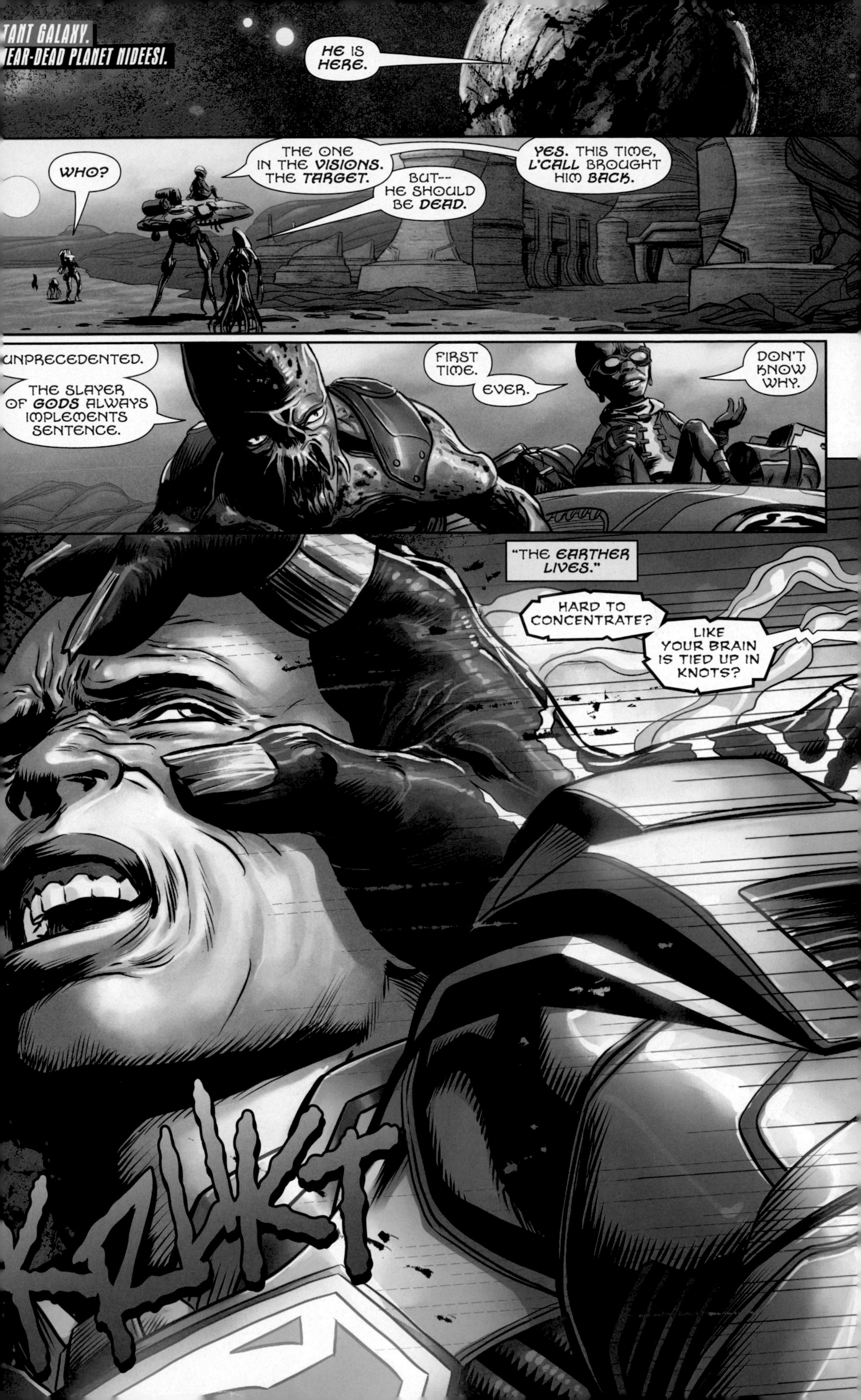

TANT GALAXY.
EAR-DEAD PLANET NIDEESI.
HE IS HERE.
WHO?
THE ONE IN THE VISIONS. THE TARGET.
BUT-- HE SHOULD BE DEAD.
YES. THIS TIME, L'CALL BROUGHT HIM BACK.
UNPRECEDENTED.
THE SLAYER OF GODS ALWAYS IMPLEMENTS SENTENCE.
FIRST TIME.
EVER.
DON'T KNOW WHY.
"THE EARTHER LIVES."
HARD TO CONCENTRATE?
LIKE YOUR BRAIN IS TIED UP IN KNOTS?
KZAKT

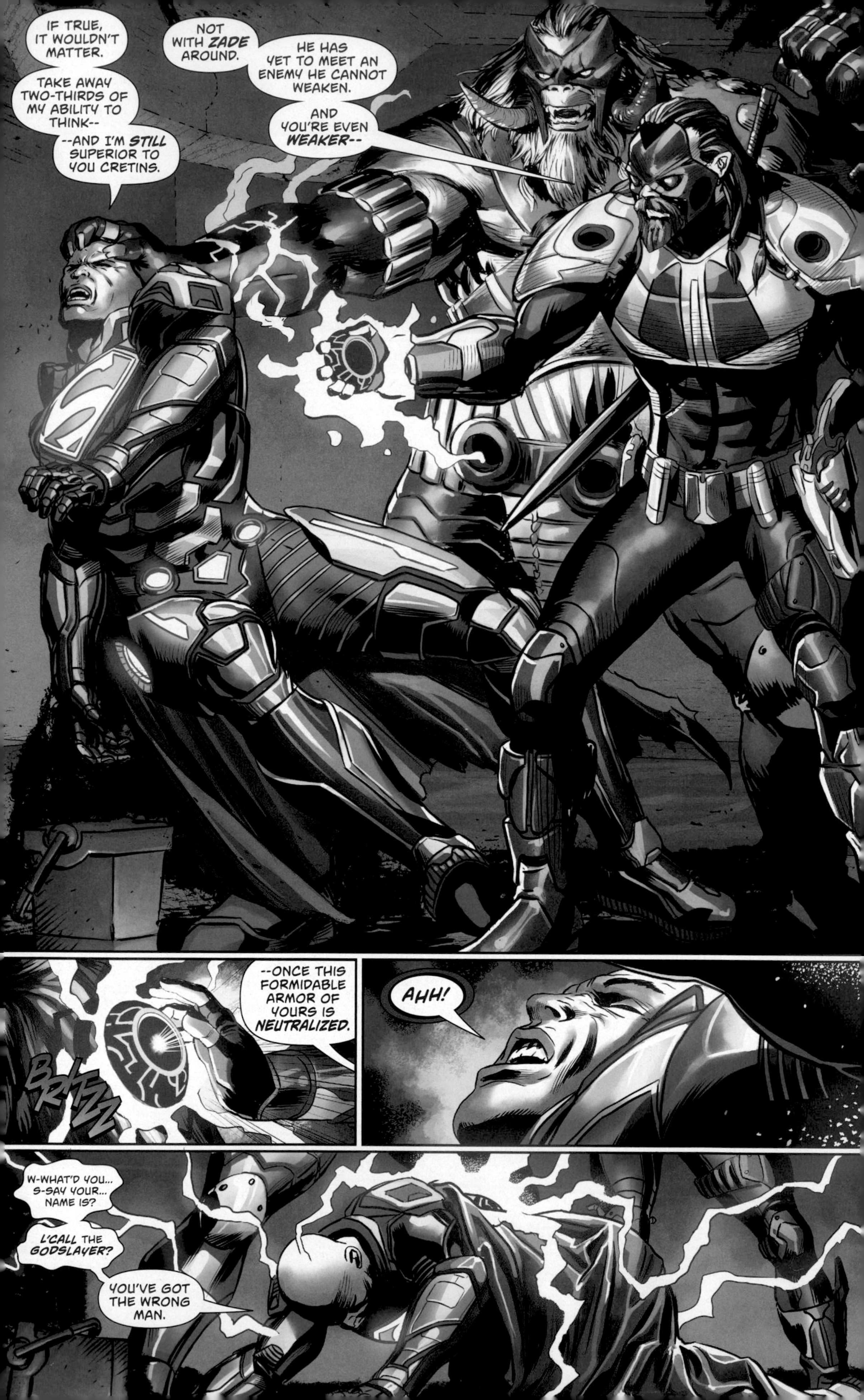
IF TRUE, IT WOULDN'T MATTER.
TAKE AWAY TWO-THIRDS OF MY ABILITY TO THINK--
--AND I'M STILL SUPERIOR TO YOU CRETINS.
NOT WITH ZADE AROUND.
HE HAS YET TO MEET AN ENEMY HE CANNOT WEAKEN.
AND YOU'RE EVEN WEAKER--
--ONCE THIS FORMIDABLE ARMOR OF YOURS IS NEUTRALIZED.
BRZZZ
AHH!
W-WHAT'D YOU... S-SAY YOUR... NAME IS?
L'CALL THE GODSLAYER?
YOU'VE GOT THE WRONG MAN.

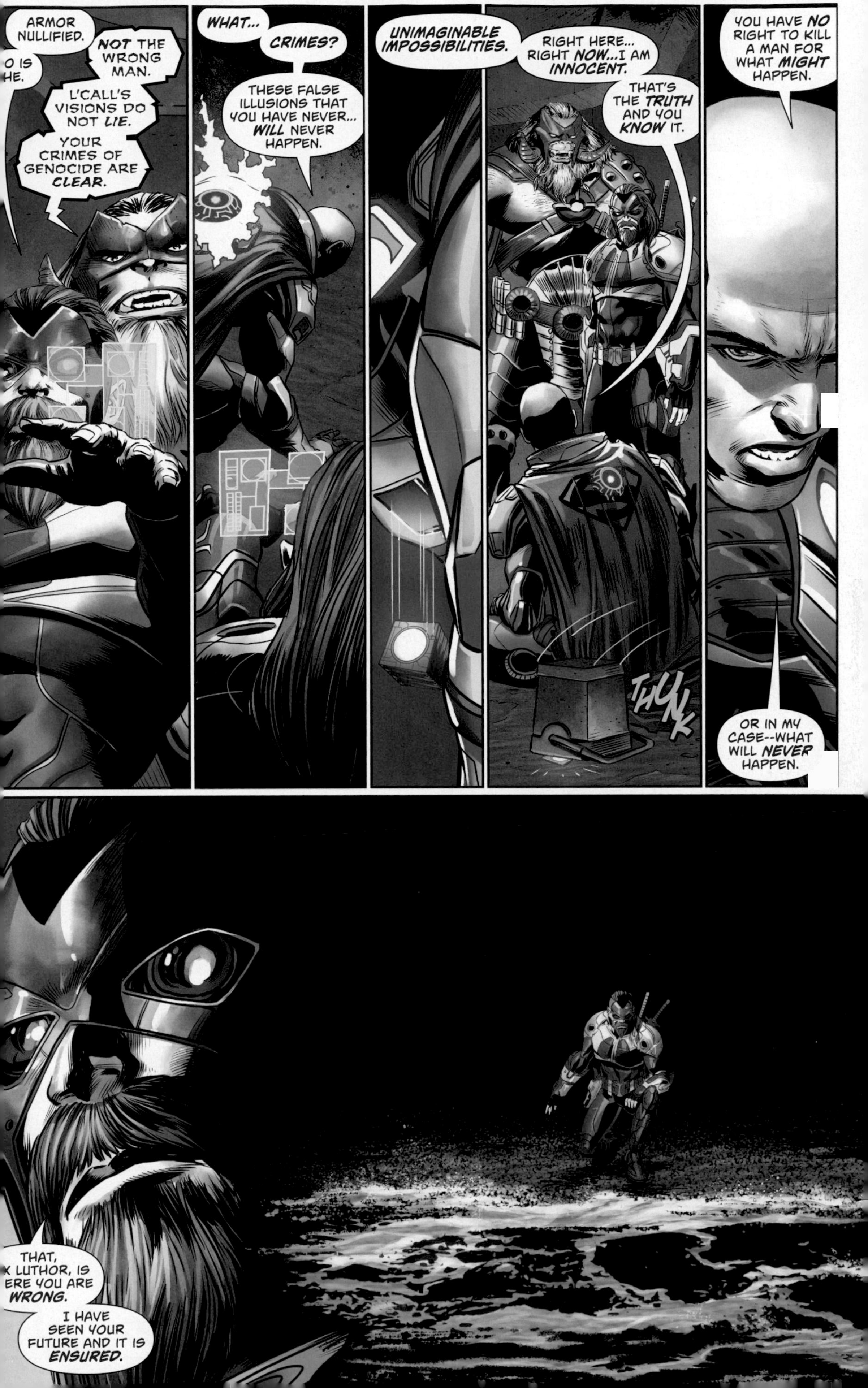

ARMOR NULLIFIED.
O IS HE.
NOT THE WRONG MAN.
L'CALL'S VISIONS DO NOT LIE.
YOUR CRIMES OF GENOCIDE ARE CLEAR.
WHAT...
CRIMES?
THESE FALSE ILLUSIONS THAT YOU HAVE NEVER... WILL NEVER HAPPEN.
UNIMAGINABLE IMPOSSIBILITIES.
RIGHT HERE... RIGHT NOW...I AM INNOCENT.
THAT'S THE TRUTH AND YOU KNOW IT.
THUNK
YOU HAVE NO RIGHT TO KILL A MAN FOR WHAT MIGHT HAPPEN.
OR IN MY CASE--WHAT WILL NEVER HAPPEN.
THAT, X LUTHOR, IS ERE YOU ARE WRONG.
I HAVE SEEN YOUR FUTURE AND IT IS ENSURED.

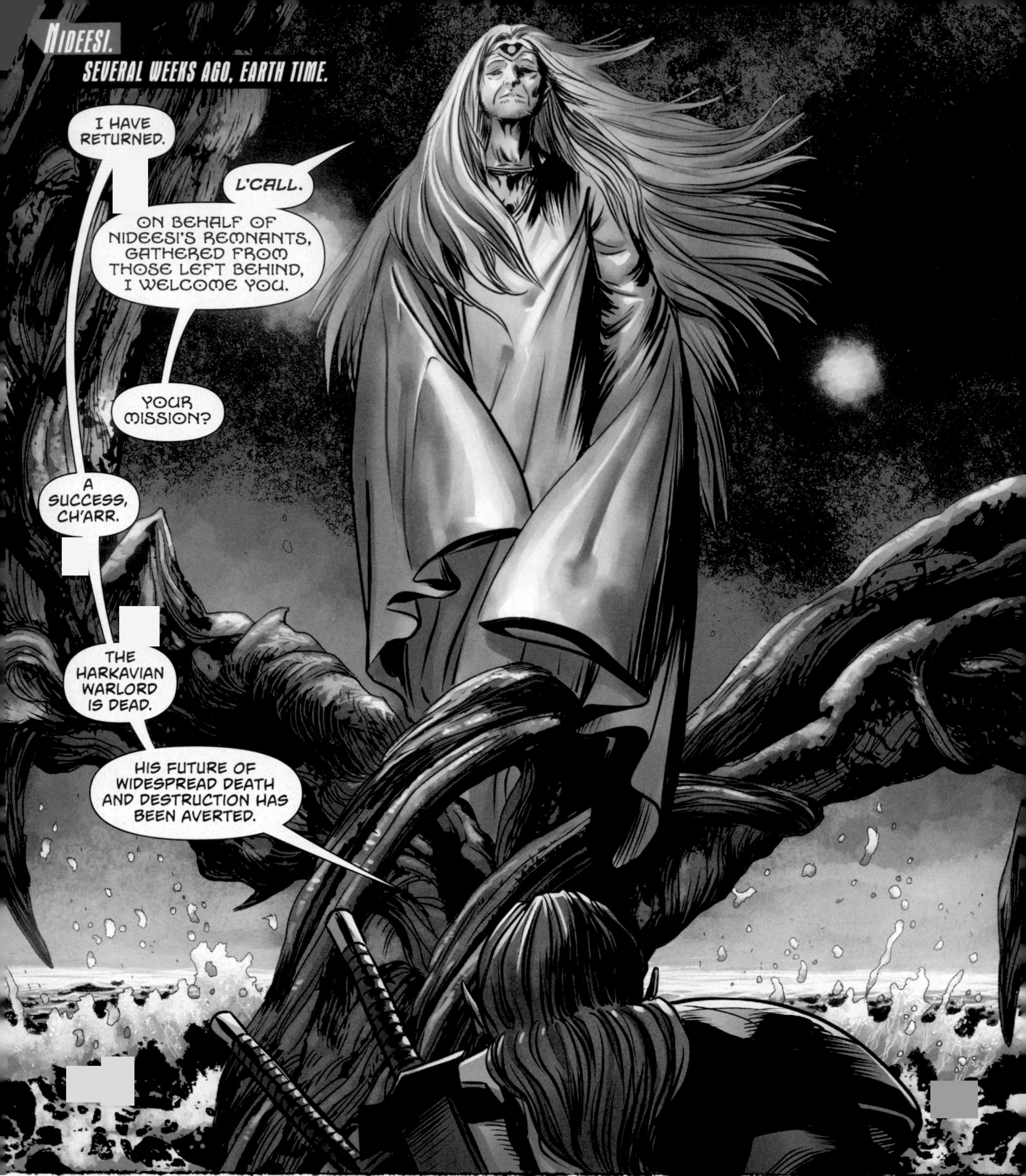
NIDEESI.
SEVERAL WEEKS AGO, EARTH TIME.
I HAVE RETURNED.
L'CALL.
ON BEHALF OF NIDEESI'S REMNANTS, GATHERED FROM THOSE LEFT BEHIND, I WELCOME YOU.
YOUR MISSION?
A SUCCESS, CH'ARR.
THE HARKAVIAN WARLORD IS DEAD.
HIS FUTURE OF WIDESPREAD DEATH AND DESTRUCTION HAS BEEN AVERTED.

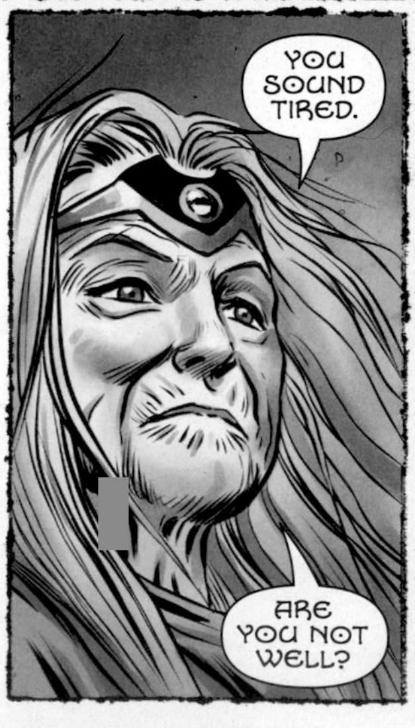
YOU SOUND TIRED.
ARE YOU NOT WELL?

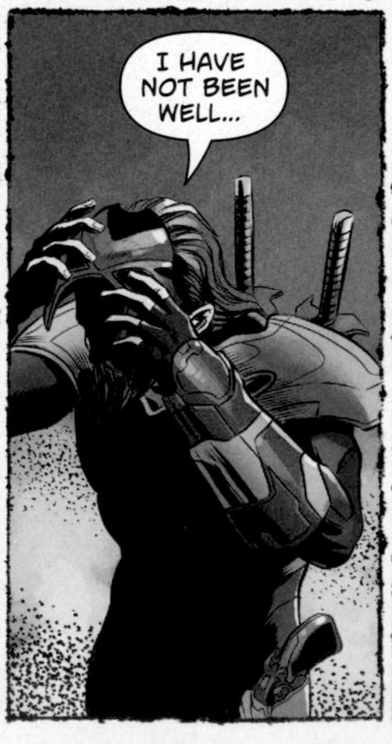
I HAVE NOT BEEN WELL...

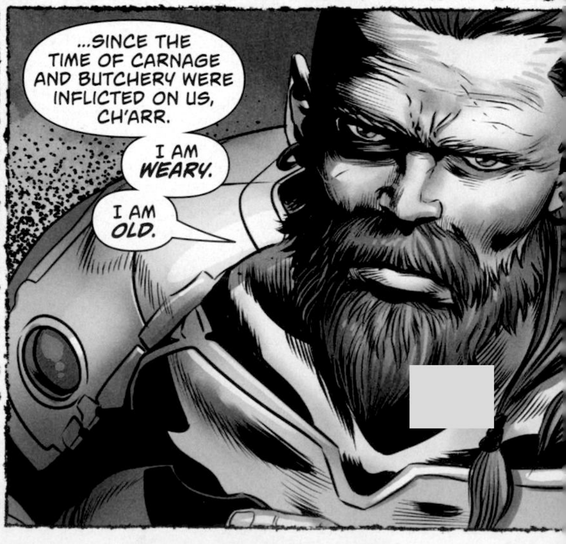
...SINCE THE TIME OF CARNAGE AND BUTCHERY WERE INFLICTED ON US, CH'ARR.
I AM *WEARY.*
I AM *OLD.*

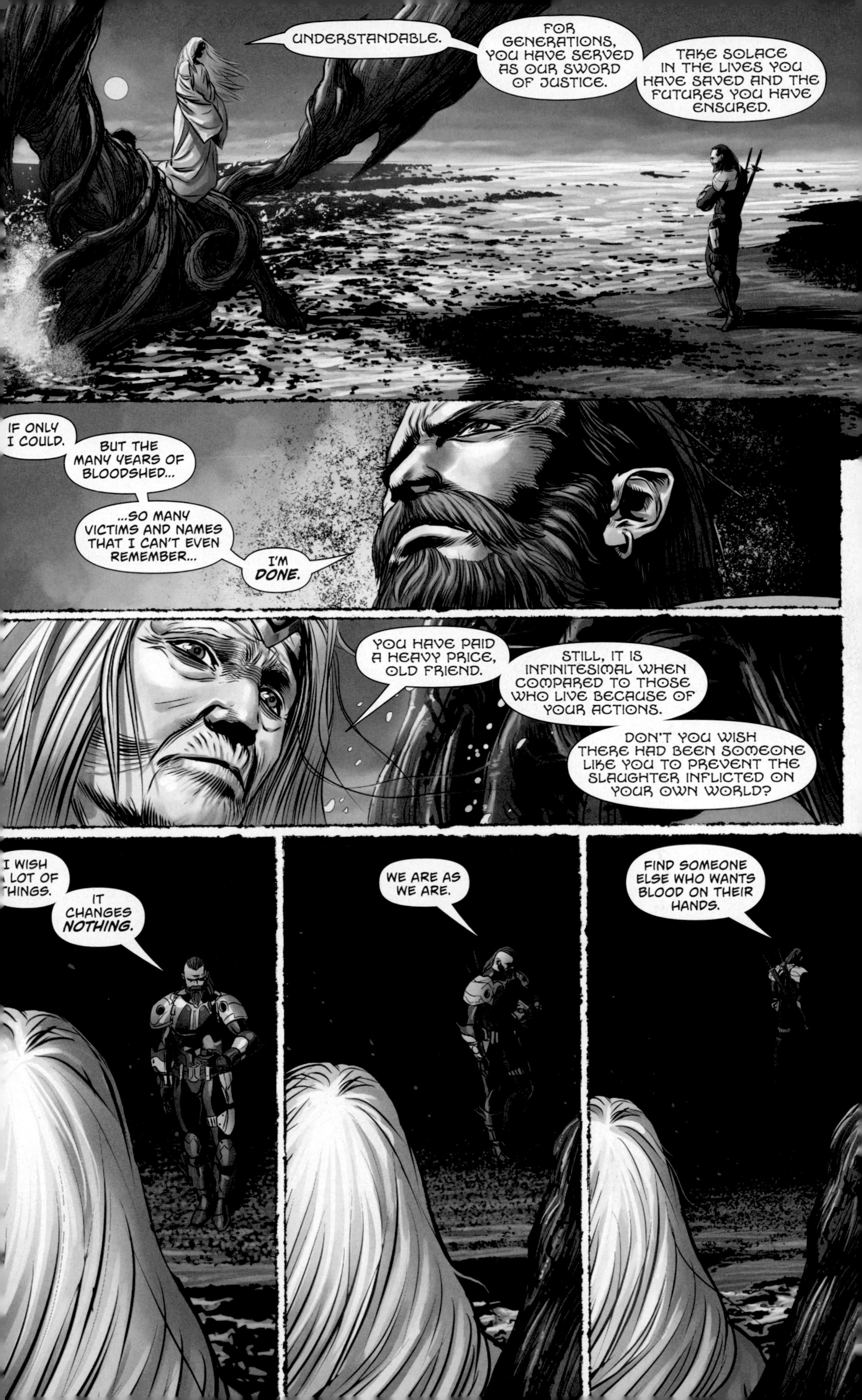
UNDERSTANDABLE.
FOR GENERATIONS, YOU HAVE SERVED AS OUR SWORD OF JUSTICE.
TAKE SOLACE IN THE LIVES YOU HAVE SAVED AND THE FUTURES YOU HAVE ENSURED.
IF ONLY I COULD.
BUT THE MANY YEARS OF BLOODSHED...
...SO MANY VICTIMS AND NAMES THAT I CAN'T EVEN REMEMBER...
I'M *DONE.*
YOU HAVE PAID A HEAVY PRICE, OLD FRIEND.
STILL, IT IS INFINITESIMAL WHEN COMPARED TO THOSE WHO LIVE BECAUSE OF YOUR ACTIONS.
DON'T YOU WISH THERE HAD BEEN SOMEONE LIKE YOU TO PREVENT THE SLAUGHTER INFLICTED ON YOUR OWN WORLD?
I WISH LOT OF HINGS.
IT CHANGES *NOTHING.*
WE ARE AS WE ARE.
FIND SOMEONE ELSE WHO WANTS BLOOD ON THEIR HANDS.

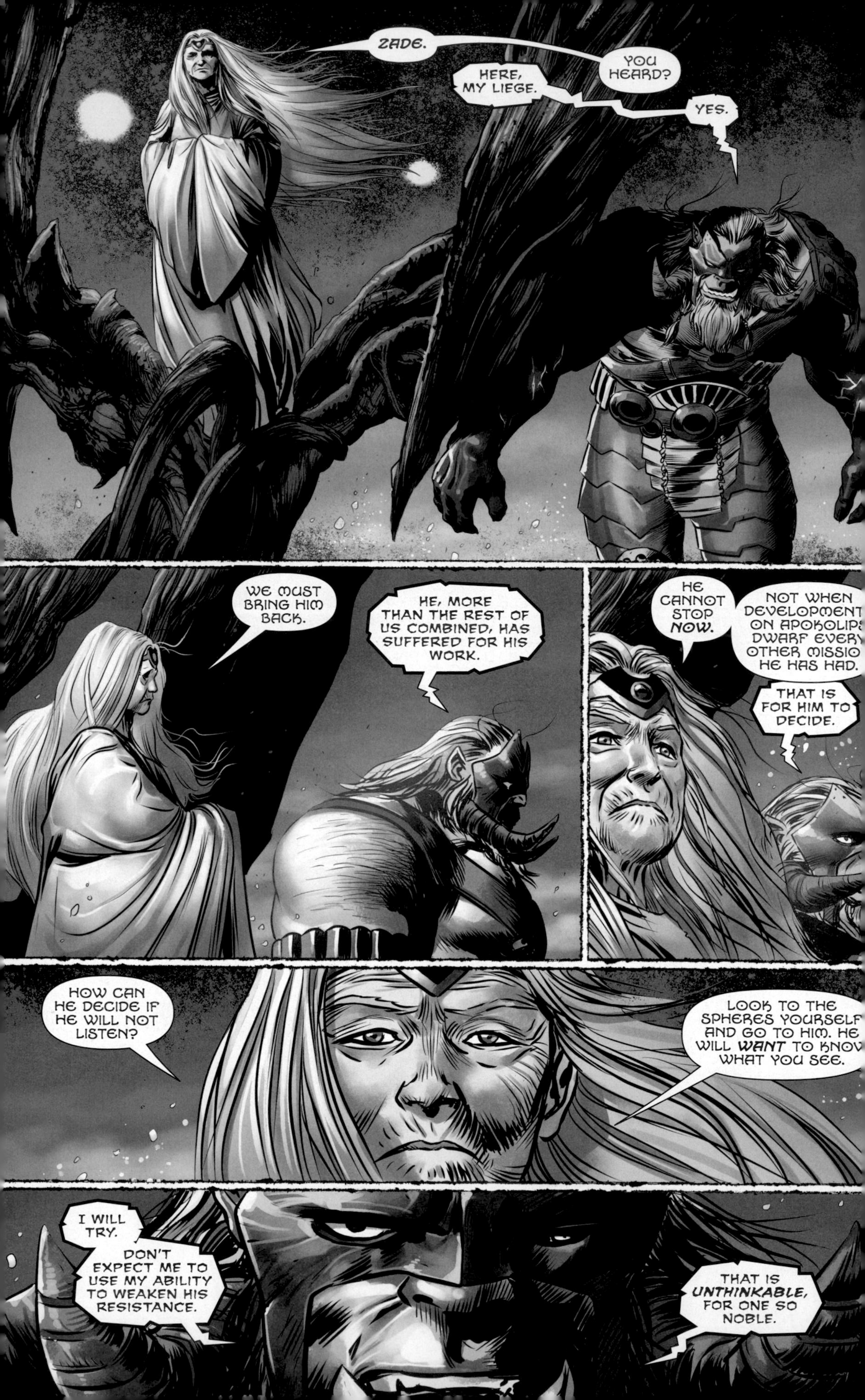
ZADE.
YOU HEARD?
HERE, MY LIEGE.
YES.
WE MUST BRING HIM BACK.
HE, MORE THAN THE REST OF US COMBINED, HAS SUFFERED FOR HIS WORK.
HE CANNOT STOP NOW.
NOT WHEN DEVELOPMENT ON APOKOLIPS DWARF EVERY OTHER MISSIO HE HAS HAD.
THAT IS FOR HIM TO DECIDE.
HOW CAN HE DECIDE IF HE WILL NOT LISTEN?
LOOK TO THE SPHERES YOURSELF AND GO TO HIM. HE WILL WANT TO KNOV WHAT YOU SEE.
I WILL TRY.
DON'T EXPECT ME TO USE MY ABILITY TO WEAKEN HIS RESISTANCE.
THAT IS UNTHINKABLE, FOR ONE SO NOBLE.

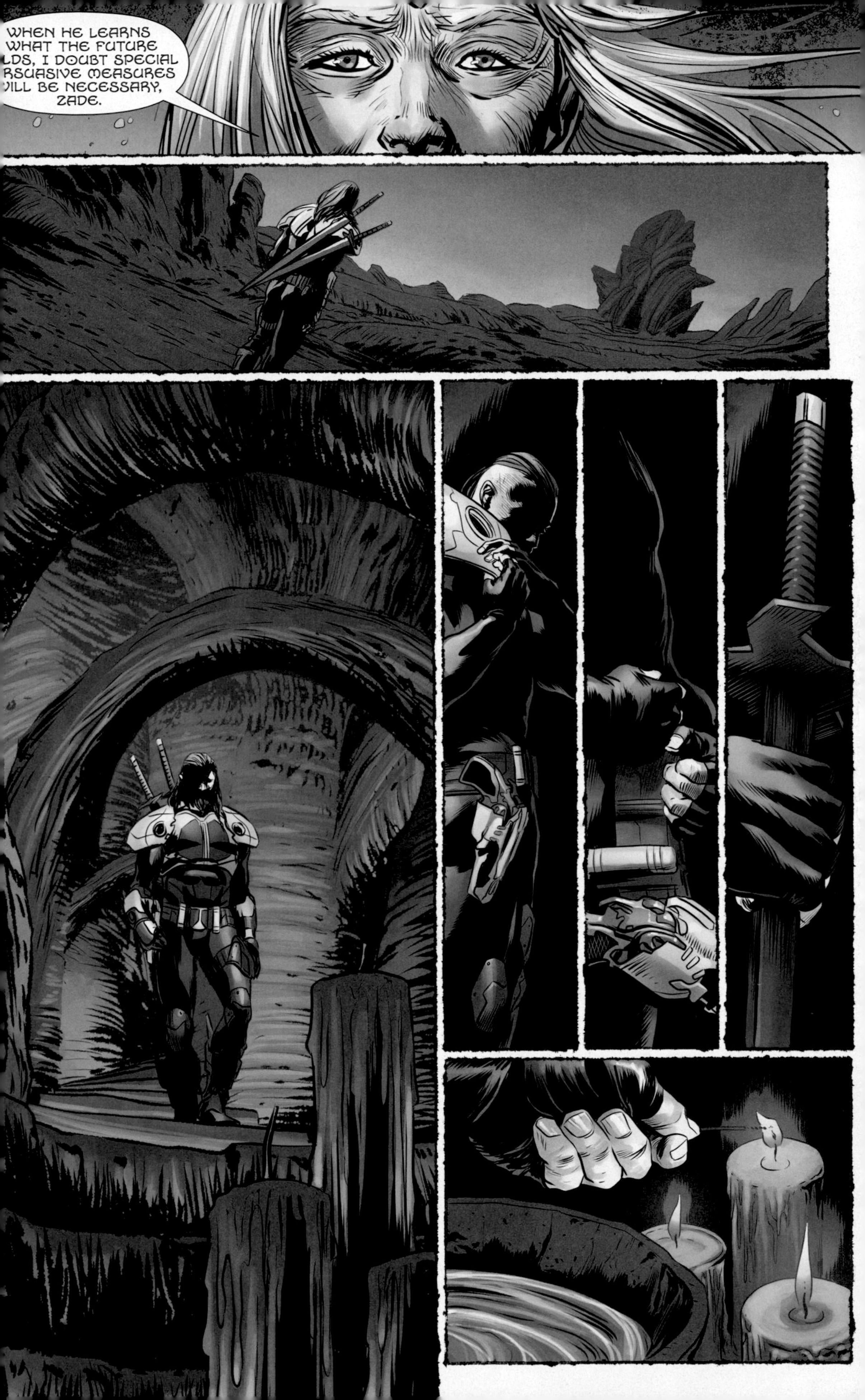
WHEN HE LEARNS WHAT THE FUTURE LDS, I DOUBT SPECIAL RSUASIVE MEASURES VILL BE NECESSARY, ZADE.

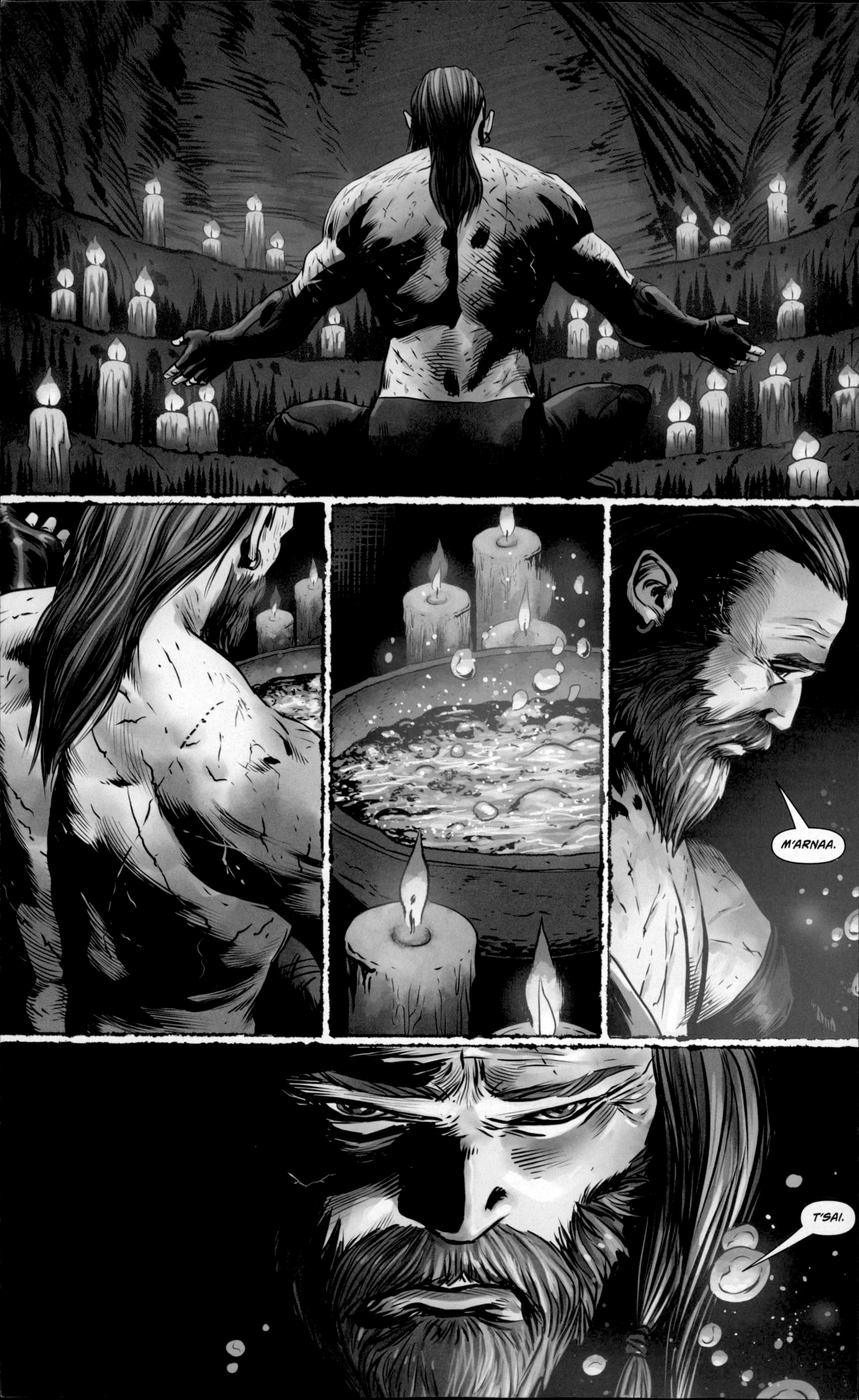
M'ARNAA.
T'SAI.

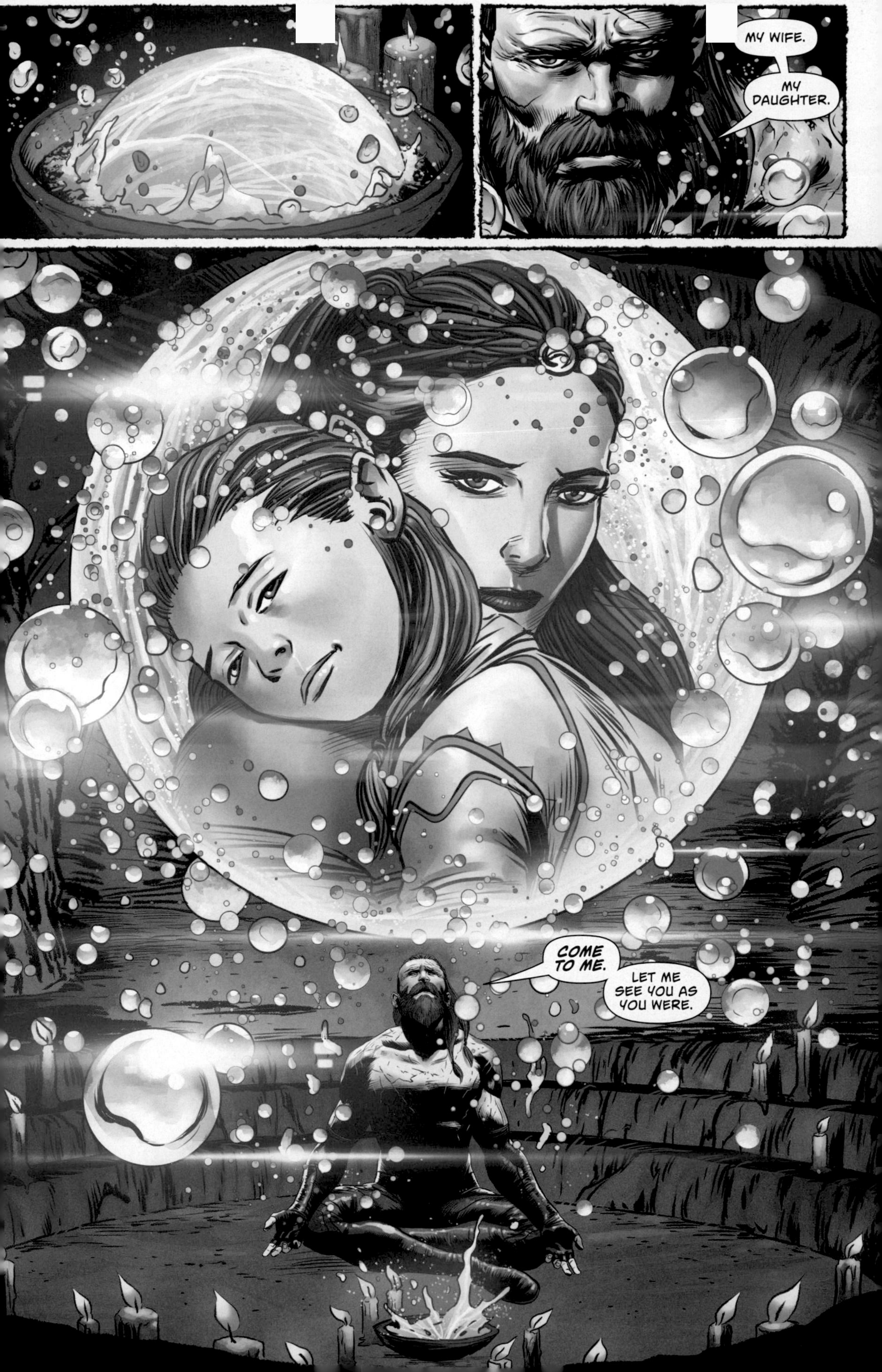

MY WIFE.
MY DAUGHTER.
COME TO ME.
LET ME SEE YOU AS YOU WERE.

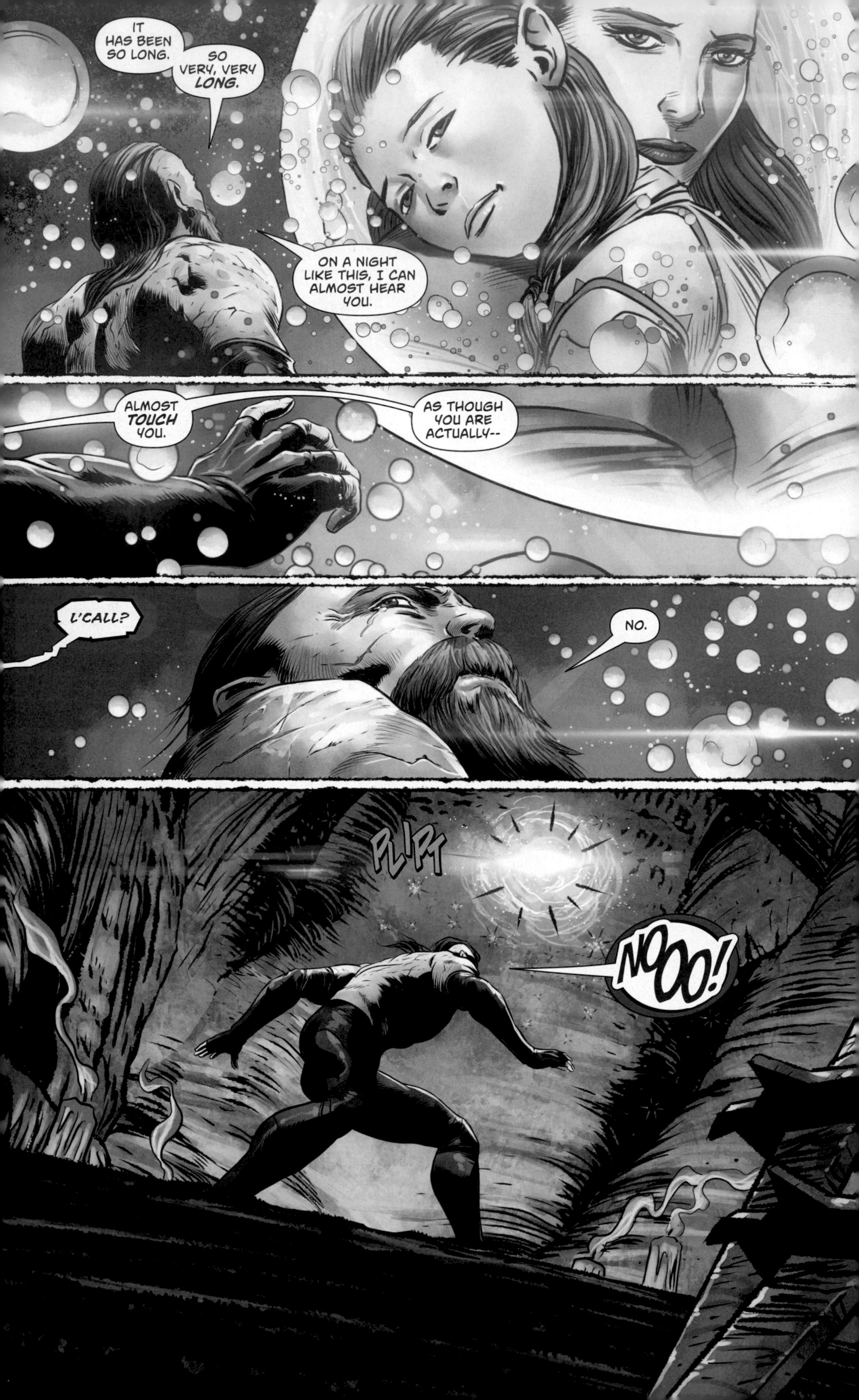
IT HAS BEEN SO LONG.
SO VERY, VERY LONG.
ON A NIGHT LIKE THIS, I CAN ALMOST HEAR YOU.
ALMOST TOUCH YOU.
AS THOUGH YOU ARE ACTUALLY--
L'CALL?
NO.
PLIPT
NOOO!

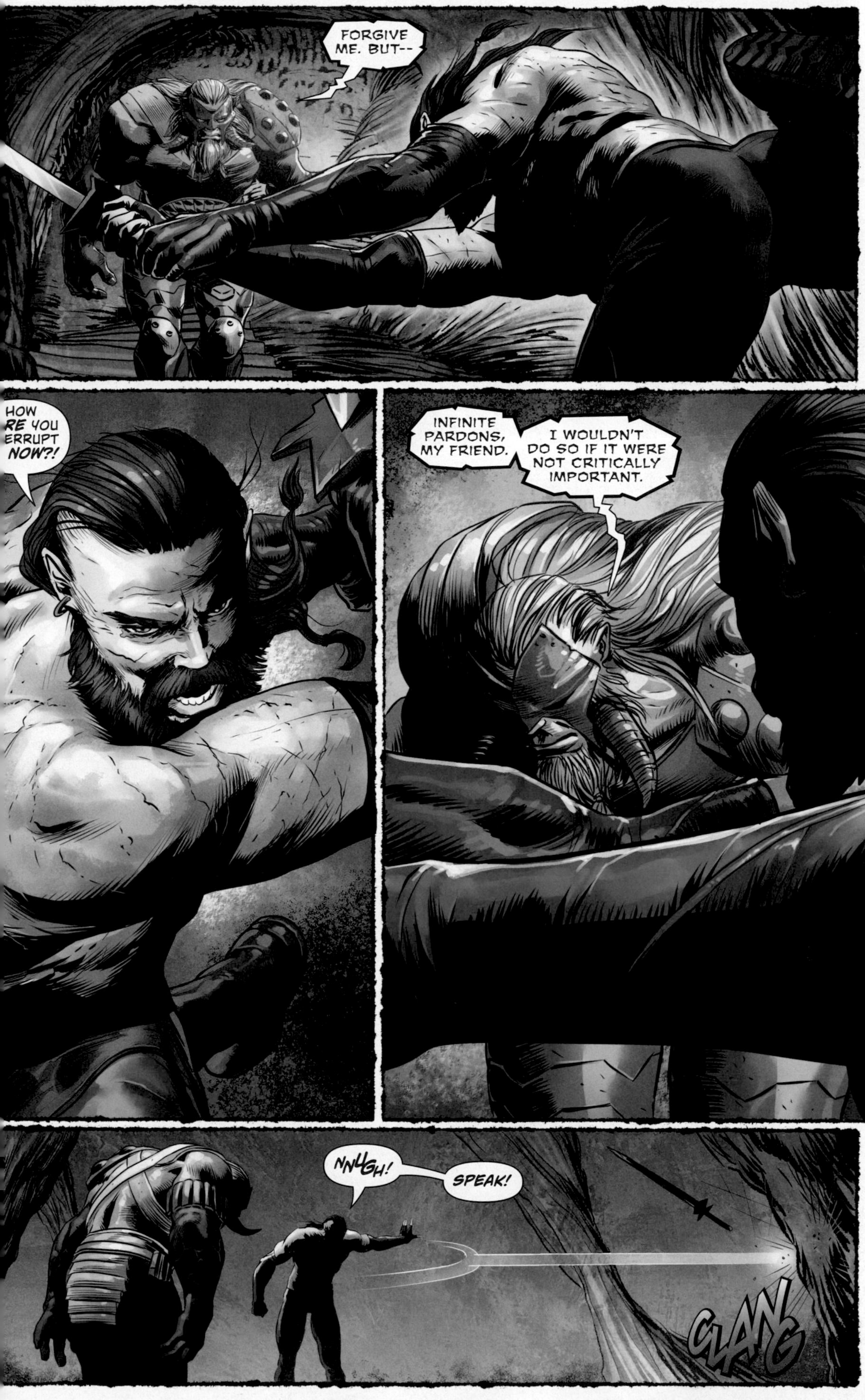
FORGIVE ME. BUT--
HOW RE YOU ERRUPT NOW?!
INFINITE PARDONS, MY FRIEND.
I WOULDN'T DO SO IF IT WERE NOT CRITICALLY IMPORTANT.
NNUGH!
SPEAK!
CLANG

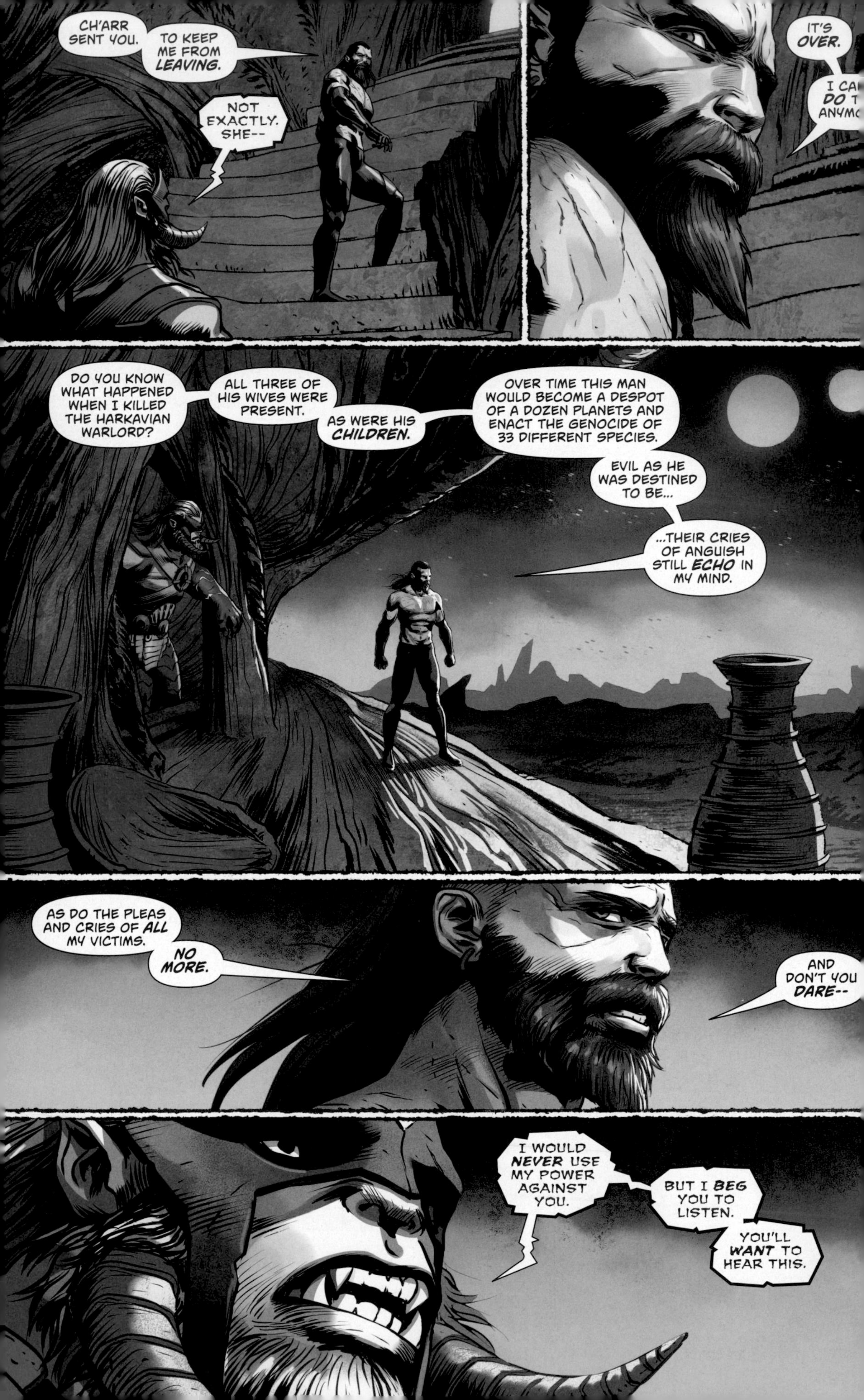
CH'ARR SENT YOU.
TO KEEP ME FROM LEAVING.
NOT EXACTLY. SHE--
IT'S OVER.
DO YOU KNOW WHAT HAPPENED WHEN I KILLED THE HARKAVIAN WARLORD?
ALL THREE OF HIS WIVES WERE PRESENT.
AS WERE HIS CHILDREN.
OVER TIME THIS MAN WOULD BECOME A DESPOT OF A DOZEN PLANETS AND ENACT THE GENOCIDE OF 33 DIFFERENT SPECIES.
EVIL AS HE WAS DESTINED TO BE...
...THEIR CRIES OF ANGUISH STILL ECHO IN MY MIND.
AS DO THE PLEAS AND CRIES OF ALL MY VICTIMS.
NO MORE.
AND DON'T YOU DARE--
I WOULD NEVER USE MY POWER AGAINST YOU.
BUT I BEG YOU TO LISTEN.
YOU'LL WANT TO HEAR THIS.

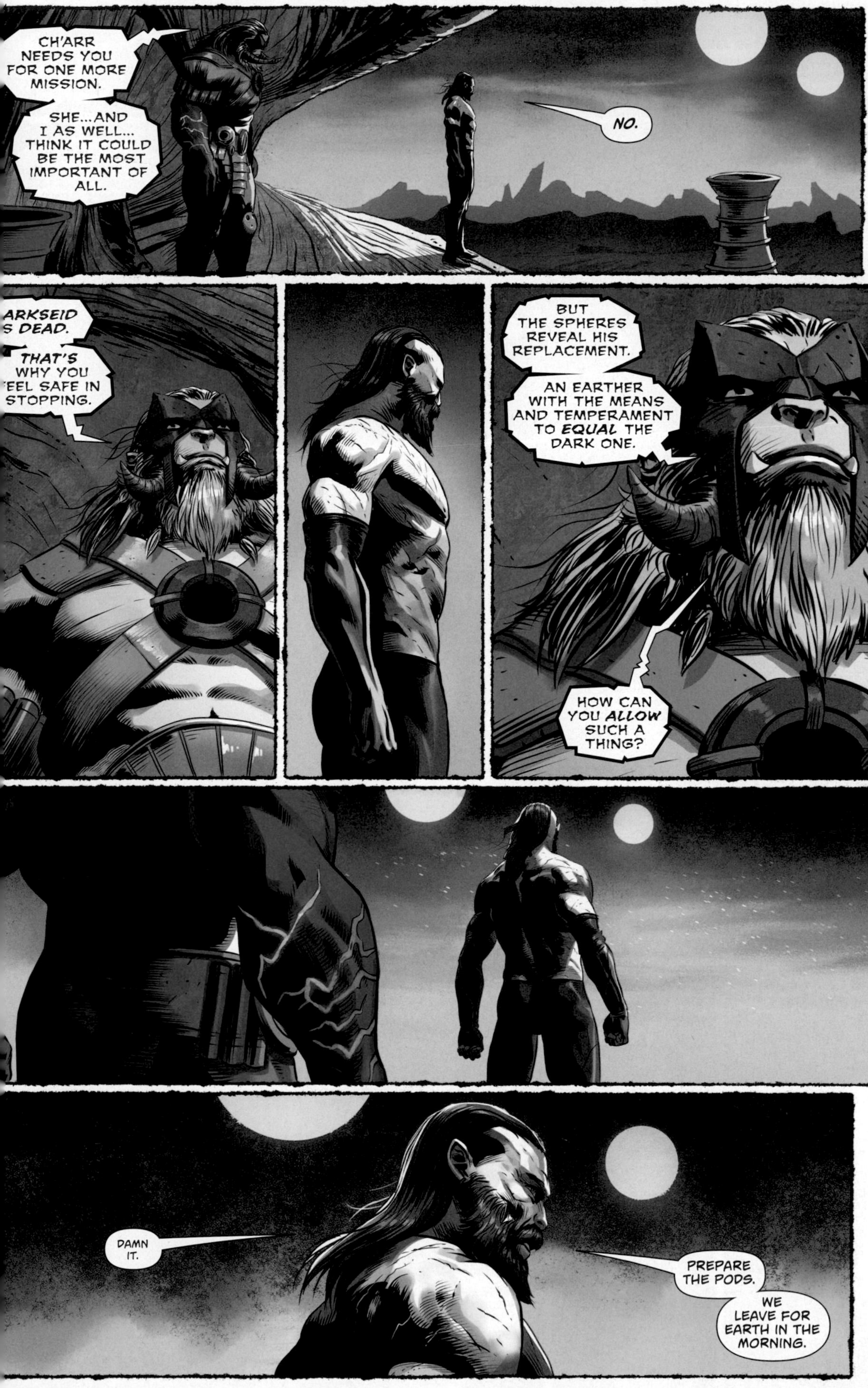
CH'ARR NEEDS YOU FOR ONE MORE MISSION.
SHE...AND I AS WELL... THINK IT COULD BE THE MOST IMPORTANT OF ALL.
NO.
ARKSEID S DEAD.
THAT'S WHY YOU FEEL SAFE IN STOPPING.
BUT THE SPHERES REVEAL HIS REPLACEMENT.
AN EARTHER WITH THE MEANS AND TEMPERAMENT TO EQUAL THE DARK ONE.
HOW CAN YOU ALLOW SUCH A THING?
DAMN IT.
PREPARE THE PODS.
WE LEAVE FOR EARTH IN THE MORNING.

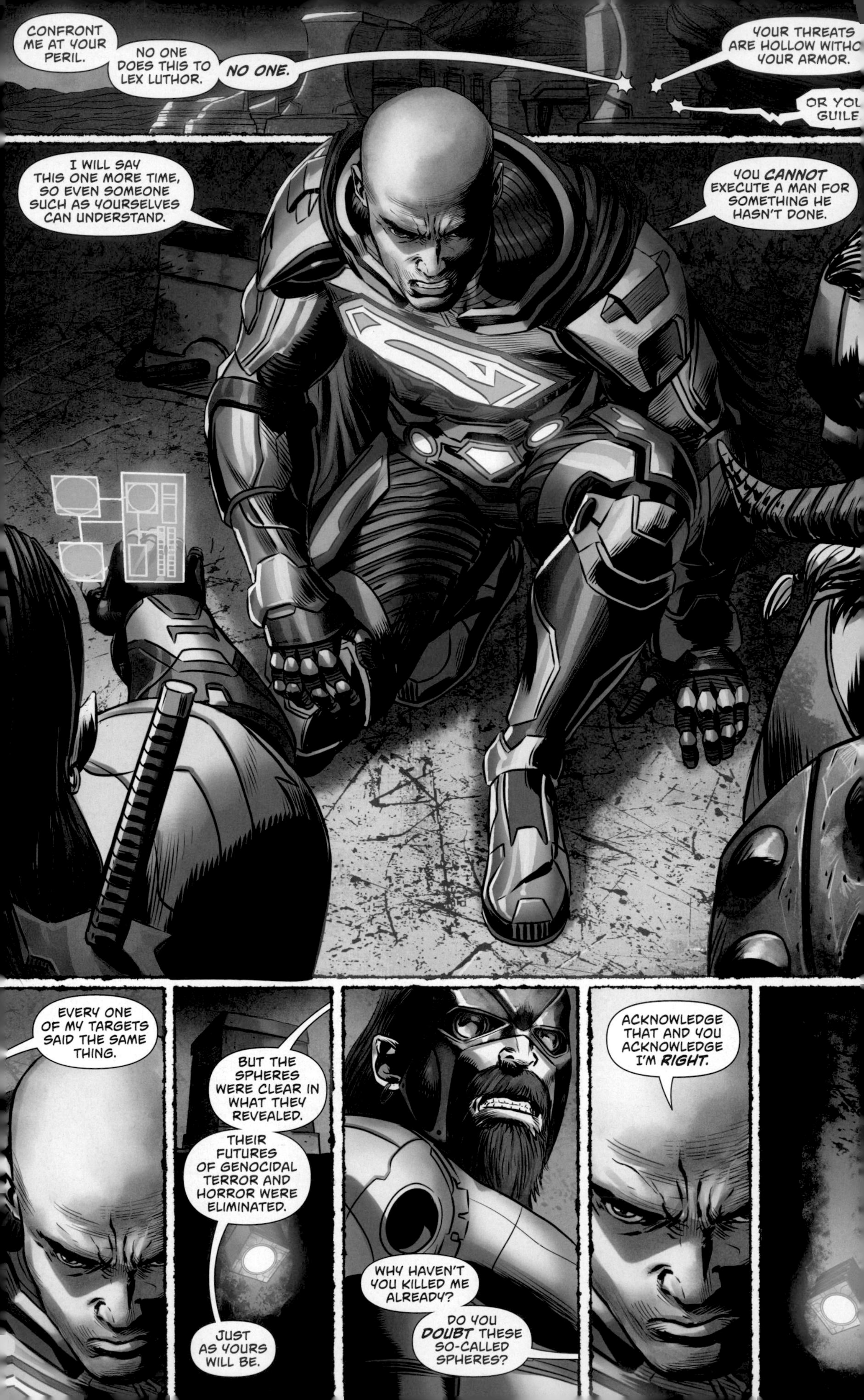
CONFRONT ME AT YOUR PERIL.
NO ONE DOES THIS TO LEX LUTHOR.
NO ONE.
YOUR THREATS ARE HOLLOW WITHO YOUR ARMOR.
OR YOU GUILE
I WILL SAY THIS ONE MORE TIME, SO EVEN SOMEONE SUCH AS YOURSELVES CAN UNDERSTAND.
YOU CANNOT EXECUTE A MAN FOR SOMETHING HE HASN'T DONE.
EVERY ONE OF MY TARGETS SAID THE SAME THING.
BUT THE SPHERES WERE CLEAR IN WHAT THEY REVEALED.
THEIR FUTURES OF GENOCIDAL TERROR AND HORROR WERE ELIMINATED.
JUST AS YOURS WILL BE.
WHY HAVEN'T YOU KILLED ME ALREADY?
DO YOU DOUBT THESE SO-CALLED SPHERES?
ACKNOWLEDGE THAT AND YOU ACKNOWLEDGE I'M RIGHT.

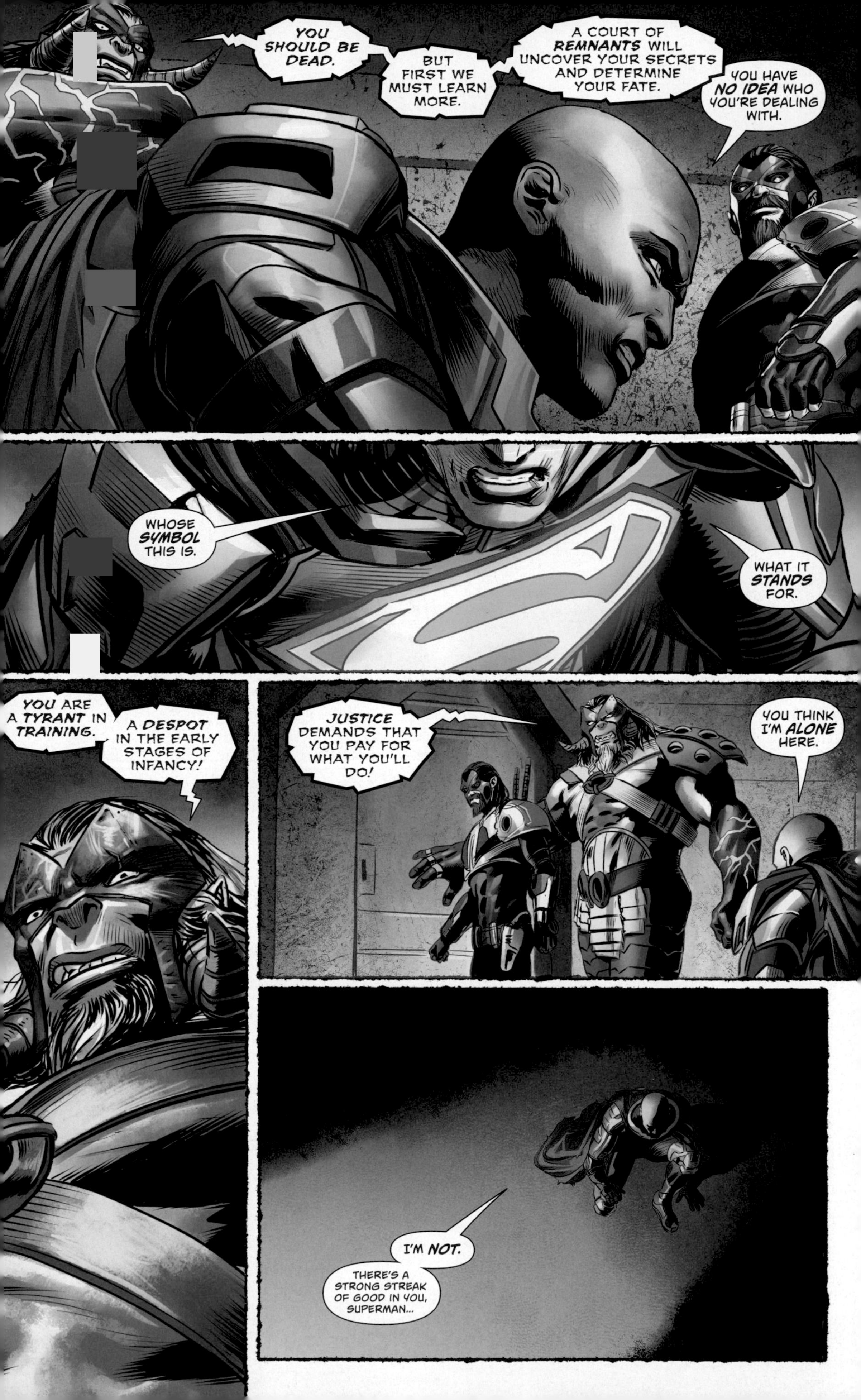
YOU SHOULD BE DEAD.
BUT FIRST WE MUST LEARN MORE.
A COURT OF REMNANTS WILL UNCOVER YOUR SECRETS AND DETERMINE YOUR FATE.
YOU HAVE NO IDEA WHO YOU'RE DEALING WITH.
WHOSE SYMBOL THIS IS.
WHAT IT STANDS FOR.
YOU ARE A TYRANT IN TRAINING.
A DESPOT IN THE EARLY STAGES OF INFANCY!
JUSTICE DEMANDS THAT YOU PAY FOR WHAT YOU'LL DO!
YOU THINK I'M ALONE HERE.
I'M NOT.
THERE'S A STRONG STREAK OF GOOD IN YOU, SUPERMAN...

"...YOU'LL COME FOR ME..."

WHEN GODSLAYER TRANSPORTS, HE EXHIBITS A UNIQUE FORM OF ENERGY.

I'VE SEEN THAT ENERGY BEFORE-- IN RESIDUAL FORM, ANYWAY.

IT WAS LEFT BEHIND AFTER THE GENETICRON BUILDING WAS TAKEN.

I COULDN'T UNDERSTAND WHY SOMEONE WOULD TAKE AN OFFICE BUILDING AND DROP IT IN THE AMAZON.

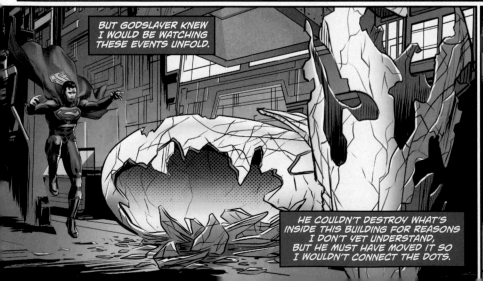

BUT GODSLAYER KNEW I WOULD BE WATCHING THESE EVENTS UNFOLD.

HE COULDN'T DESTROY WHAT'S INSIDE THIS BUILDING FOR REASONS I DON'T YET UNDERSTAND, BUT HE MUST HAVE MOVED IT SO I WOULDN'T CONNECT THE DOTS.

AND REALIZE HE BEEN HERE, JU AS DOOMSDAY W

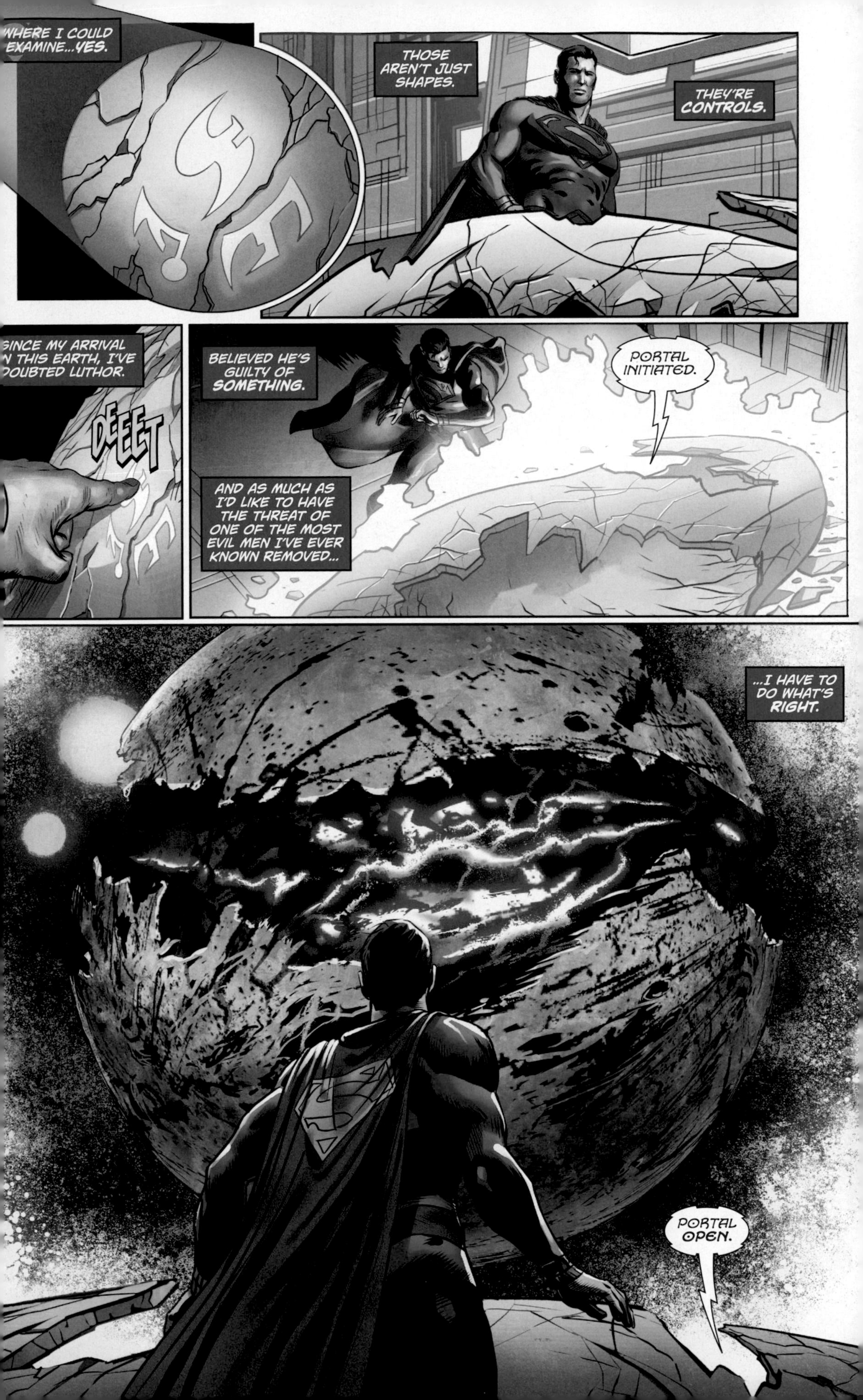
WHERE I COULD EXAMINE...YES.
THOSE AREN'T JUST SHAPES.
THEY'RE CONTROLS.
SINCE MY ARRIVAL ON THIS EARTH, I'VE DOUBTED LUTHOR.
DEEET
BELIEVED HE'S GUILTY OF SOMETHING.
PORTAL INITIATED.
AND AS MUCH AS I'D LIKE TO HAVE THE THREAT OF ONE OF THE MOST EVIL MEN I'VE EVER KNOWN REMOVED...
...I HAVE TO DO WHAT'S RIGHT.
PORTAL OPEN.

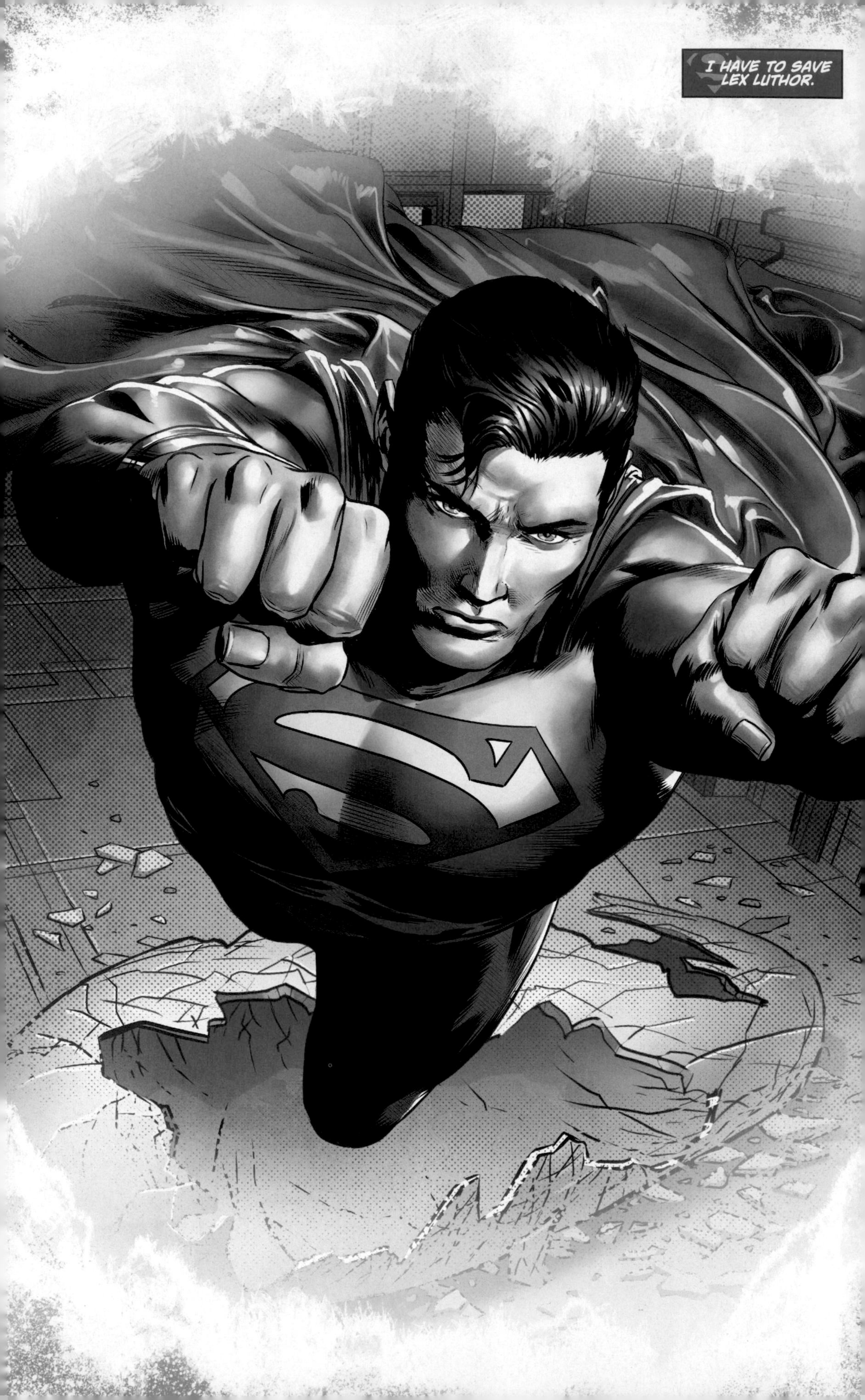
I HAVE TO SAVE LEX LUTHOR.

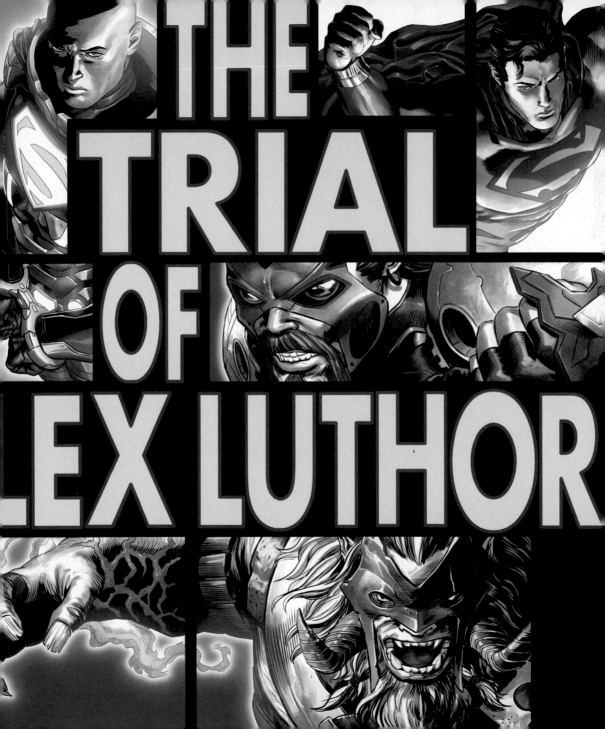

THE TRIAL OF LEX LUTHOR

MEN OF STEEL PART 4
PATCH ZIRCHER artist * **ULISES ARREOLA** colorist
PATCH ZIRCHER ARIF PRIANTO cover artists

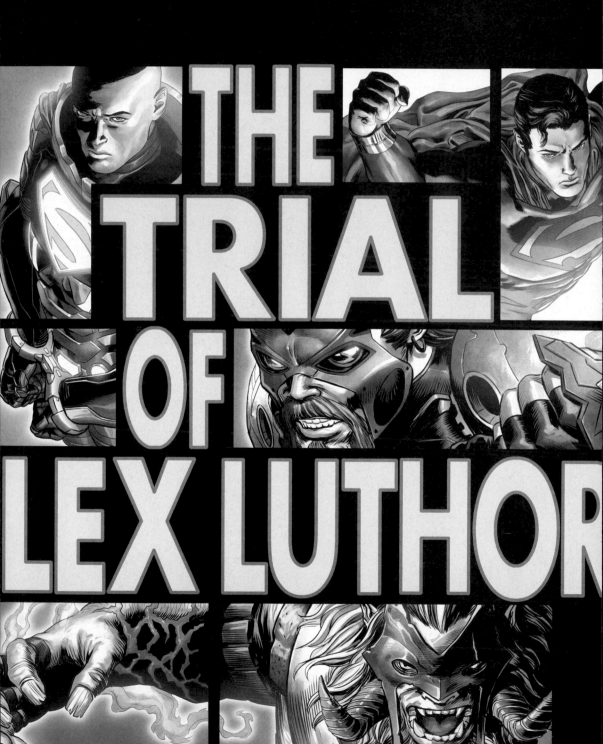

THE TRIAL OF LEX LUTHOR

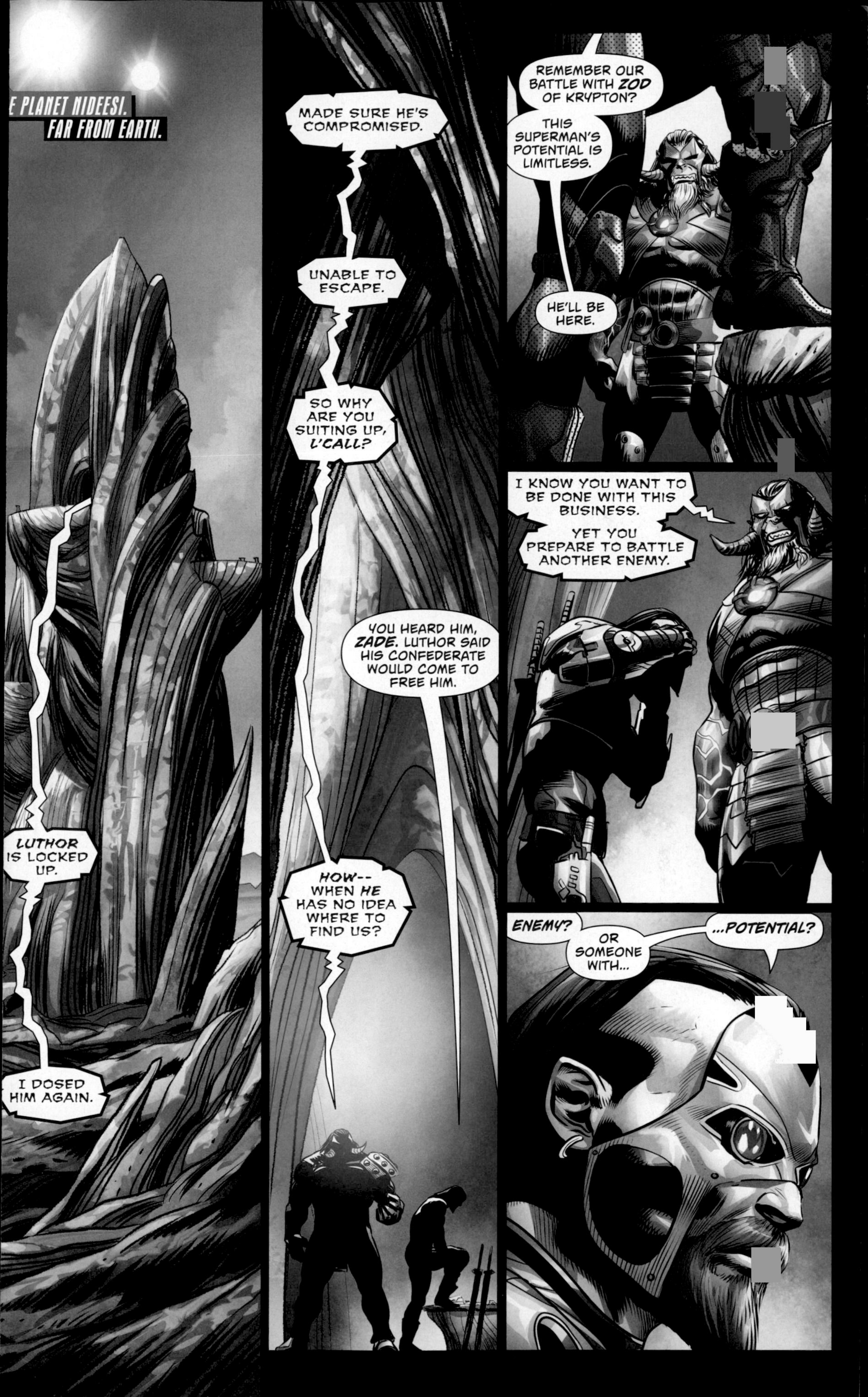
E PLANET NIDEESI.
FAR FROM EARTH.
LUTHOR IS LOCKED UP.
I DOSED HIM AGAIN.
MADE SURE HE'S COMPROMISED.
UNABLE TO ESCAPE.
SO WHY ARE YOU SUITING UP, L'CALL?
YOU HEARD HIM, ZADE. LUTHOR SAID HIS CONFEDERATE WOULD COME TO FREE HIM.
HOW--WHEN HE HAS NO IDEA WHERE TO FIND US?
REMEMBER OUR BATTLE WITH ZOD OF KRYPTON?
THIS SUPERMAN'S POTENTIAL IS LIMITLESS.
HE'LL BE HERE.
I KNOW YOU WANT TO BE DONE WITH THIS BUSINESS.
YET YOU PREPARE TO BATTLE ANOTHER ENEMY.
ENEMY?
OR SOMEONE WITH...
...POTENTIAL?

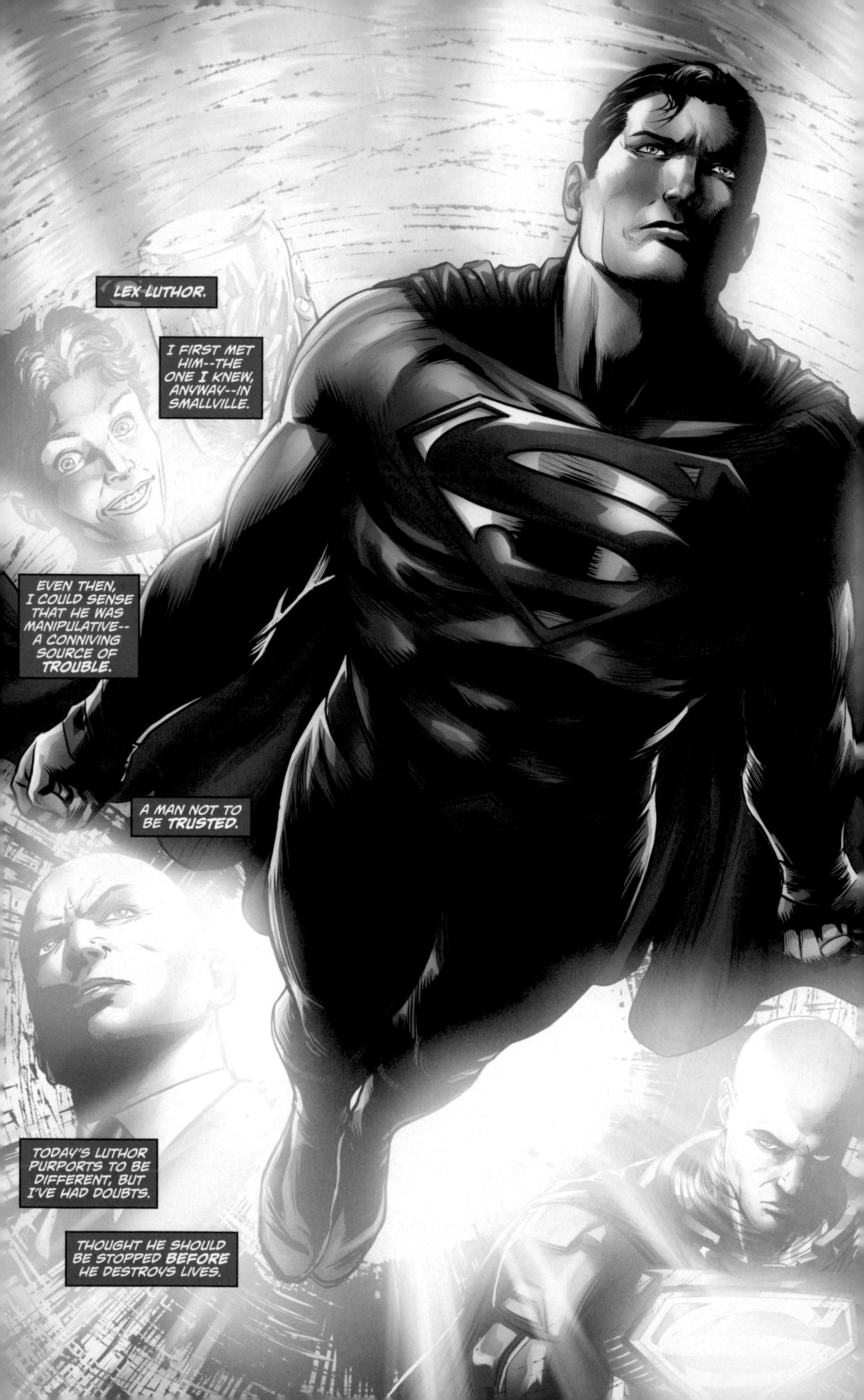
LEX LUTHOR.
I FIRST MET HIM--THE ONE I KNEW, ANYWAY--IN SMALLVILLE.
EVEN THEN, I COULD SENSE THAT HE WAS MANIPULATIVE--A CONNIVING SOURCE OF TROUBLE.
A MAN NOT TO BE TRUSTED.
TODAY'S LUTHOR PURPORTS TO BE DIFFERENT, BUT I'VE HAD DOUBTS.
THOUGHT HE SHOULD BE STOPPED BEFORE HE DESTROYS LIVES.

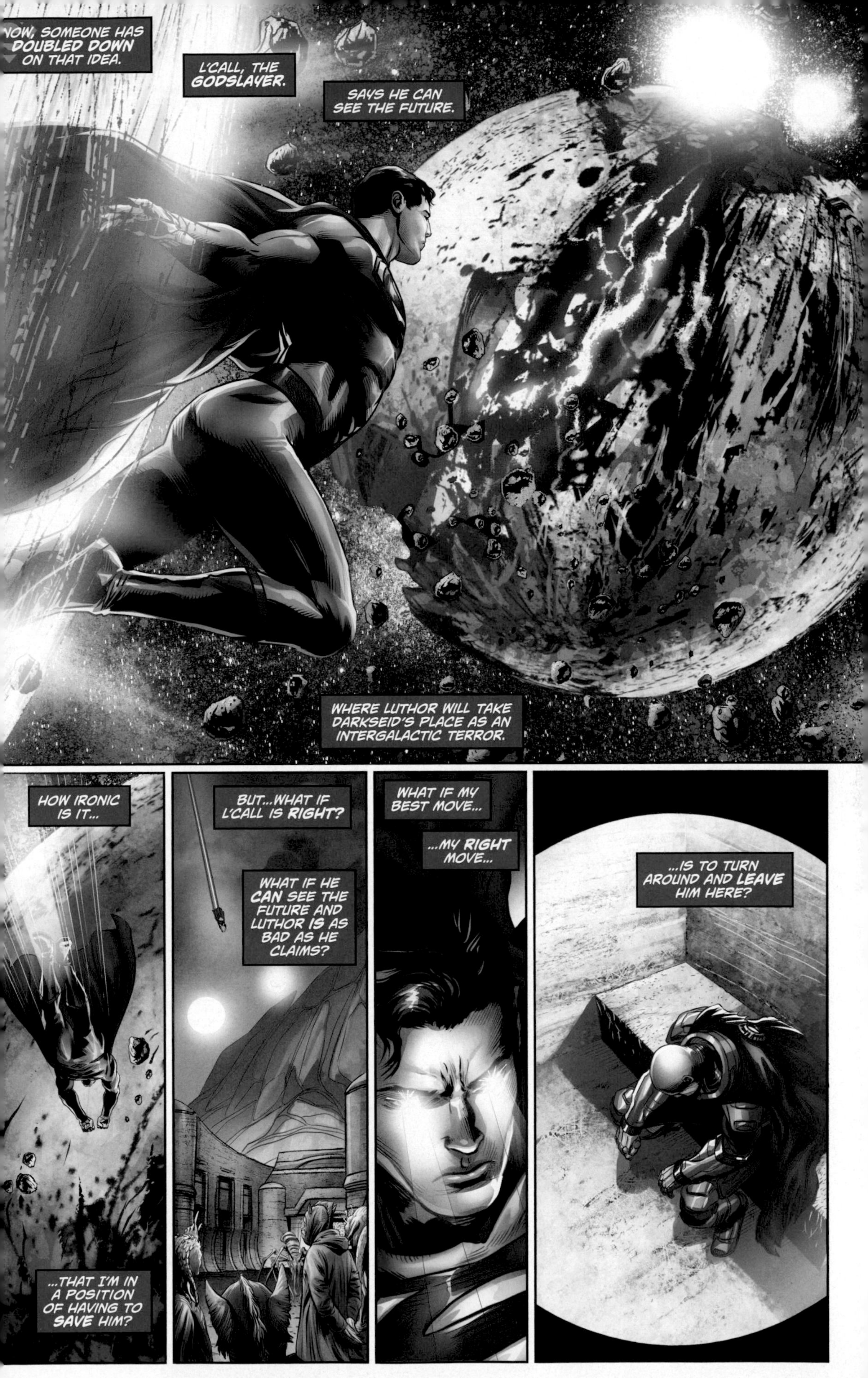
NOW, SOMEONE HAS DOUBLED DOWN ON THAT IDEA.
L'CALL, THE GODSLAYER.
SAYS HE CAN SEE THE FUTURE.
WHERE LUTHOR WILL TAKE DARKSEID'S PLACE AS AN INTERGALACTIC TERROR.
HOW IRONIC IS IT...
...THAT I'M IN A POSITION OF HAVING TO SAVE HIM?
BUT...WHAT IF L'CALL IS RIGHT?
WHAT IF HE CAN SEE THE FUTURE AND LUTHOR IS AS BAD AS HE CLAIMS?
WHAT IF MY BEST MOVE...
...MY RIGHT MOVE...
...IS TO TURN AROUND AND LEAVE HIM HERE?

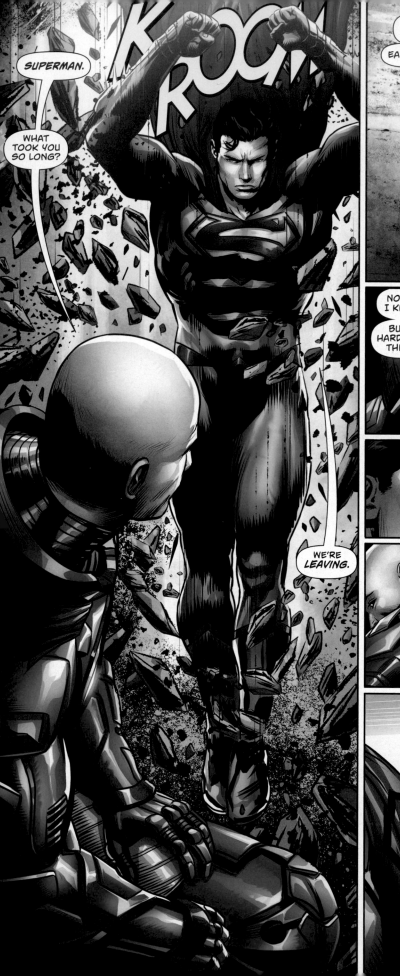

SUPERMAN.

WHAT TOOK YOU SO LONG?

WE'RE LEAVING.

TO GO... HOME?

EARTH...

WHAT'S WRONG WITH YOU?

ARE YOU DRUGGED OR--

NOT...THAT I KNOW OF.

BUT... HARD TO... THINK.

ZADE. HE WAS HERE...

HE DID SOMETHING TO WEAKEN ME ON EARTH.

I DON'T KNOW HOW YET, BUT EFFECTIVE.

EVEN MY ARMOR IS... COMPROMISED.

I THINK I KNOW THE CULPRIT.

SOME KIND OF NULLIFIER.

YOU SHOULD BE FINE NOW.

NGH!

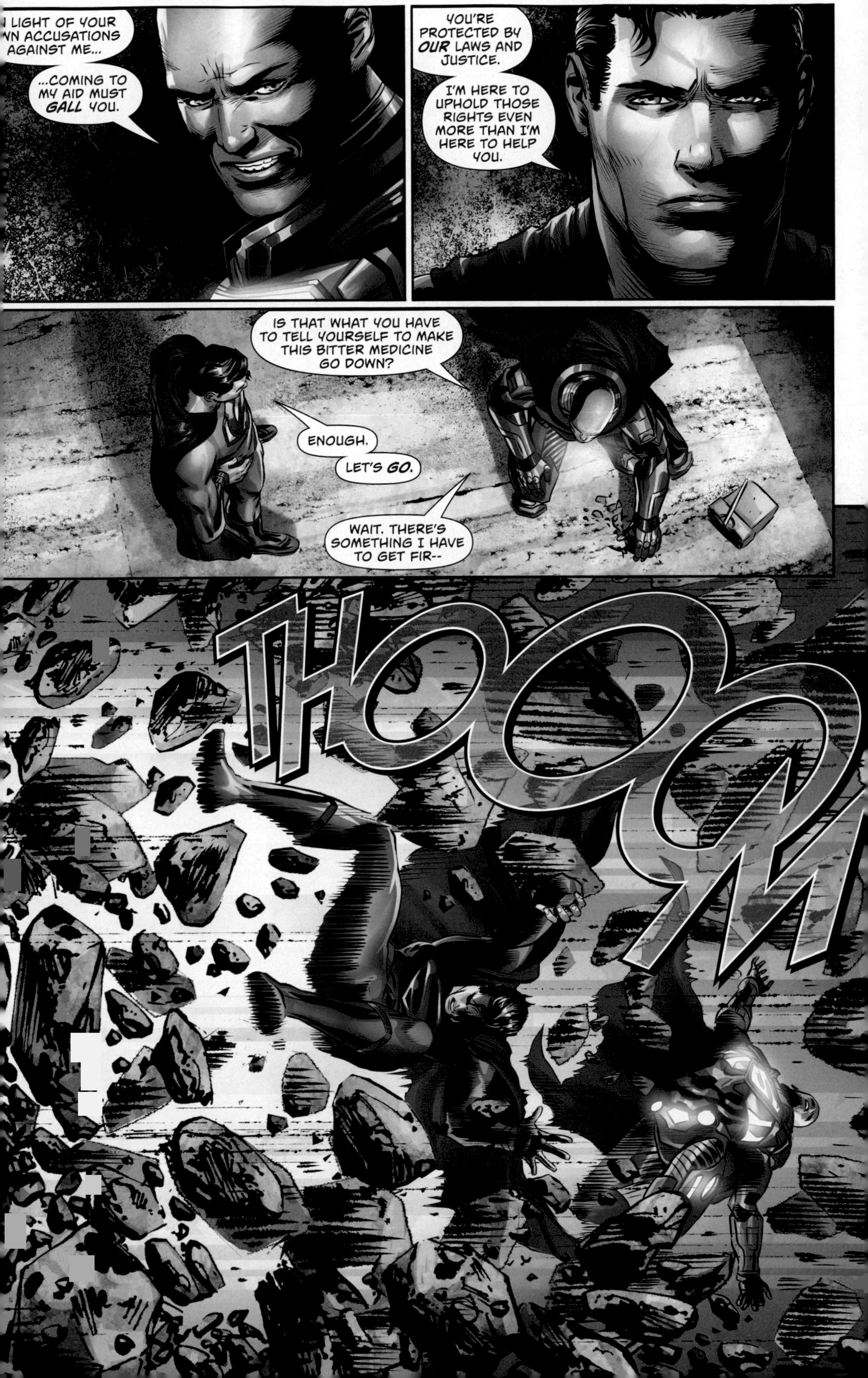

N LIGHT OF YOUR
WN ACCUSATIONS
AGAINST ME...
...COMING TO MY AID MUST GALL YOU.
YOU'RE PROTECTED BY OUR LAWS AND JUSTICE.
I'M HERE TO UPHOLD THOSE RIGHTS EVEN MORE THAN I'M HERE TO HELP YOU.
IS THAT WHAT YOU HAVE TO TELL YOURSELF TO MAKE THIS BITTER MEDICINE GO DOWN?
ENOUGH.
LET'S GO.
WAIT. THERE'S SOMETHING I HAVE TO GET FIR--
THOOOM

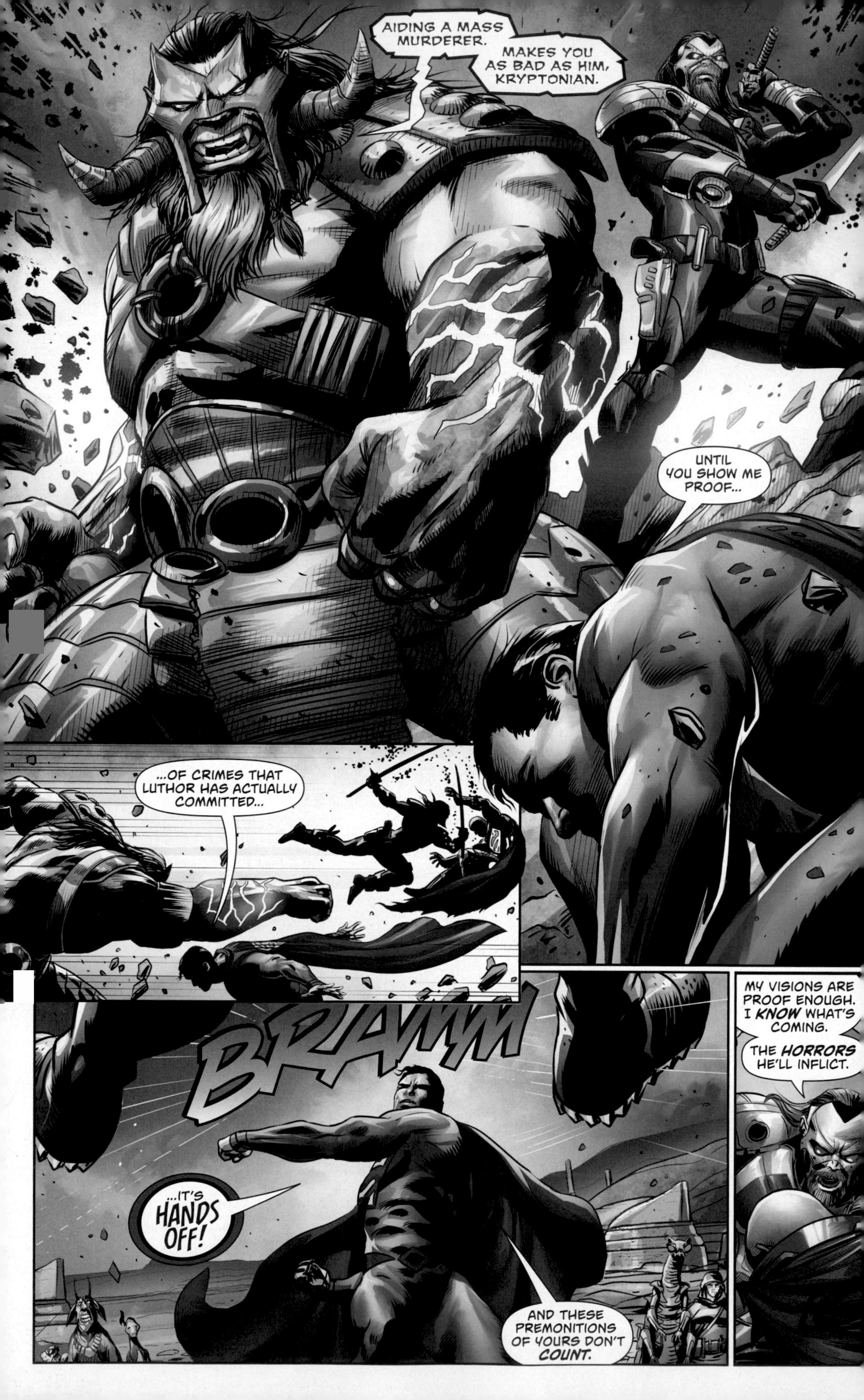
AIDING A MASS MURDERER.
MAKES YOU AS BAD AS HIM, KRYPTONIAN.
UNTIL YOU SHOW ME PROOF...
...OF CRIMES THAT LUTHOR HAS ACTUALLY COMMITTED...
BRAMM
...IT'S HANDS OFF!
AND THESE PREMONITIONS OF YOURS DON'T COUNT.
MY VISIONS ARE PROOF ENOUGH. I KNOW WHAT'S COMING.
THE HORRORS HE'LL INFLICT.

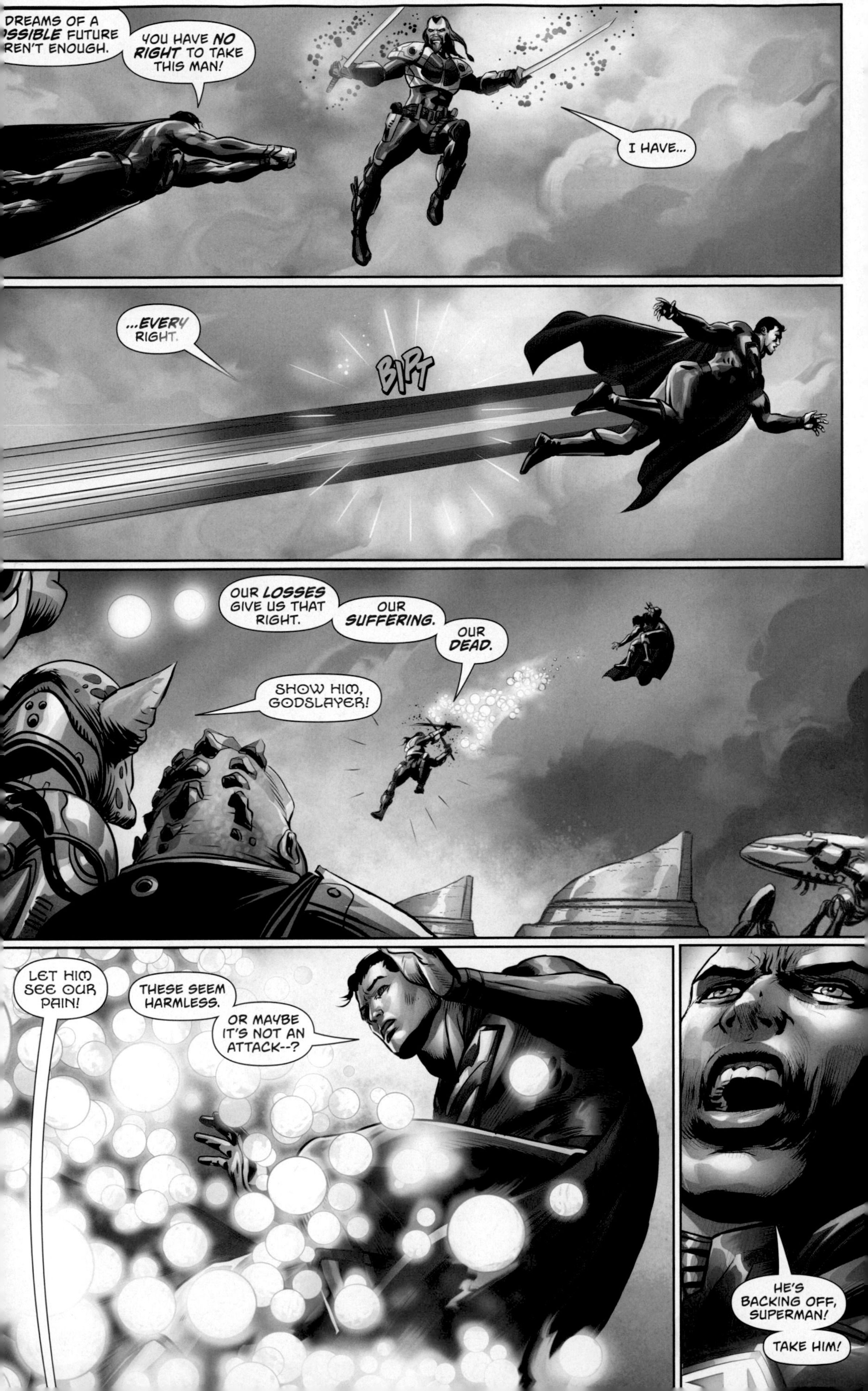

DREAMS OF A
...SSIBLE FUTURE
...REN'T ENOUGH.
YOU HAVE NO RIGHT TO TAKE THIS MAN!
I HAVE...
...EVERY RIGHT.
BIPT
OUR LOSSES GIVE US THAT RIGHT.
OUR SUFFERING.
OUR DEAD.
SHOW HIM, GODSLAYER!
LET HIM SEE OUR PAIN!
THESE SEEM HARMLESS.
OR MAYBE IT'S NOT AN ATTACK--?
HE'S BACKING OFF, SUPERMAN!
TAKE HIM!

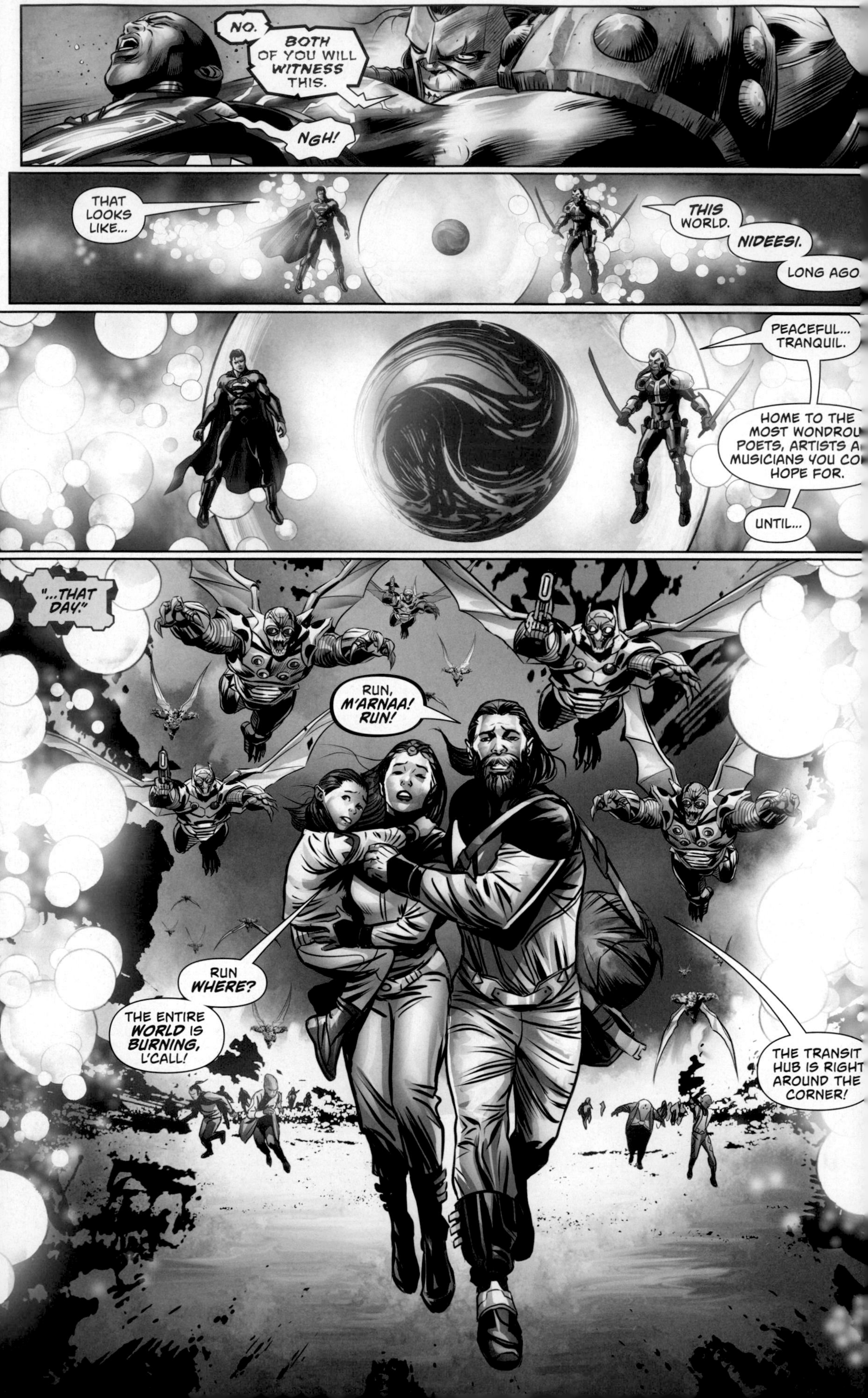
NO.
BOTH OF YOU WILL WITNESS THIS.
NGH!
THAT LOOKS LIKE...
THIS WORLD.
NIDEESI.
LONG AGO
PEACEFUL... TRANQUIL.
HOME TO THE MOST WONDROU POETS, ARTISTS A MUSICIANS YOU CO HOPE FOR.
UNTIL...
"...THAT DAY."
RUN, M'ARNAA! RUN!
RUN WHERE?
THE ENTIRE WORLD IS BURNING, L'CALL!
THE TRANSIT HUB IS RIGHT AROUND THE CORNER!

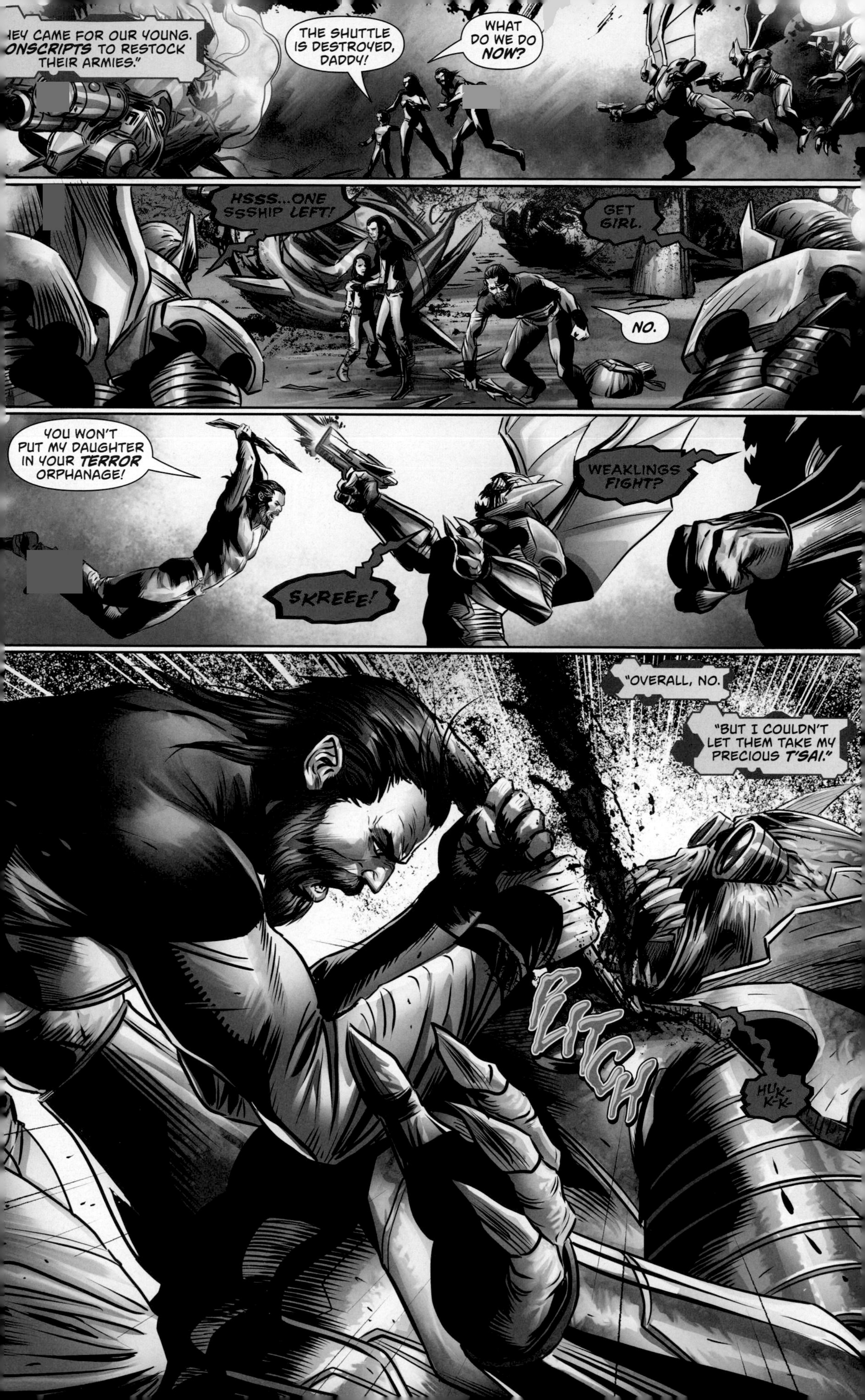
HEY CAME FOR OUR YOUNG. *ONSCRIPTS* TO RESTOCK THEIR ARMIES."
THE SHUTTLE IS DESTROYED, DADDY!
WHAT DO WE DO *NOW?*
HSSS...ONE SSSHIP *LEFT!*
GET GIRL.
NO.
YOU WON'T PUT MY DAUGHTER IN YOUR *TERROR* ORPHANAGE!
WEAKLINGS *FIGHT?*
SKREEE!
"OVERALL, NO.
"BUT I COULDN'T LET THEM TAKE MY PRECIOUS *T'SAI.*"
PLTCH
HUK-K-K-

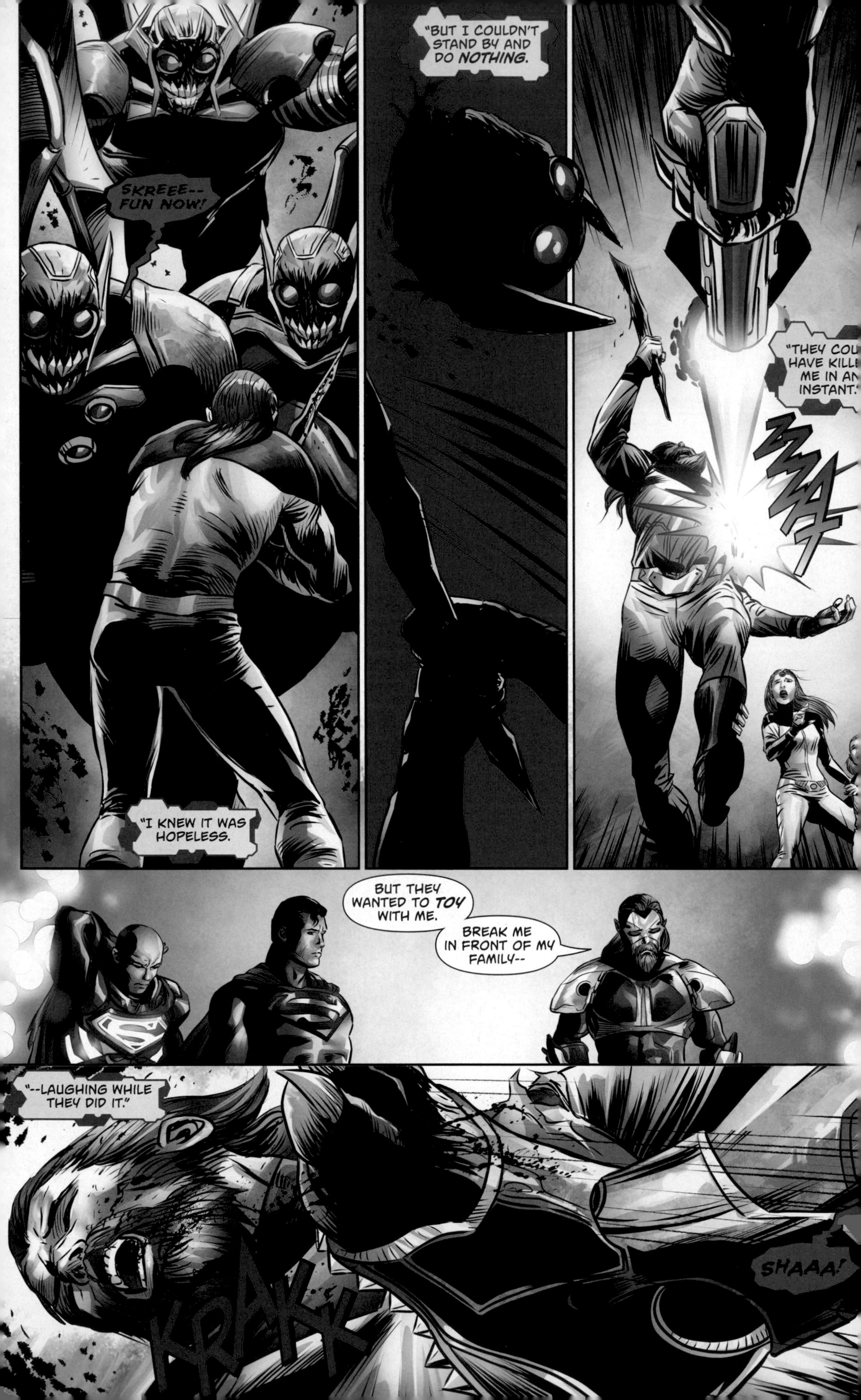
SKREEE-- FUN NOW!
"I KNEW IT WAS HOPELESS.
"BUT I COULDN'T STAND BY AND DO NOTHING.
BUT THEY WANTED TO TOY WITH ME.
BREAK ME IN FRONT OF MY FAMILY--
"--LAUGHING WHILE THEY DID IT."
KRAKK
SHAAA!

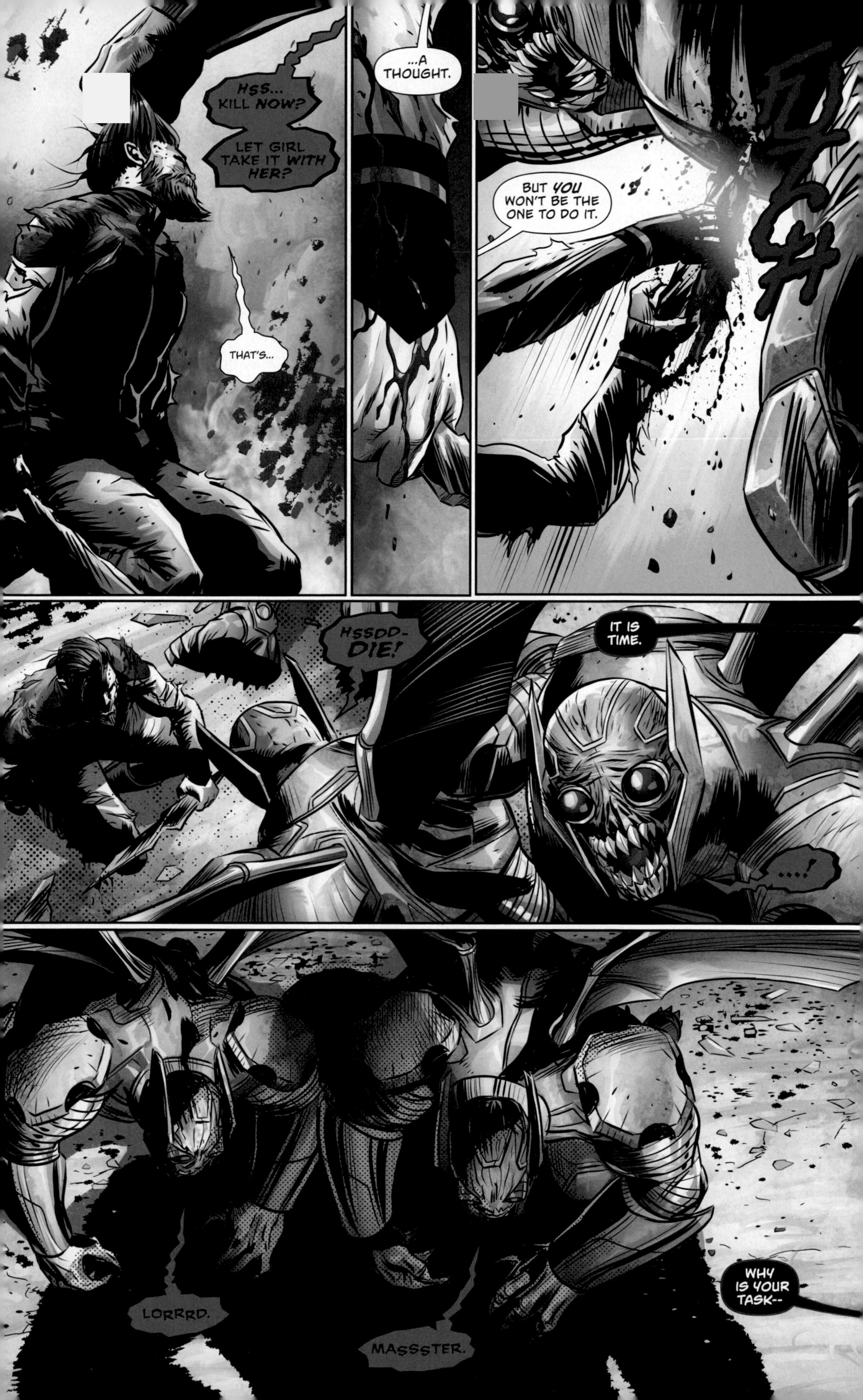
HSS... KILL NOW?
LET GIRL TAKE IT WITH HER?
THAT'S...
...A THOUGHT.
BUT YOU WON'T BE THE ONE TO DO IT.
HSSDD-DIE!
IT IS TIME.
...!
LORRRD.
MASSSTER.
WHY IS YOUR TASK--

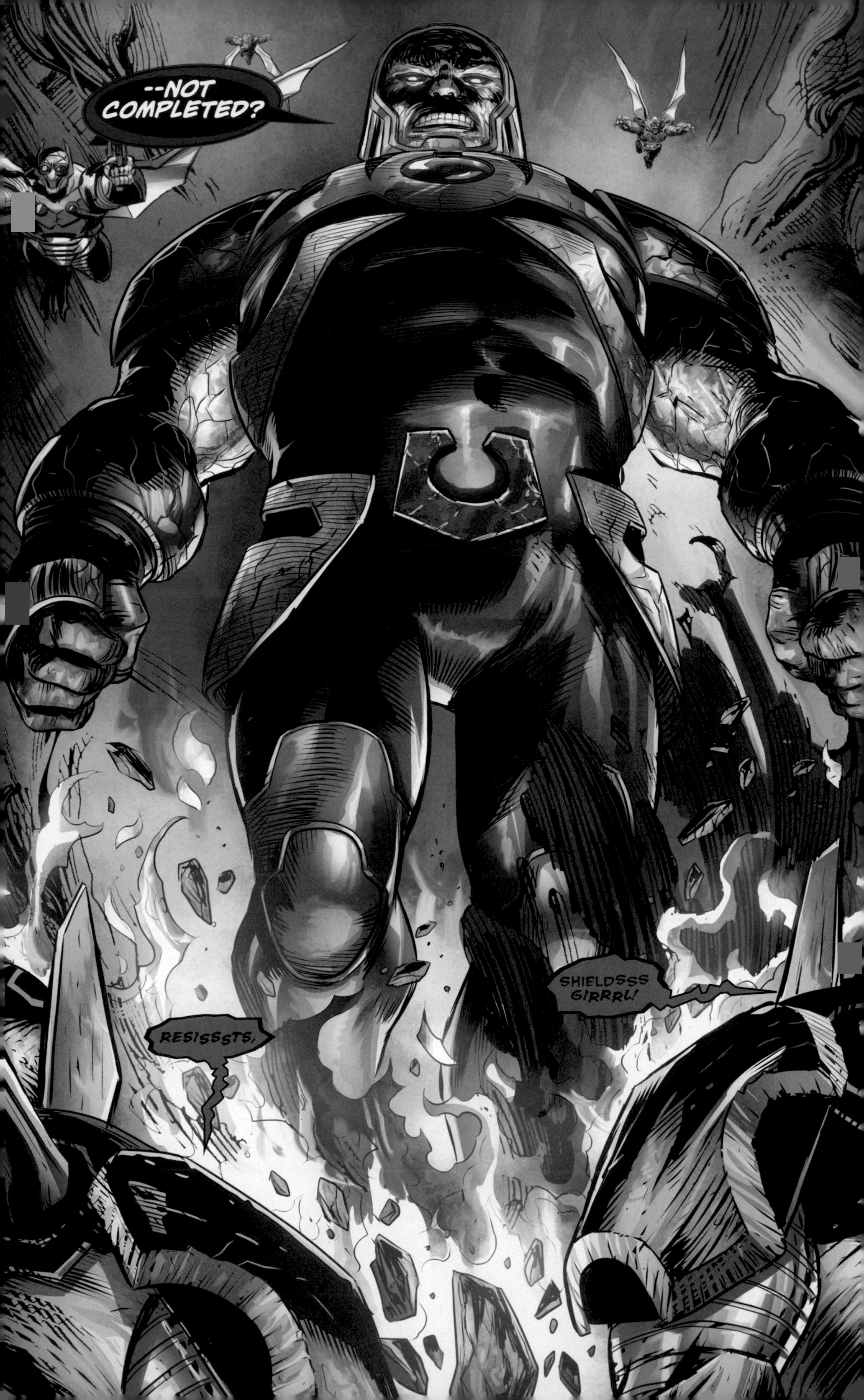
--NOT COMPLETED?
SHIELDSSS GIRRRL!
RESISSSTS.

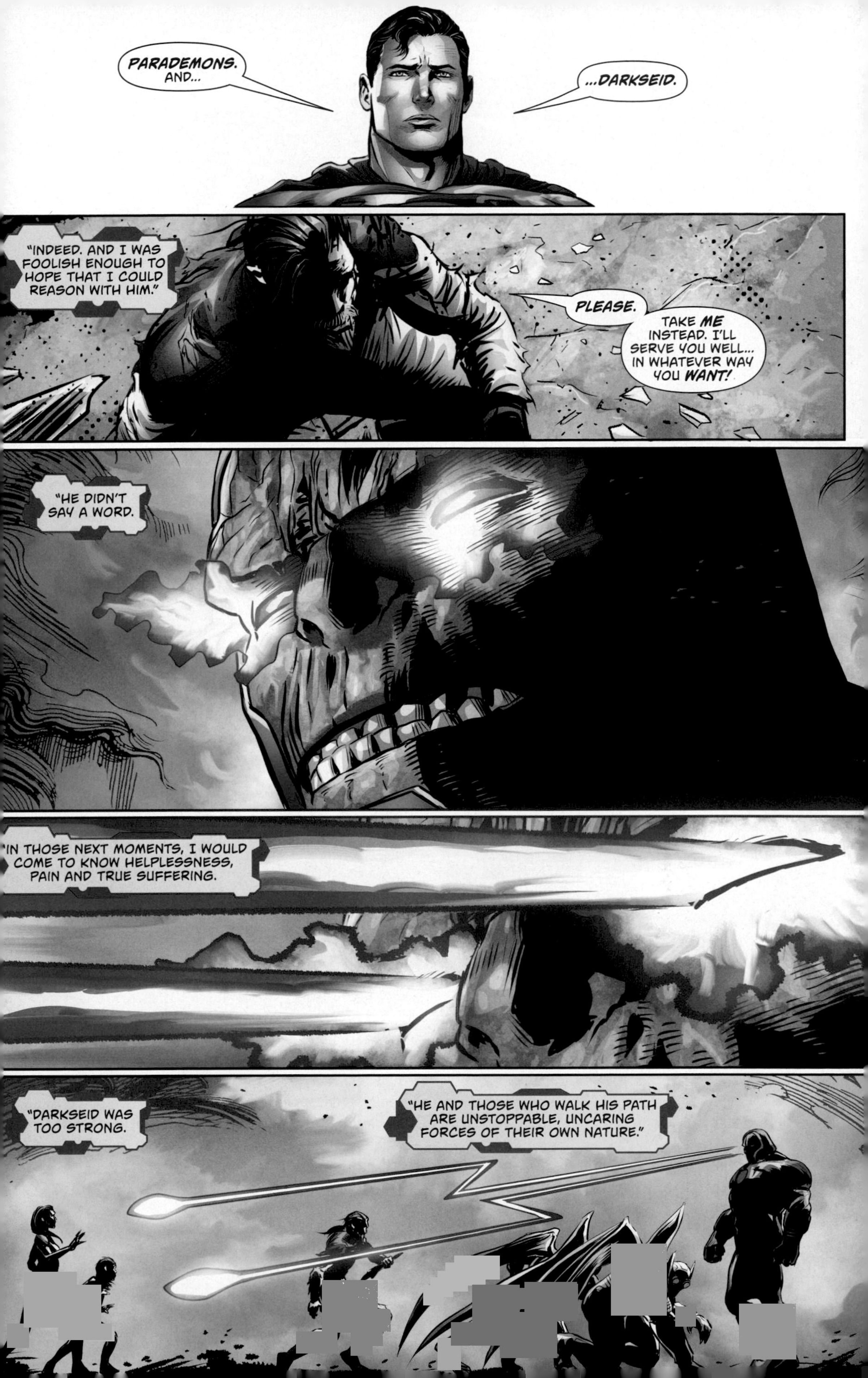
PARADEMONS. AND...
...DARKSEID.
"INDEED. AND I WAS FOOLISH ENOUGH TO HOPE THAT I COULD REASON WITH HIM."
PLEASE.
TAKE ME INSTEAD. I'LL SERVE YOU WELL... IN WHATEVER WAY YOU WANT!
"HE DIDN'T SAY A WORD.
"IN THOSE NEXT MOMENTS, I WOULD COME TO KNOW HELPLESSNESS, PAIN AND TRUE SUFFERING.
"DARKSEID WAS TOO STRONG.
"HE AND THOSE WHO WALK HIS PATH ARE UNSTOPPABLE, UNCARING FORCES OF THEIR OWN NATURE."

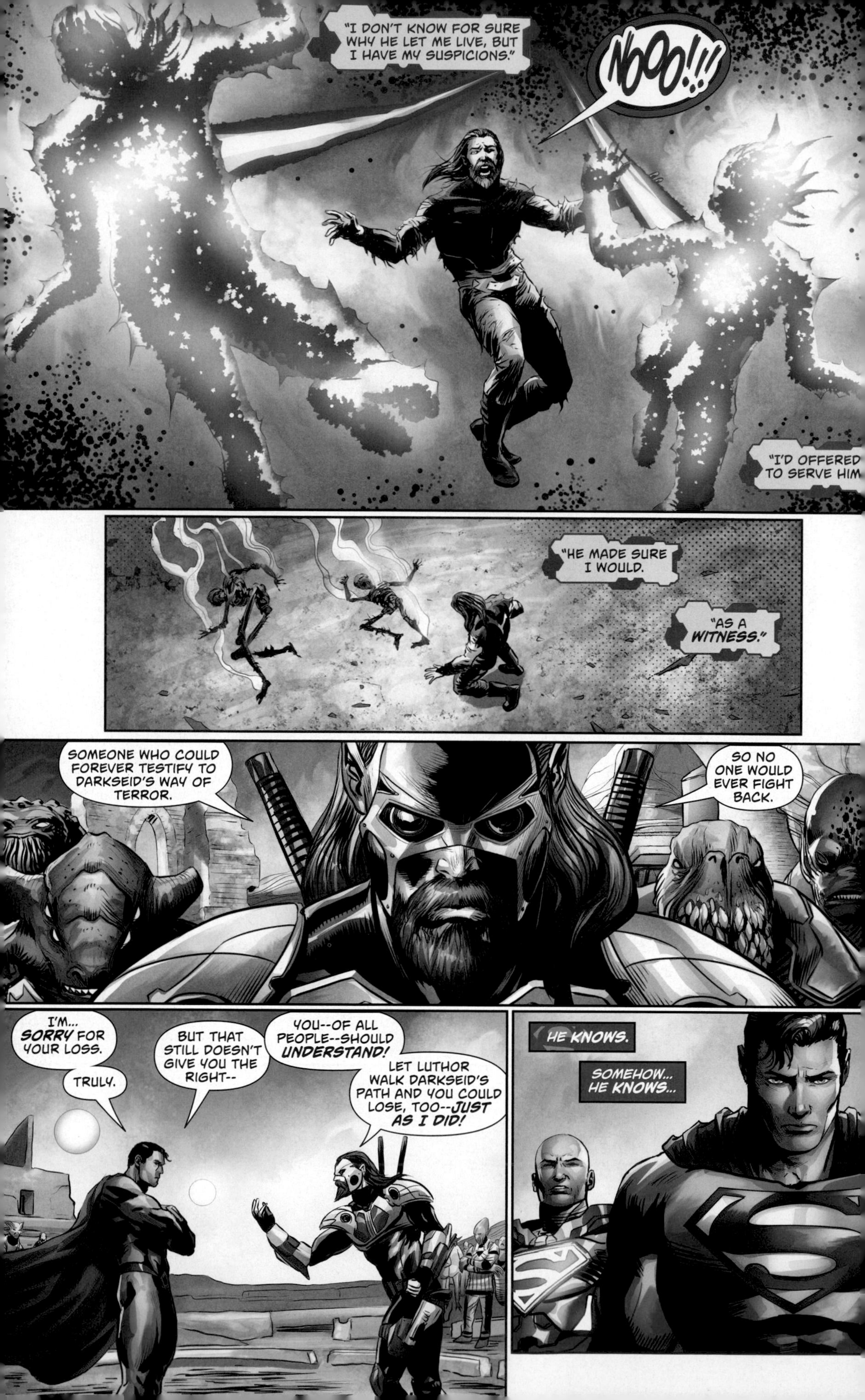
"I DON'T KNOW FOR SURE WHY HE LET ME LIVE, BUT I HAVE MY SUSPICIONS."
NOOO!!!
"I'D OFFERED TO SERVE HIM
"HE MADE SURE I WOULD.
"AS A WITNESS."
SOMEONE WHO COULD FOREVER TESTIFY TO DARKSEID'S WAY OF TERROR.
SO NO ONE WOULD EVER FIGHT BACK.
I'M... SORRY FOR YOUR LOSS.
TRULY.
BUT THAT STILL DOESN'T GIVE YOU THE RIGHT--
YOU--OF ALL PEOPLE--SHOULD UNDERSTAND!
LET LUTHOR WALK DARKSEID'S PATH AND YOU COULD LOSE, TOO--JUST AS I DID!
HE KNOWS.
SOMEHOW... HE KNOWS...

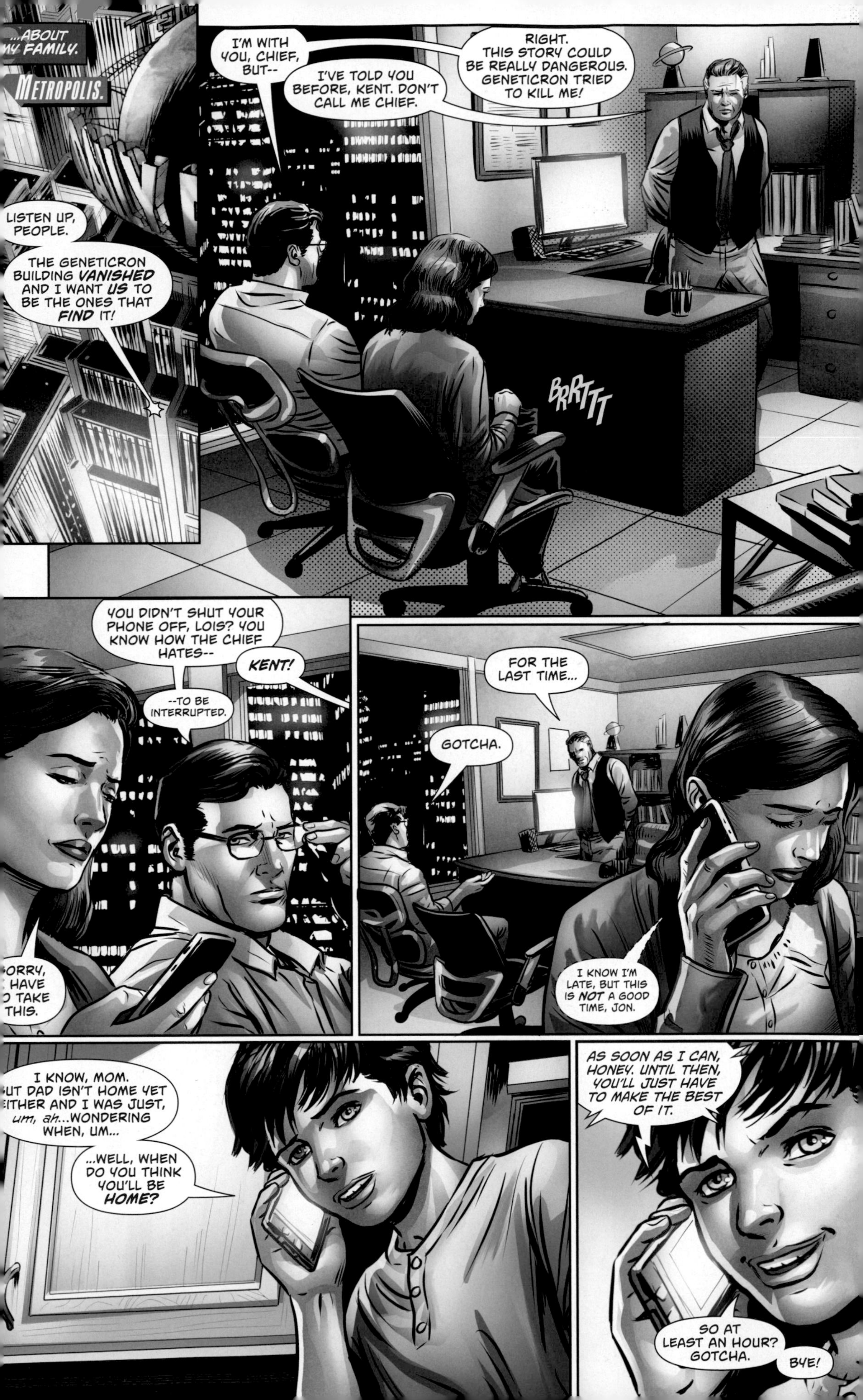
...ABOUT
MY FAMILY.
METROPOLIS.
LISTEN UP, PEOPLE.
THE GENETICRON BUILDING VANISHED AND I WANT US TO BE THE ONES THAT FIND IT!
I'M WITH YOU, CHIEF, BUT--
I'VE TOLD YOU BEFORE, KENT. DON'T CALL ME CHIEF.
RIGHT. THIS STORY COULD BE REALLY DANGEROUS. GENETICRON TRIED TO KILL ME!
BRRTTT
YOU DIDN'T SHUT YOUR PHONE OFF, LOIS? YOU KNOW HOW THE CHIEF HATES--
KENT!
--TO BE INTERRUPTED.
ORRY, HAVE TAKE THIS.
FOR THE LAST TIME...
GOTCHA.
I KNOW I'M LATE, BUT THIS IS NOT A GOOD TIME, JON.
I KNOW, MOM. UT DAD ISN'T HOME YET EITHER AND I WAS JUST, um, ah...WONDERING WHEN, UM...
...WELL, WHEN DO YOU THINK YOU'LL BE HOME?
AS SOON AS I CAN, HONEY. UNTIL THEN, YOU'LL JUST HAVE TO MAKE THE BEST OF IT.
SO AT LEAST AN HOUR? GOTCHA.
BYE!

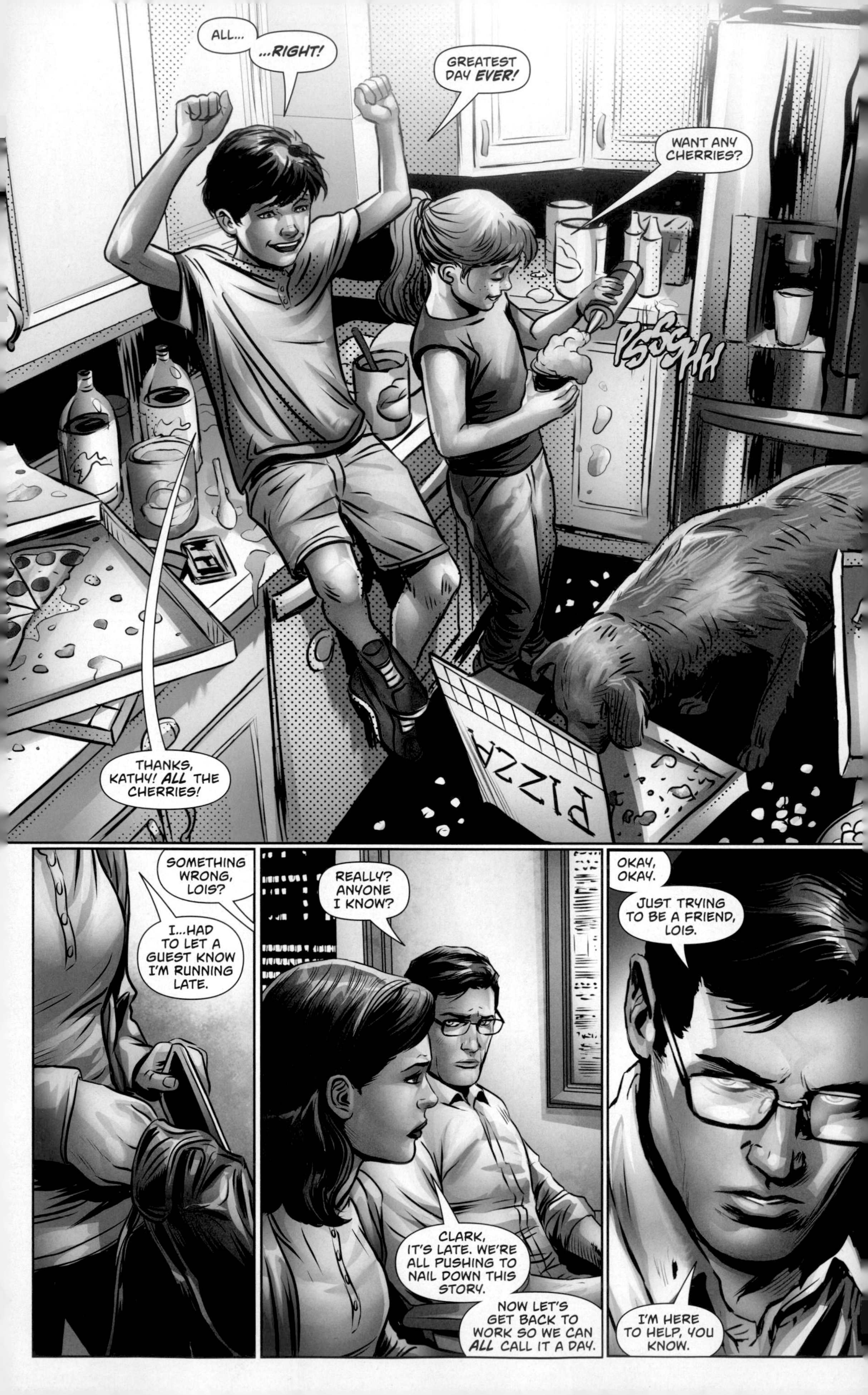
ALL...
...RIGHT!
GREATEST DAY EVER!
WANT ANY CHERRIES?
PSSSHH
THANKS, KATHY! ALL THE CHERRIES!
PIZZA
SOMETHING WRONG, LOIS?
I...HAD TO LET A GUEST KNOW I'M RUNNING LATE.
REALLY? ANYONE I KNOW?
CLARK, IT'S LATE. WE'RE ALL PUSHING TO NAIL DOWN THIS STORY.
NOW LET'S GET BACK TO WORK SO WE CAN ALL CALL IT A DAY.
OKAY, OKAY.
JUST TRYING TO BE A FRIEND, LOIS.
I'M HERE TO HELP, YOU KNOW.

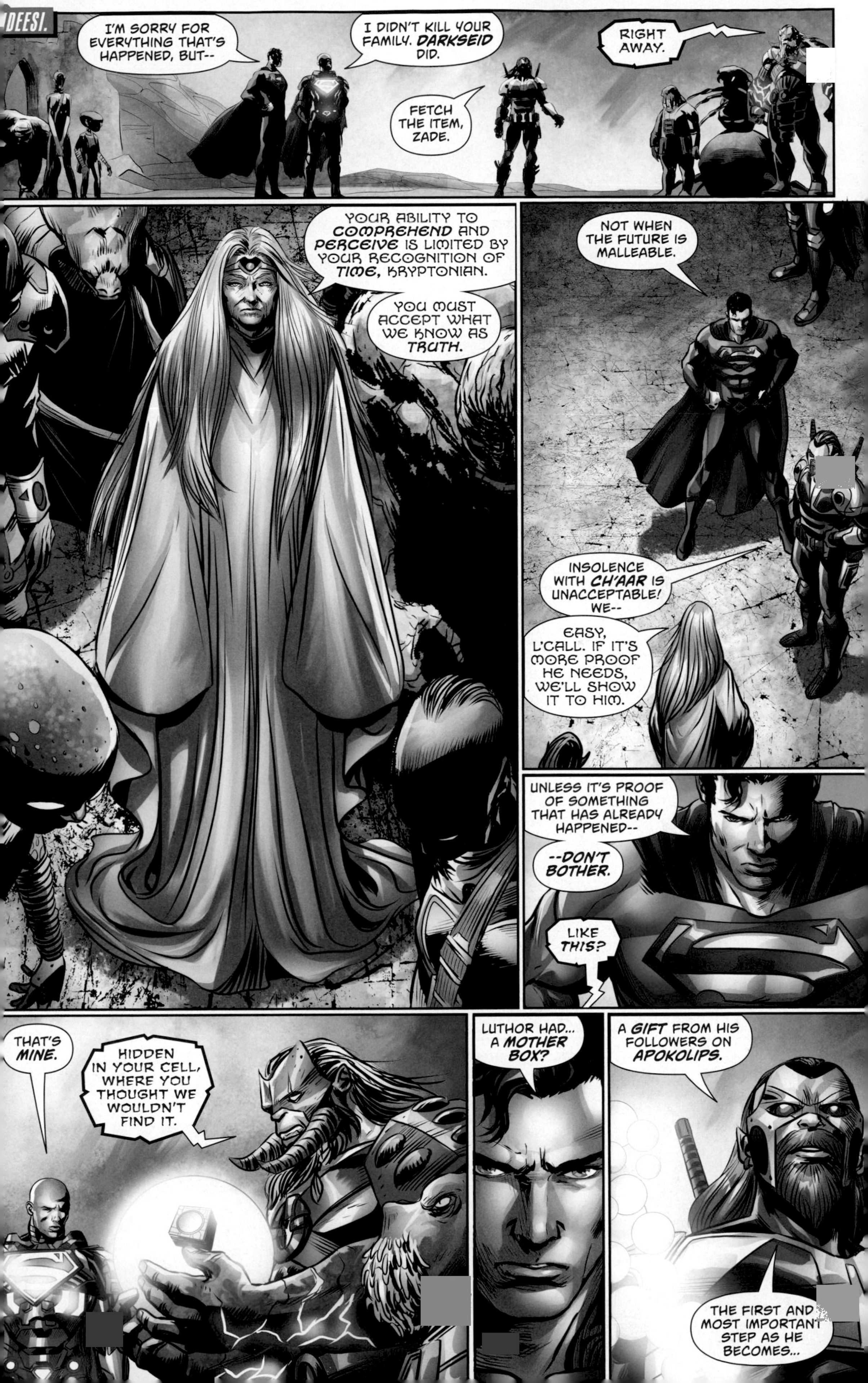
DEESI.
I'M SORRY FOR EVERYTHING THAT'S HAPPENED, BUT--
I DIDN'T KILL YOUR FAMILY. **DARKSEID** DID.
FETCH THE ITEM, ZADE.
RIGHT AWAY.
YOUR ABILITY TO **COMPREHEND** AND **PERCEIVE** IS LIMITED BY YOUR RECOGNITION OF **TIME,** KRYPTONIAN.
YOU MUST ACCEPT WHAT WE KNOW AS **TRUTH.**
NOT WHEN THE FUTURE IS MALLEABLE.
INSOLENCE WITH **CH'AAR** IS UNACCEPTABLE! WE--
EASY, L'CALL. IF IT'S MORE PROOF HE NEEDS, WE'LL SHOW IT TO HIM.
UNLESS IT'S PROOF OF SOMETHING THAT HAS ALREADY HAPPENED--
--DON'T BOTHER.
LIKE **THIS?**
THAT'S **MINE.**
HIDDEN IN YOUR CELL, WHERE YOU THOUGHT WE WOULDN'T FIND IT.
LUTHOR HAD... A **MOTHER BOX?**
A **GIFT** FROM HIS FOLLOWERS ON **APOKOLIPS.**
THE FIRST AND MOST IMPORTANT STEP AS HE BECOMES...

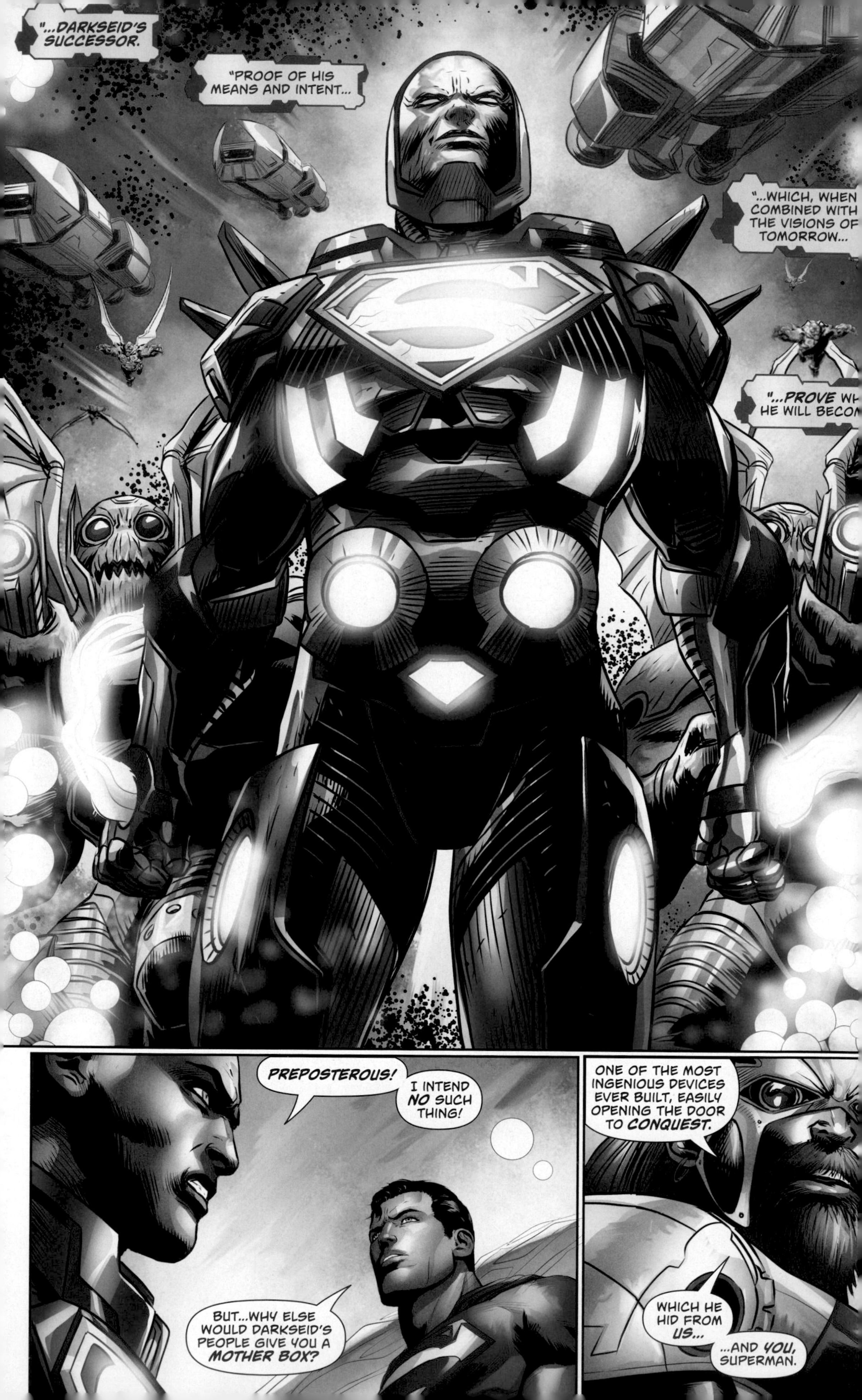
"...DARKSEID'S SUCCESSOR.
"PROOF OF HIS MEANS AND INTENT...
"...WHICH, WHEN COMBINED WITH THE VISIONS OF TOMORROW...
"...PROVE WH HE WILL BECOM
PREPOSTEROUS!
I INTEND NO SUCH THING!
BUT...WHY ELSE WOULD DARKSEID'S PEOPLE GIVE YOU A MOTHER BOX?
ONE OF THE MOST INGENIOUS DEVICES EVER BUILT, EASILY OPENING THE DOOR TO CONQUEST.
WHICH HE HID FROM US...
...AND YOU, SUPERMAN.

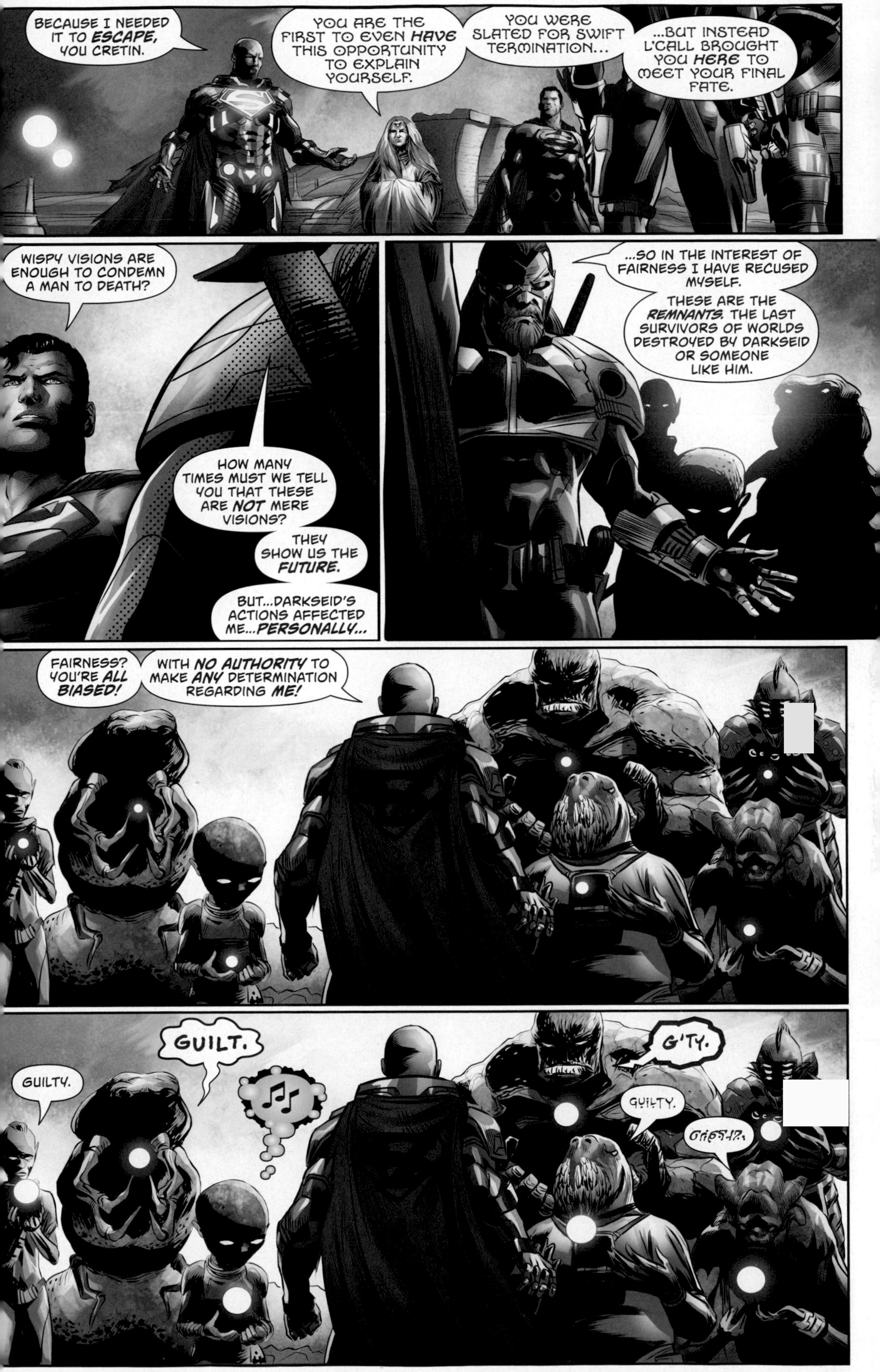
BECAUSE I NEEDED IT TO ESCAPE, YOU CRETIN.
YOU ARE THE FIRST TO EVEN HAVE THIS OPPORTUNITY TO EXPLAIN YOURSELF.
YOU WERE SLATED FOR SWIFT TERMINATION...
...BUT INSTEAD L'CALL BROUGHT YOU HERE TO MEET YOUR FINAL FATE.
WISPY VISIONS ARE ENOUGH TO CONDEMN A MAN TO DEATH?
HOW MANY TIMES MUST WE TELL YOU THAT THESE ARE NOT MERE VISIONS?
THEY SHOW US THE FUTURE.
BUT...DARKSEID'S ACTIONS AFFECTED ME...PERSONALLY...
...SO IN THE INTEREST OF FAIRNESS I HAVE RECUSED MYSELF.
THESE ARE THE REMNANTS. THE LAST SURVIVORS OF WORLDS DESTROYED BY DARKSEID OR SOMEONE LIKE HIM.
FAIRNESS? YOU'RE ALL BIASED!
WITH NO AUTHORITY TO MAKE ANY DETERMINATION REGARDING ME!
GUILTY.
GUILT.
G'TY.
GUILTY.

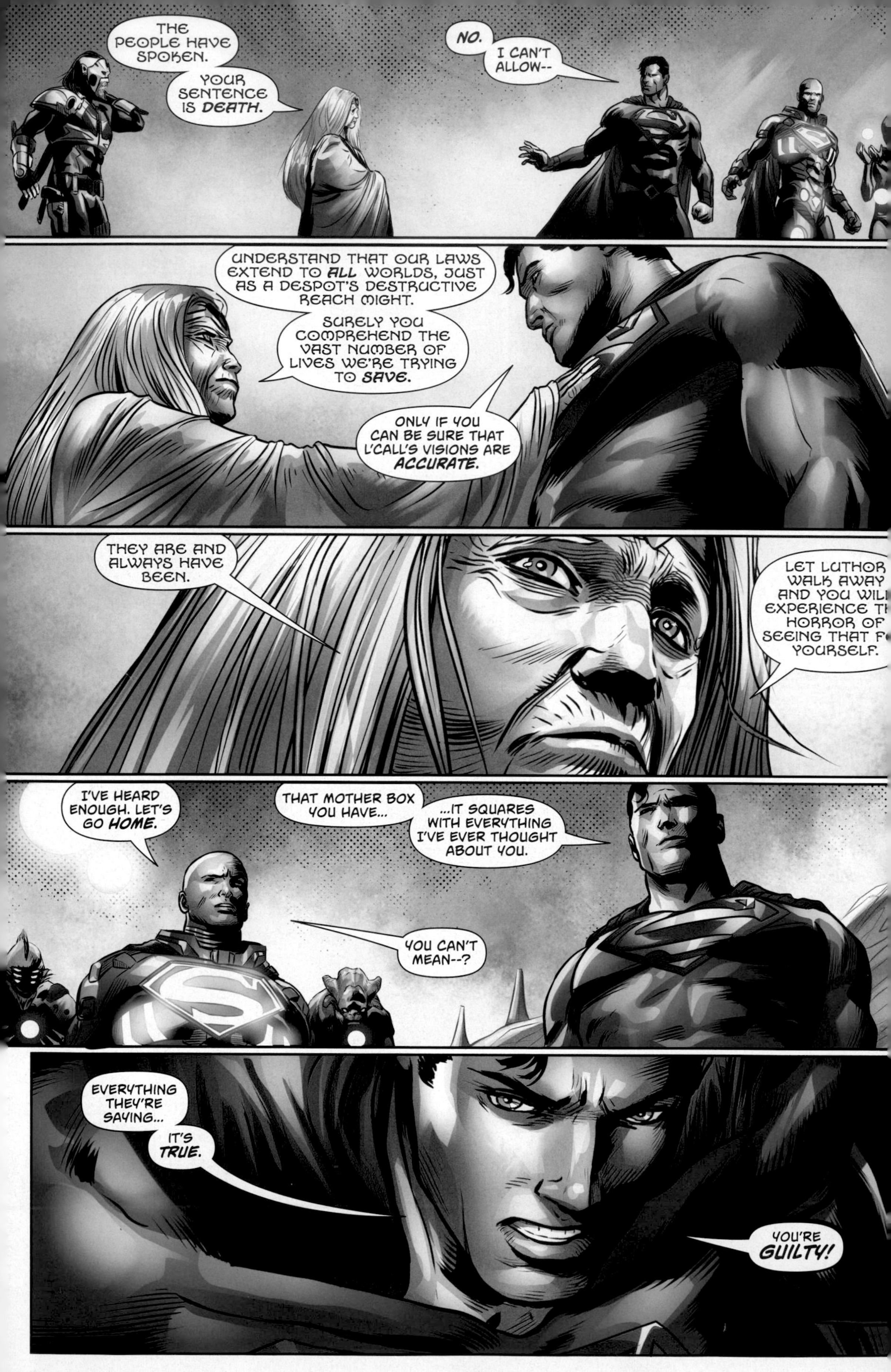
THE PEOPLE HAVE SPOKEN.
YOUR SENTENCE IS DEATH.
NO.
I CAN'T ALLOW--
UNDERSTAND THAT OUR LAWS EXTEND TO ALL WORLDS, JUST AS A DESPOT'S DESTRUCTIVE REACH MIGHT.
SURELY YOU COMPREHEND THE VAST NUMBER OF LIVES WE'RE TRYING TO SAVE.
ONLY IF YOU CAN BE SURE THAT L'CALL'S VISIONS ARE ACCURATE.
THEY ARE AND ALWAYS HAVE BEEN.
LET LUTHOR WALK AWAY AND YOU WIL EXPERIENCE TH HORROR OF SEEING THAT F YOURSELF.
I'VE HEARD ENOUGH. LET'S GO HOME.
THAT MOTHER BOX YOU HAVE...
...IT SQUARES WITH EVERYTHING I'VE EVER THOUGHT ABOUT YOU.
YOU CAN'T MEAN--?
EVERYTHING THEY'RE SAYING...
IT'S TRUE.
YOU'RE GUILTY!

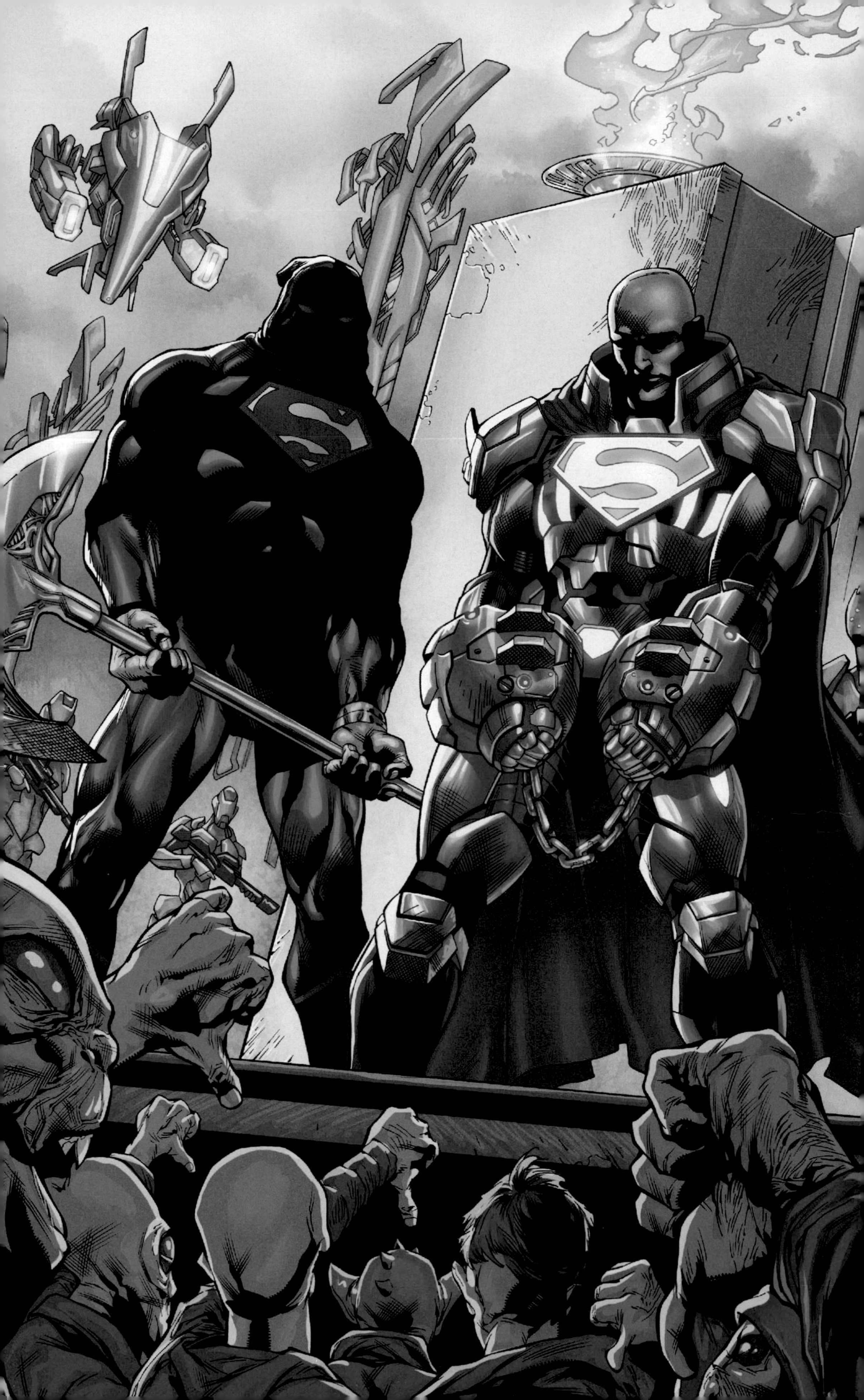

MEN OF STEEL PART 5

STEPHEN SEGOVIA penciller * ART THIBERT inker * ARIF PRIANTO colorist

STEPHEN SEGOVIA ART THIBERT HI-FI cover artists

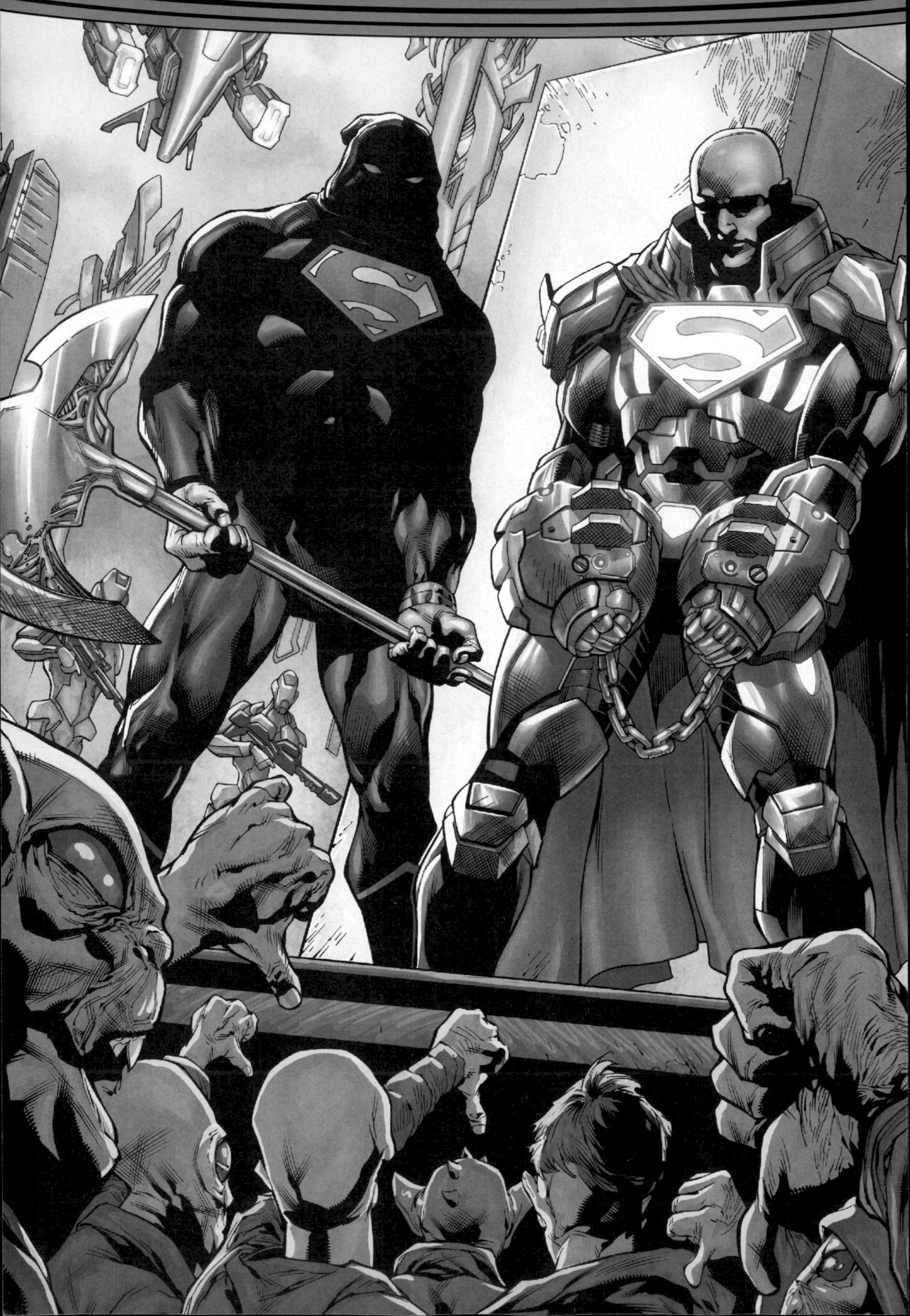

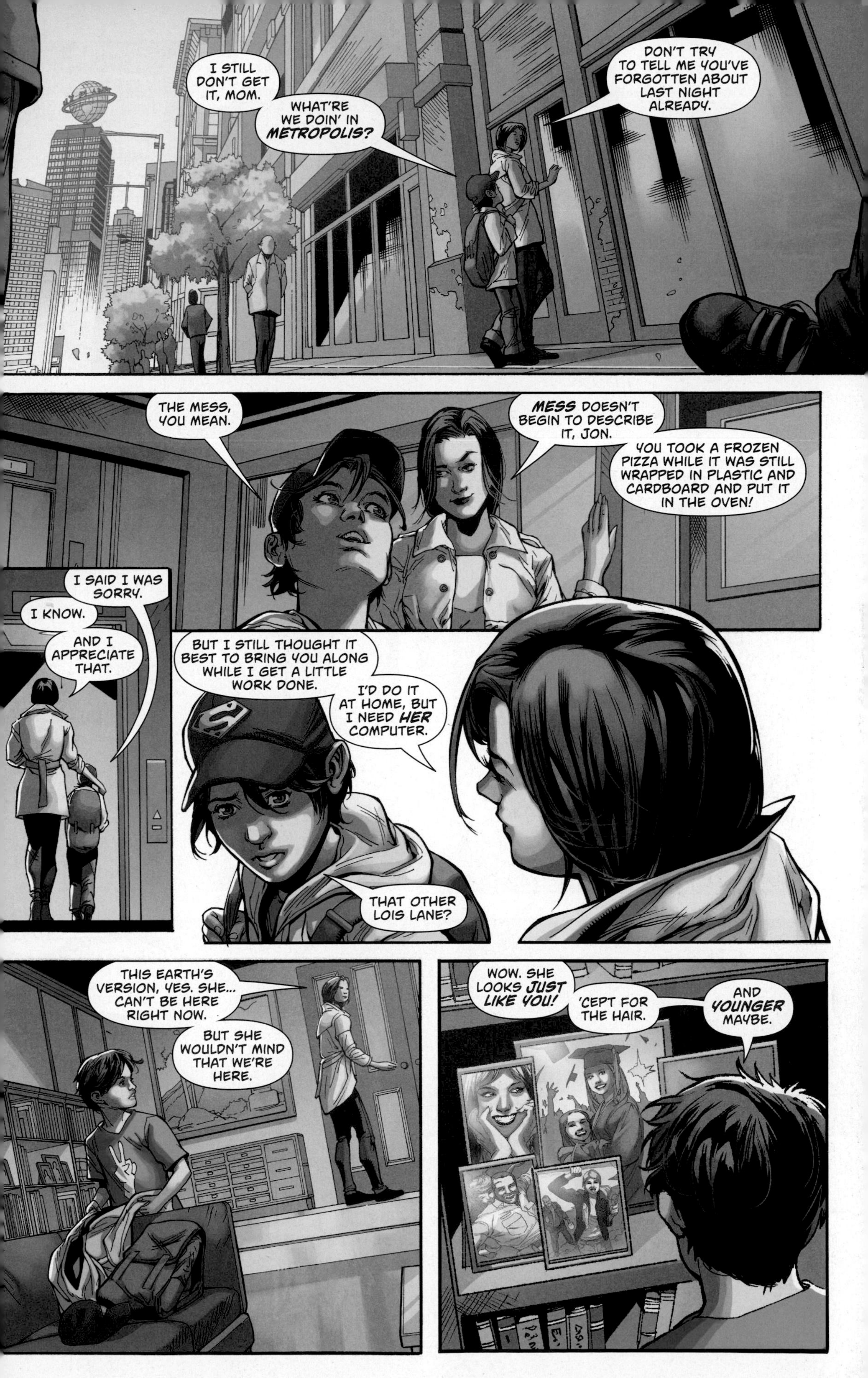
I STILL DON'T GET IT, MOM.
WHAT'RE WE DOIN' IN METROPOLIS?
DON'T TRY TO TELL ME YOU'VE FORGOTTEN ABOUT LAST NIGHT ALREADY.
THE MESS, YOU MEAN.
MESS DOESN'T BEGIN TO DESCRIBE IT, JON.
YOU TOOK A FROZEN PIZZA WHILE IT WAS STILL WRAPPED IN PLASTIC AND CARDBOARD AND PUT IT IN THE OVEN!
I SAID I WAS SORRY.
I KNOW.
AND I APPRECIATE THAT.
BUT I STILL THOUGHT IT BEST TO BRING YOU ALONG WHILE I GET A LITTLE WORK DONE.
I'D DO IT AT HOME, BUT I NEED HER COMPUTER.
THAT OTHER LOIS LANE?
THIS EARTH'S VERSION, YES. SHE... CAN'T BE HERE RIGHT NOW.
BUT SHE WOULDN'T MIND THAT WE'RE HERE.
WOW. SHE LOOKS JUST LIKE YOU!
'CEPT FOR THE HAIR.
AND YOUNGER MAYBE.

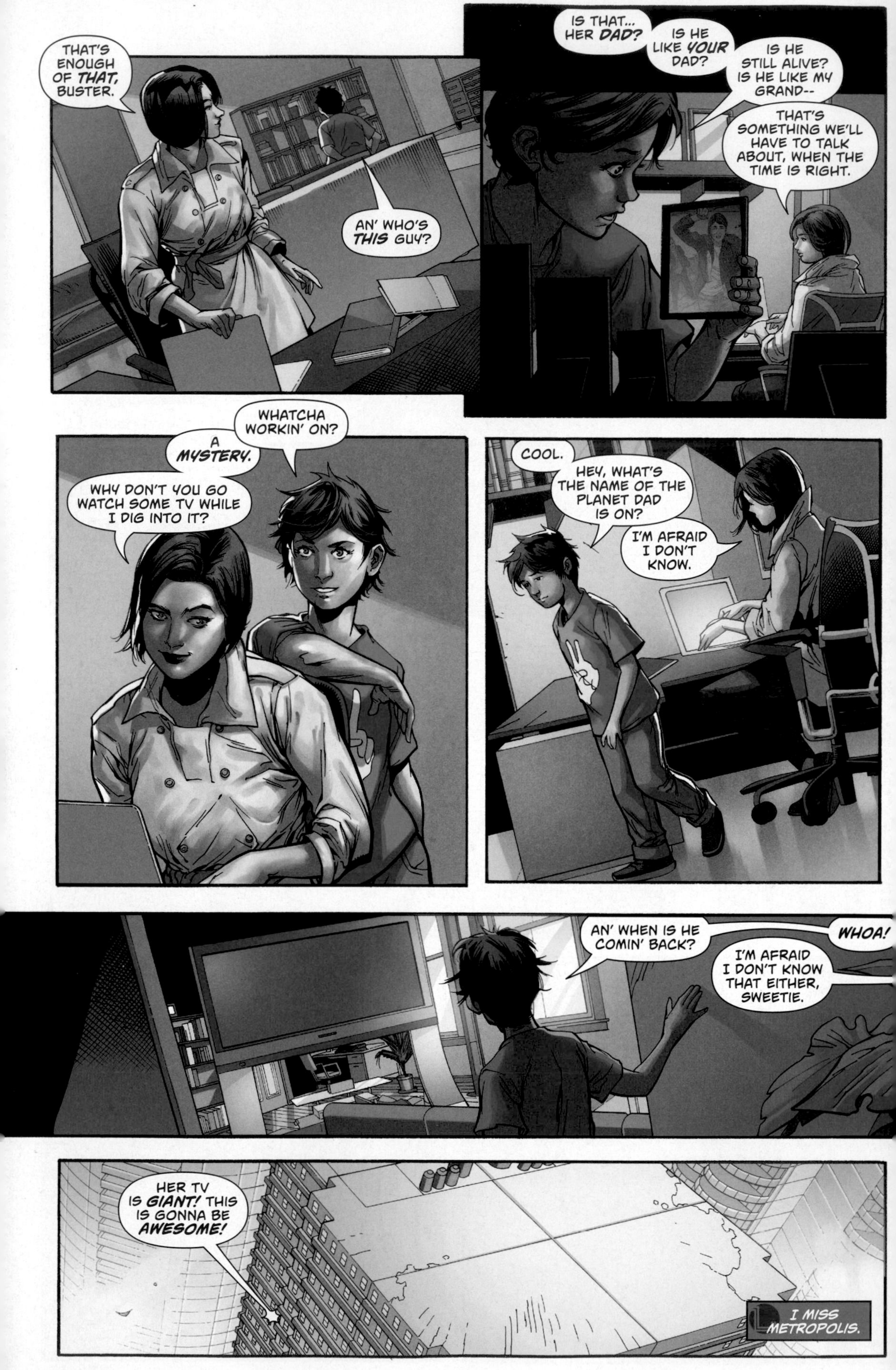
THAT'S ENOUGH OF *THAT,* BUSTER.
AN' WHO'S *THIS* GUY?
IS THAT... HER *DAD?*
IS HE LIKE *YOUR* DAD?
IS HE STILL ALIVE? IS HE LIKE MY GRAND--
THAT'S SOMETHING WE'LL HAVE TO TALK ABOUT, WHEN THE TIME IS RIGHT.
WHATCHA WORKIN' ON?
A *MYSTERY.*
WHY DON'T YOU GO WATCH SOME TV WHILE I DIG INTO IT?
COOL.
HEY, WHAT'S THE NAME OF THE PLANET DAD IS ON?
I'M AFRAID I DON'T KNOW.
AN' WHEN IS HE COMIN' BACK?
I'M AFRAID I DON'T KNOW THAT EITHER, SWEETIE.
WHOA!
HER TV IS *GIANT!* THIS IS GONNA BE *AWESOME!*
I MISS METROPOLIS.

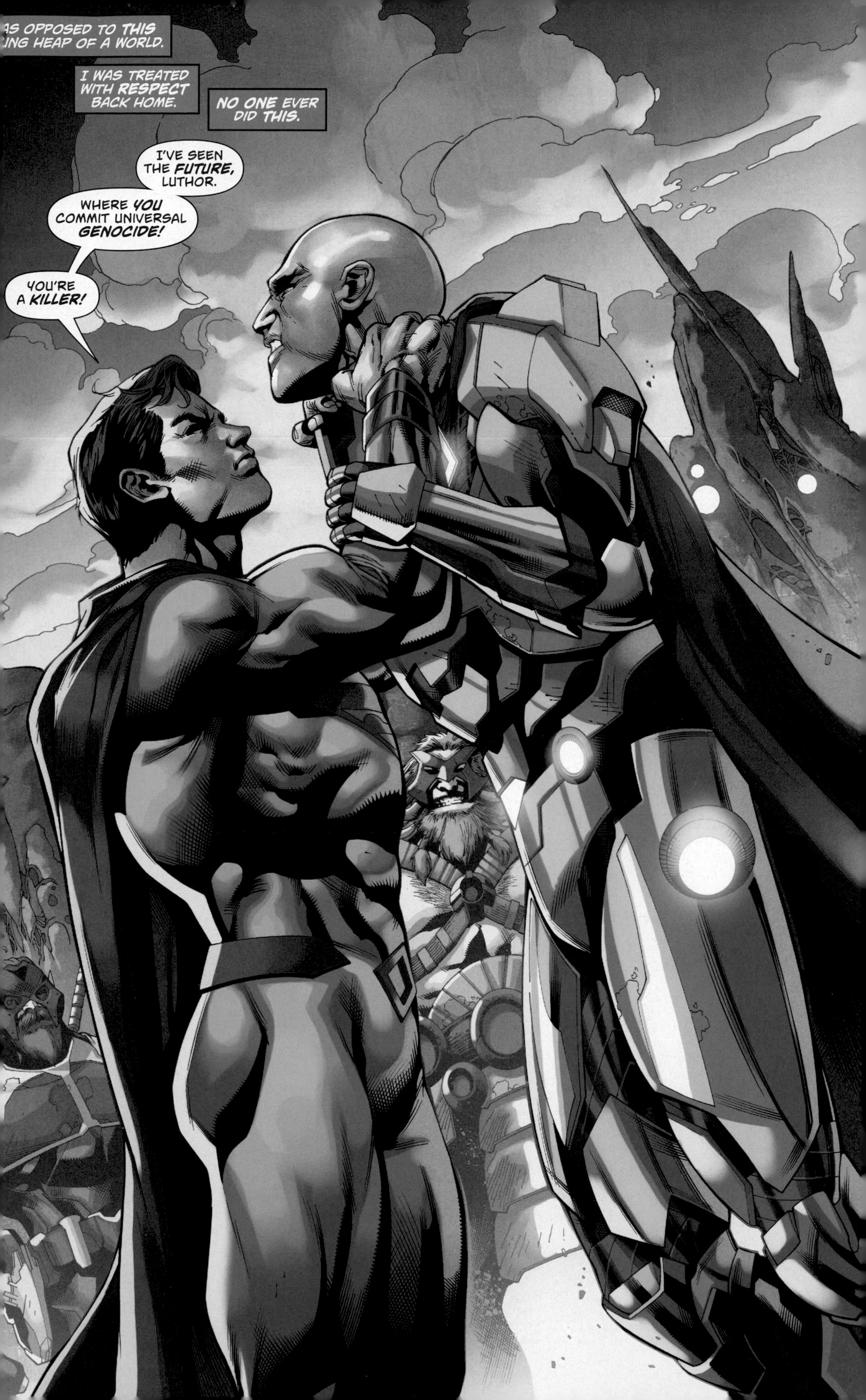
OPPOSED TO THIS
HEAP OF A WORLD.
I WAS TREATED WITH RESPECT BACK HOME.
NO ONE EVER DID THIS.
I'VE SEEN THE FUTURE, LUTHOR.
WHERE YOU COMMIT UNIVERSAL GENOCIDE!
YOU'RE A KILLER!

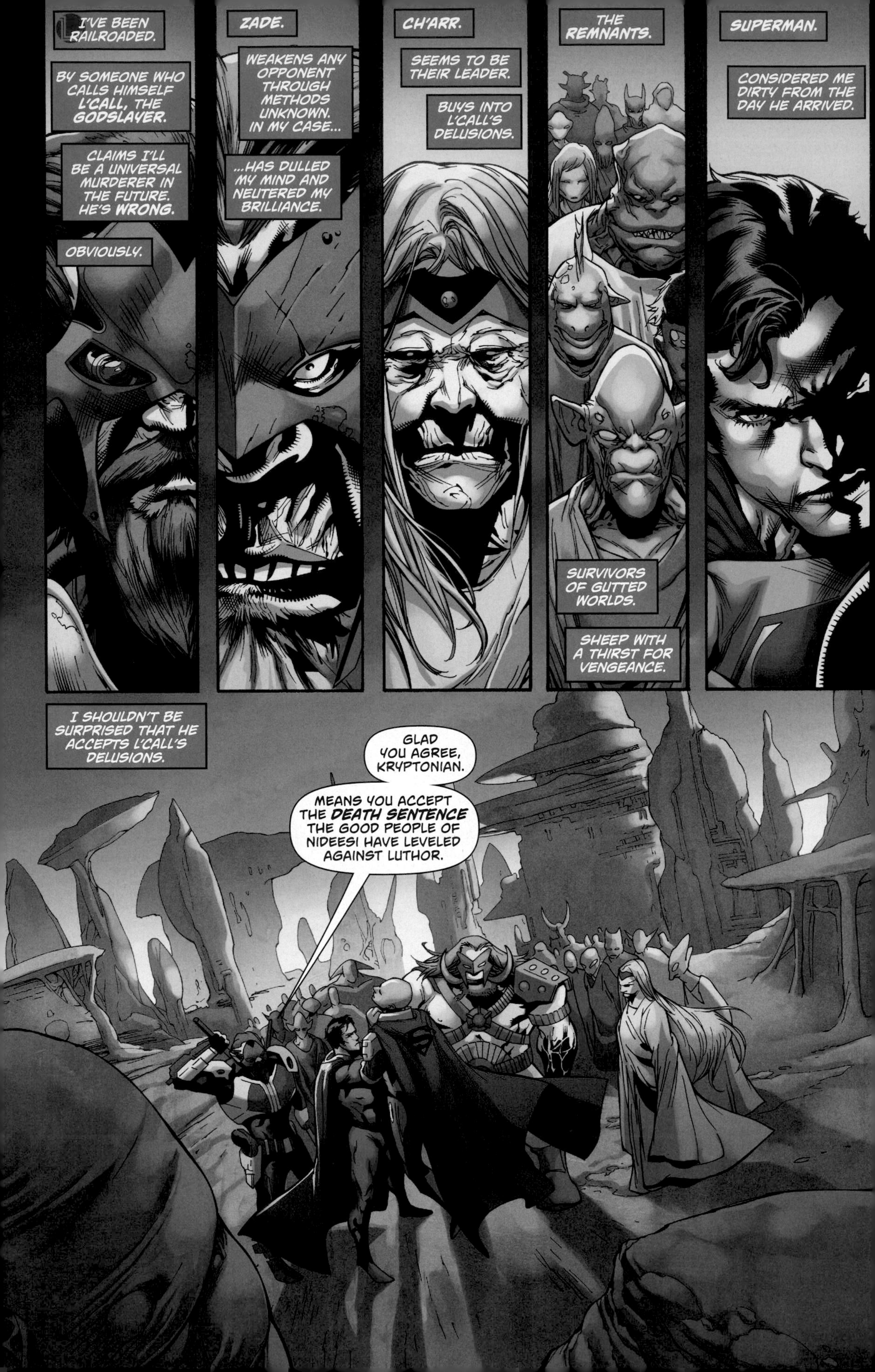
I'VE BEEN RAILROADED.
BY SOMEONE WHO CALLS HIMSELF L'CALL, THE GODSLAYER.
CLAIMS I'LL BE A UNIVERSAL MURDERER IN THE FUTURE. HE'S WRONG.
OBVIOUSLY.
ZADE.
WEAKENS ANY OPPONENT THROUGH METHODS UNKNOWN. IN MY CASE...
...HAS DULLED MY MIND AND NEUTERED MY BRILLIANCE.
CH'ARR.
SEEMS TO BE THEIR LEADER.
BUYS INTO L'CALL'S DELUSIONS.
THE REMNANTS.
SURVIVORS OF GUTTED WORLDS.
SHEEP WITH A THIRST FOR VENGEANCE.
SUPERMAN.
CONSIDERED ME DIRTY FROM THE DAY HE ARRIVED.
I SHOULDN'T BE SURPRISED THAT HE ACCEPTS L'CALL'S DELUSIONS.
GLAD YOU AGREE, KRYPTONIAN.
MEANS YOU ACCEPT THE DEATH SENTENCE THE GOOD PEOPLE OF NIDEESI HAVE LEVELED AGAINST LUTHOR.

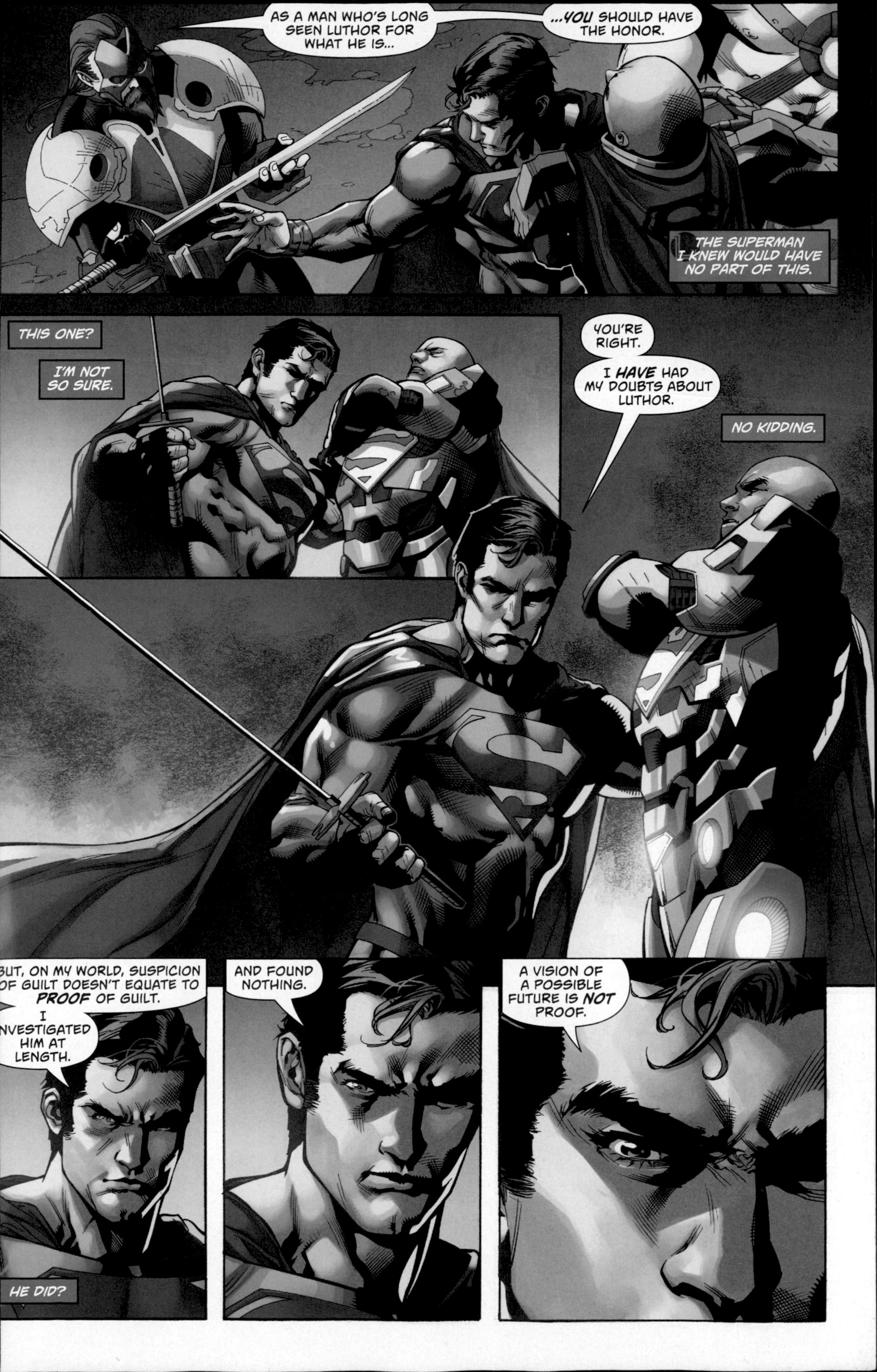
AS A MAN WHO'S LONG SEEN LUTHOR FOR WHAT HE IS...
...YOU SHOULD HAVE THE HONOR.
THE SUPERMAN I KNEW WOULD HAVE NO PART OF THIS.
THIS ONE?
I'M NOT SO SURE.
YOU'RE RIGHT.
I HAVE HAD MY DOUBTS ABOUT LUTHOR.
NO KIDDING.
BUT, ON MY WORLD, SUSPICION OF GUILT DOESN'T EQUATE TO PROOF OF GUILT.
I INVESTIGATED HIM AT LENGTH.
HE DID?
AND FOUND NOTHING.
A VISION OF A POSSIBLE FUTURE IS NOT PROOF.

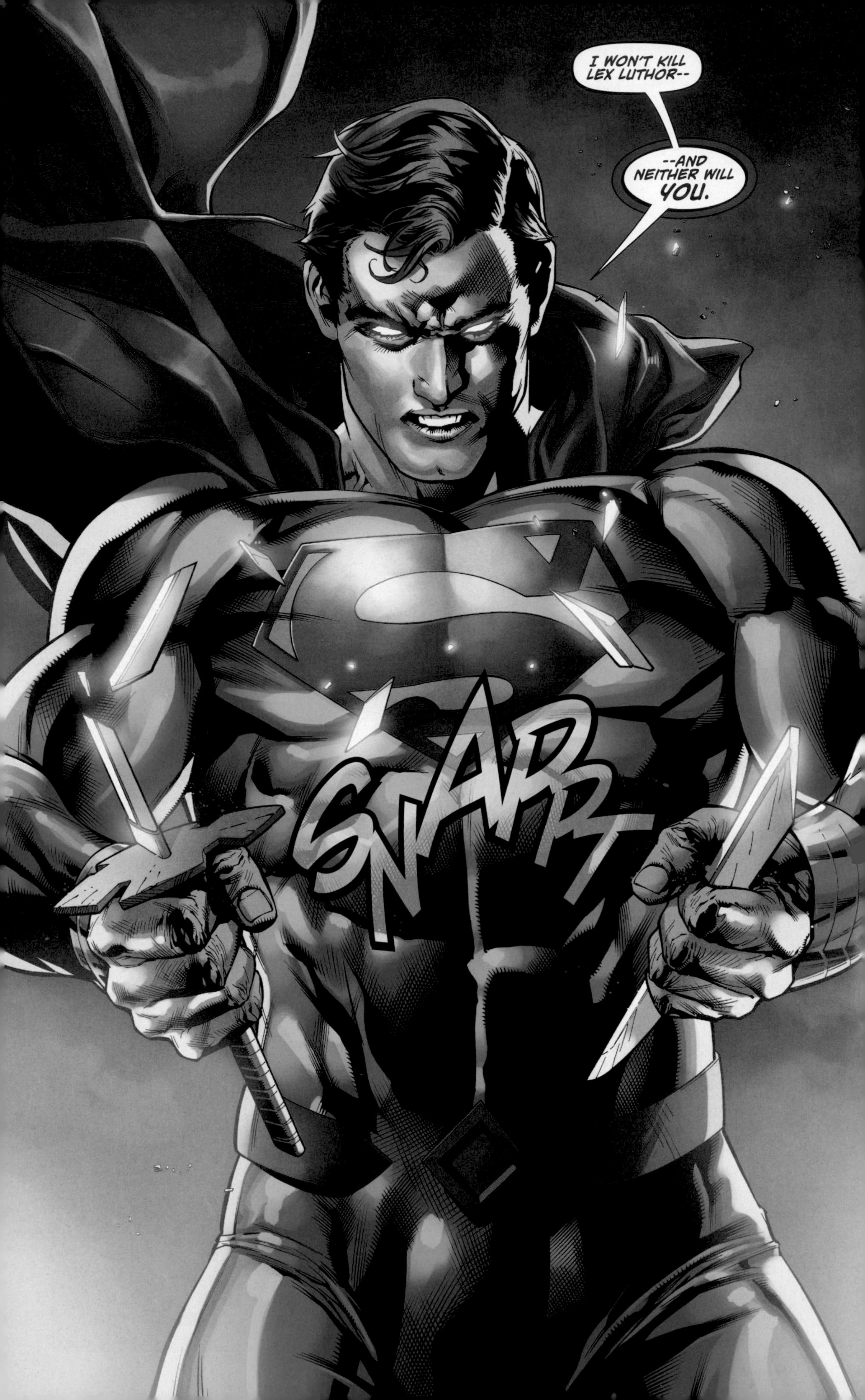
I WON'T KILL LEX LUTHOR--
--AND NEITHER WILL YOU.
SNAP

GET READY.

I SHOULD HAVE KNOWN.

HE WAS PLAYING THEM. BUYING TIME.

OF COURSE.

SETTING ME FEAR OF ZADE?

PROBABLY HOPES DISTANCE WILL CLEAR MY MIND.

SMART.

YOU'VE OVERSTEPPED YOUR BOUNDS.

LUTHOR ISN'T SUBJECT TO YOUR JUDGMENT!

ZADE WEAKENED SUPERMAN AS WELL.

IF DISTANCE IS A FACTOR, COULD IT BE...

OF COURSE.

PHEROMONES.

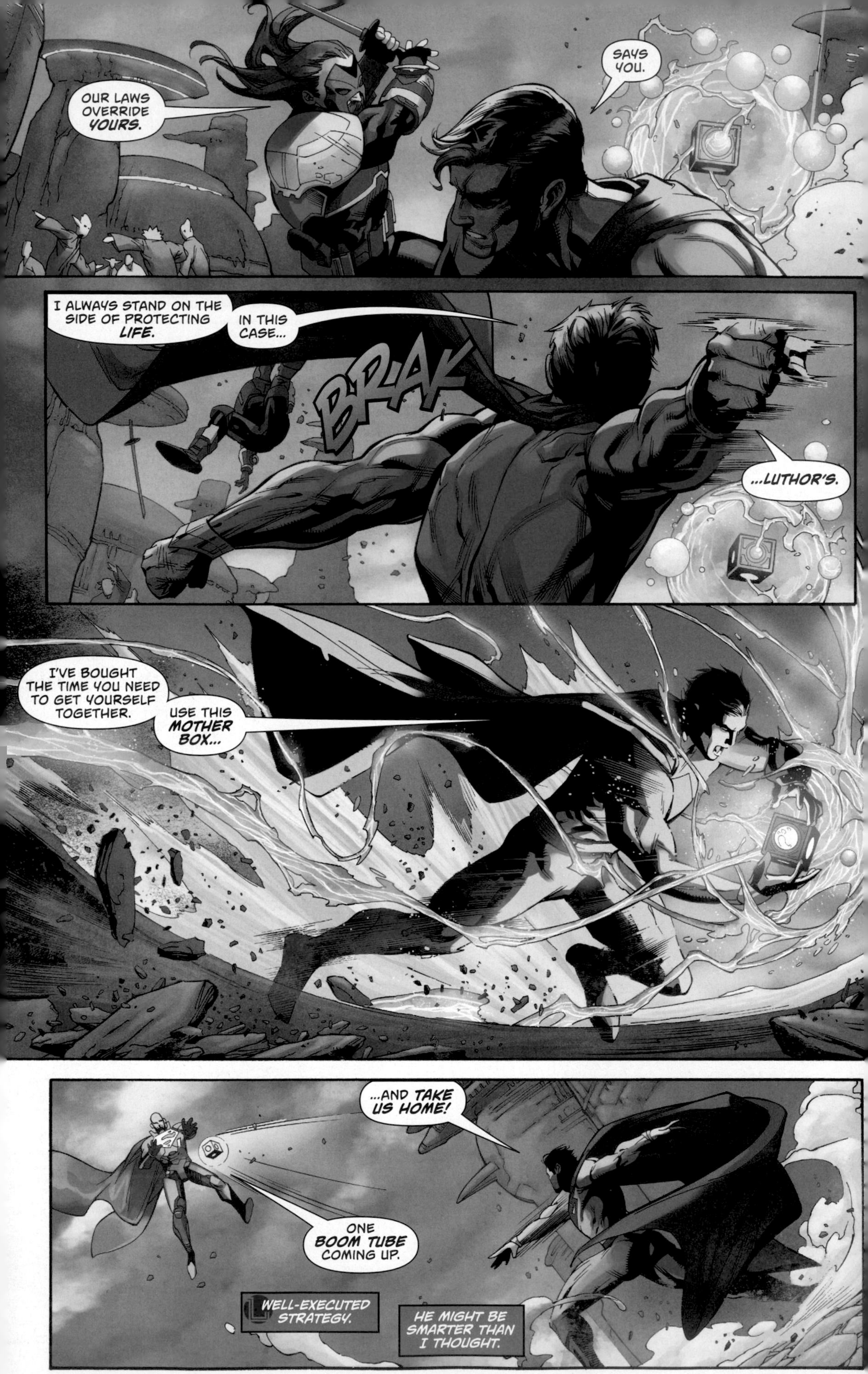
OUR LAWS OVERRIDE YOURS.
SAYS YOU.
I ALWAYS STAND ON THE SIDE OF PROTECTING LIFE.
IN THIS CASE...
BRAK
...LUTHOR'S.
I'VE BOUGHT THE TIME YOU NEED TO GET YOURSELF TOGETHER.
USE THIS MOTHER BOX...
...AND TAKE US HOME!
ONE BOOM TUBE COMING UP.
WELL-EXECUTED STRATEGY.
HE MIGHT BE SMARTER THAN I THOUGHT.

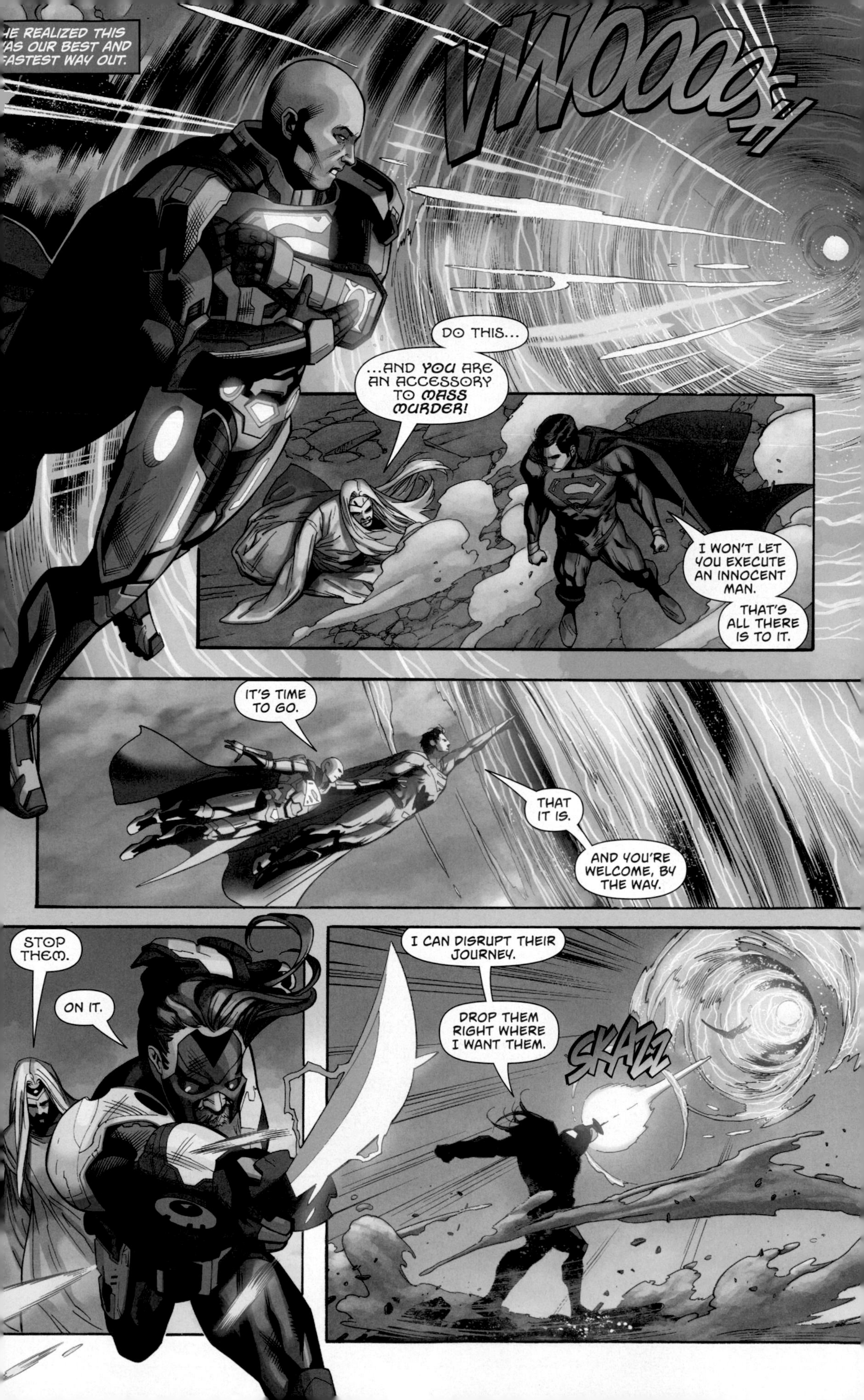

HE REALIZED THIS WAS OUR BEST AND FASTEST WAY OUT.
VWOOOOSH
DO THIS...
...AND YOU ARE AN ACCESSORY TO MASS MURDER!
I WON'T LET YOU EXECUTE AN INNOCENT MAN.
THAT'S ALL THERE IS TO IT.
IT'S TIME TO GO.
THAT IT IS.
AND YOU'RE WELCOME, BY THE WAY.
STOP THEM.
ON IT.
I CAN DISRUPT THEIR JOURNEY.
DROP THEM RIGHT WHERE I WANT THEM.
SKAZZ

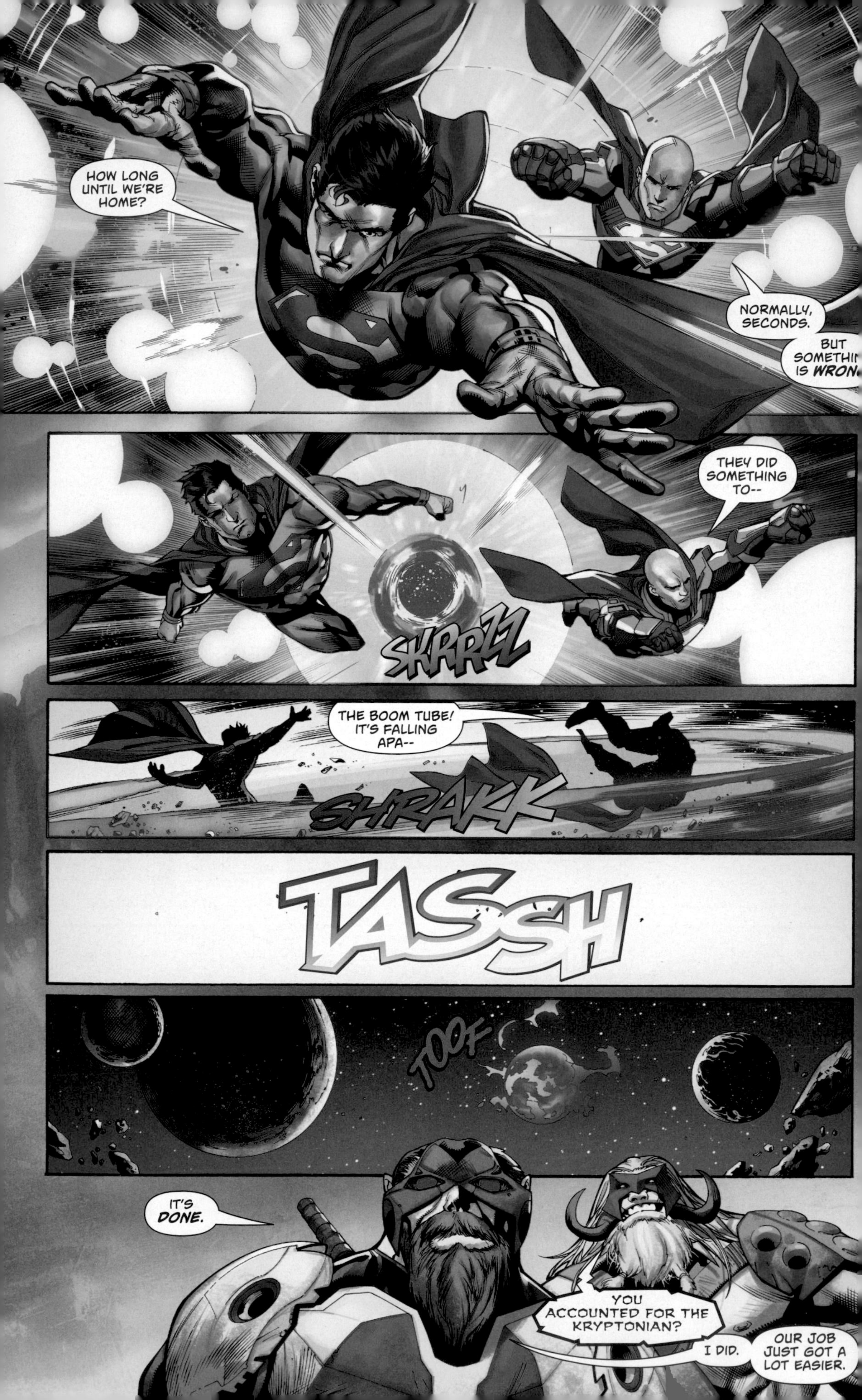
HOW LONG UNTIL WE'RE HOME?
NORMALLY, SECONDS.
BUT SOMETHIN IS WRON
THEY DID SOMETHING TO--
SKRRZZ
THE BOOM TUBE! IT'S FALLING APA--
SHRAKK
TASSH
TOOF
IT'S DONE.
YOU ACCOUNTED FOR THE KRYPTONIAN?
I DID.
OUR JOB JUST GOT A LOT EASIER.

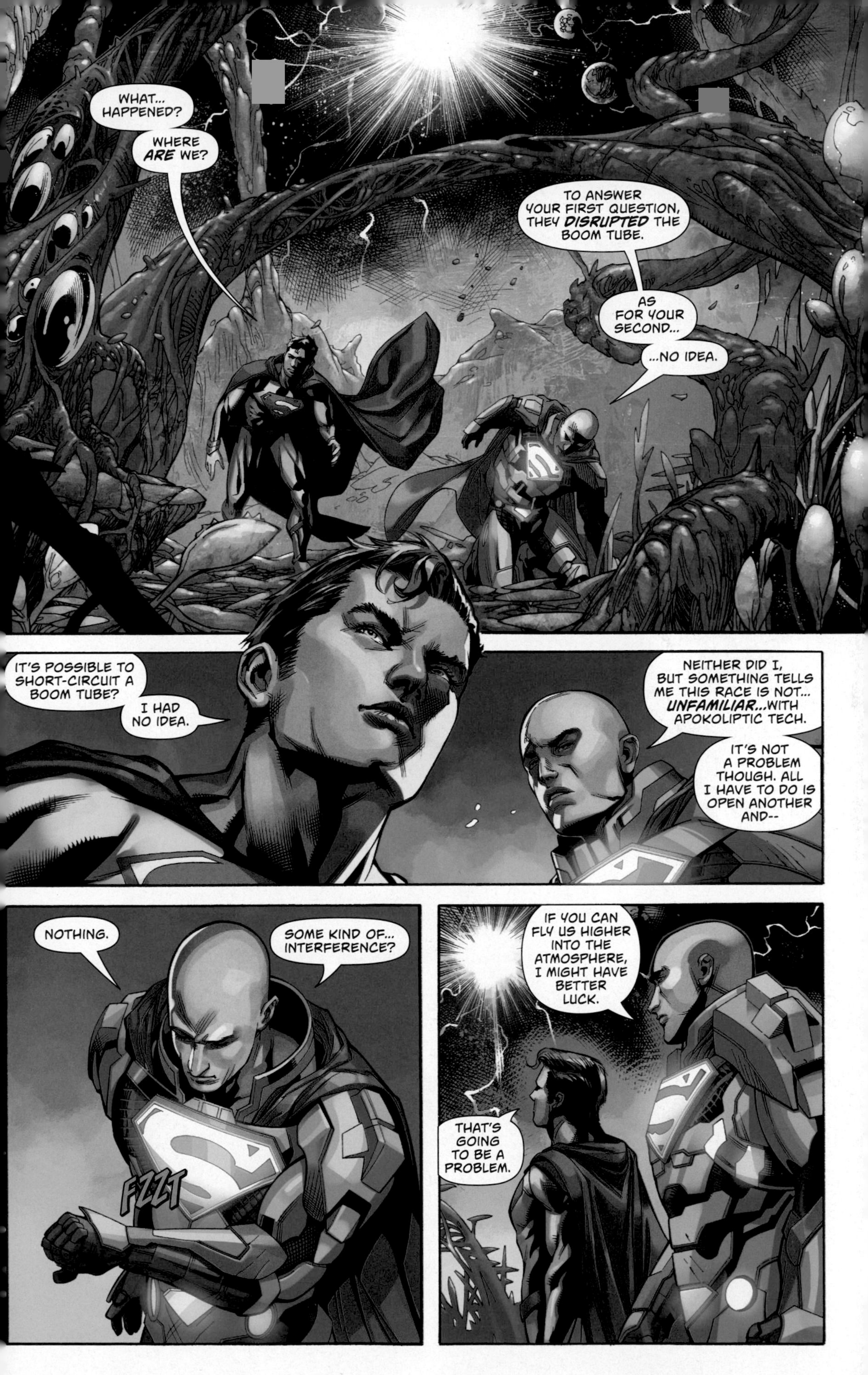
WHAT... HAPPENED?
WHERE *ARE* WE?
TO ANSWER YOUR FIRST QUESTION, THEY *DISRUPTED* THE BOOM TUBE.
AS FOR YOUR SECOND...
...NO IDEA.
IT'S POSSIBLE TO SHORT-CIRCUIT A BOOM TUBE?
I HAD NO IDEA.
NEITHER DID I, BUT SOMETHING TELLS ME THIS RACE IS NOT... *UNFAMILIAR...*WITH APOKOLIPTIC TECH.
IT'S NOT A PROBLEM THOUGH. ALL I HAVE TO DO IS OPEN ANOTHER AND--
NOTHING.
SOME KIND OF... INTERFERENCE?
FZZT
IF YOU CAN FLY US HIGHER INTO THE ATMOSPHERE, I MIGHT HAVE BETTER LUCK.
THAT'S GOING TO BE A PROBLEM.

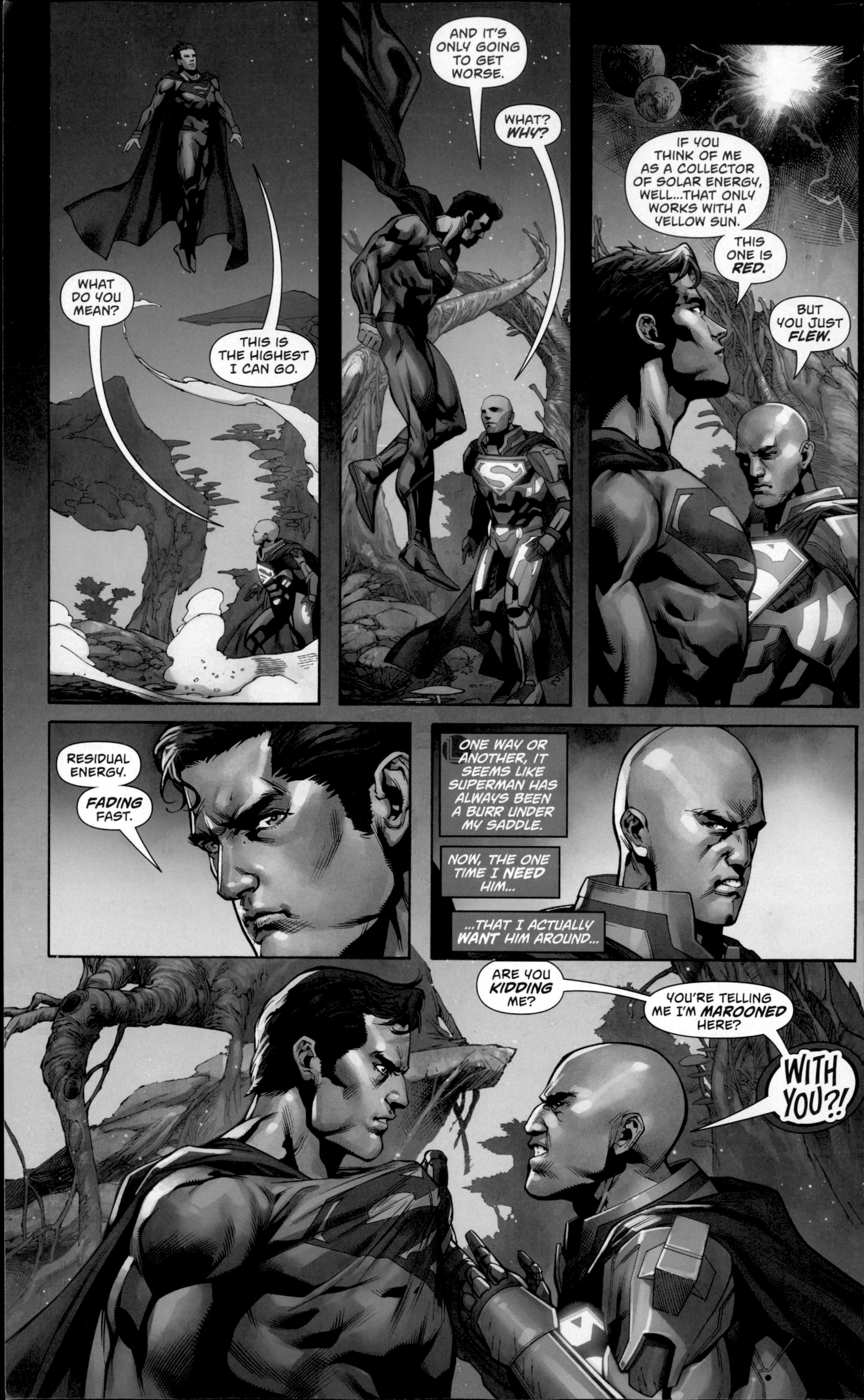

WHAT DO YOU MEAN?
THIS IS THE HIGHEST I CAN GO.
AND IT'S ONLY GOING TO GET WORSE.
WHAT? WHY?
IF YOU THINK OF ME AS A COLLECTOR OF SOLAR ENERGY, WELL...THAT ONLY WORKS WITH A YELLOW SUN.
THIS ONE IS RED.
BUT YOU JUST FLEW.
RESIDUAL ENERGY.
FADING FAST.
ONE WAY OR ANOTHER, IT SEEMS LIKE SUPERMAN HAS ALWAYS BEEN A BURR UNDER MY SADDLE.
NOW, THE ONE TIME I NEED HIM...
...THAT I ACTUALLY WANT HIM AROUND...
ARE YOU KIDDING ME?
YOU'RE TELLING ME I'M MAROONED HERE?
WITH YOU?!

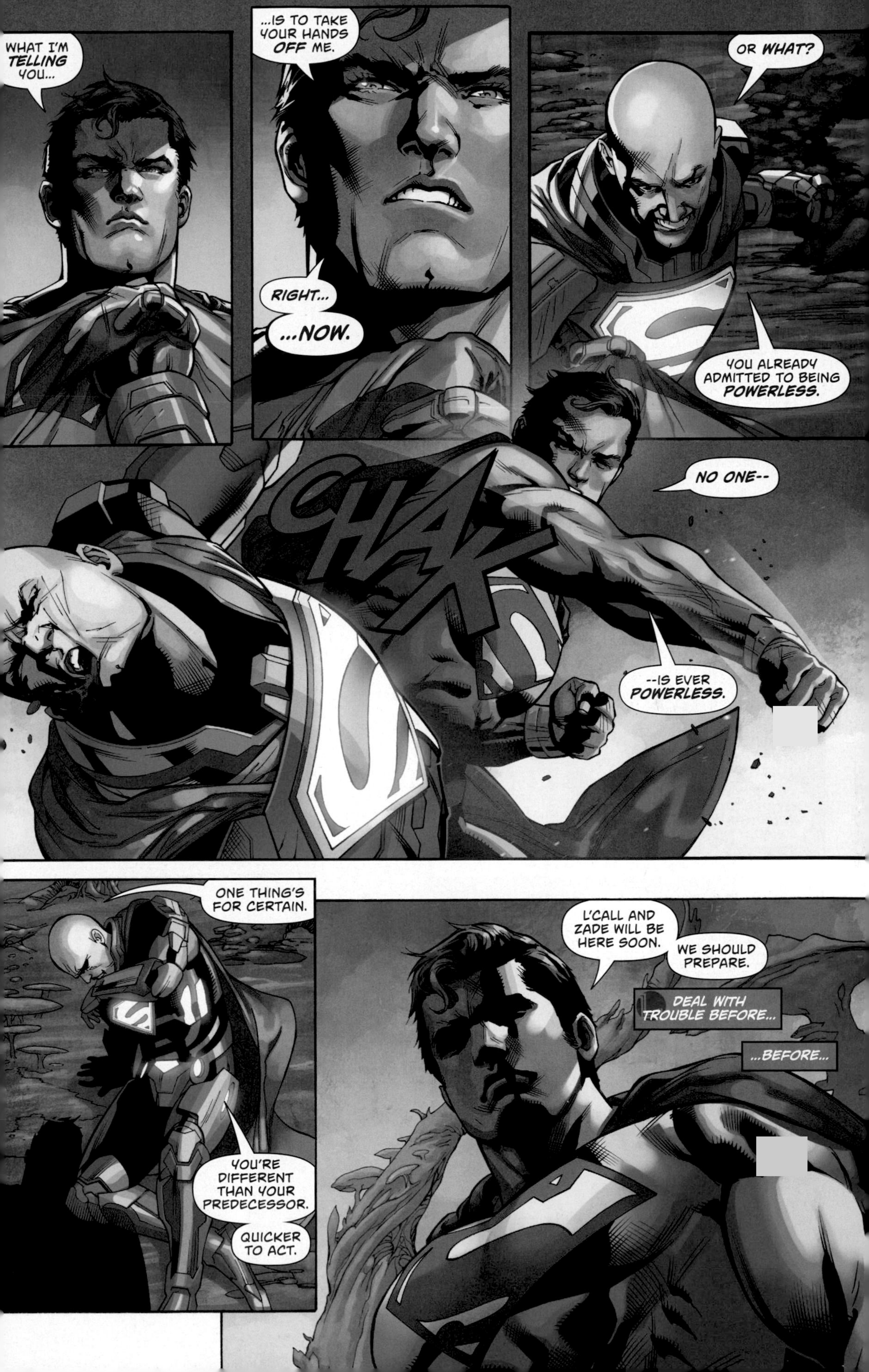
WHAT I'M TELLING YOU...
...IS TO TAKE YOUR HANDS OFF ME.
RIGHT...
...NOW.
OR WHAT?
YOU ALREADY ADMITTED TO BEING POWERLESS.
CHAK
NO ONE--
--IS EVER POWERLESS.
ONE THING'S FOR CERTAIN.
YOU'RE DIFFERENT THAN YOUR PREDECESSOR.
QUICKER TO ACT.
L'CALL AND ZADE WILL BE HERE SOON.
WE SHOULD PREPARE.
DEAL WITH TROUBLE BEFORE...
...BEFORE...

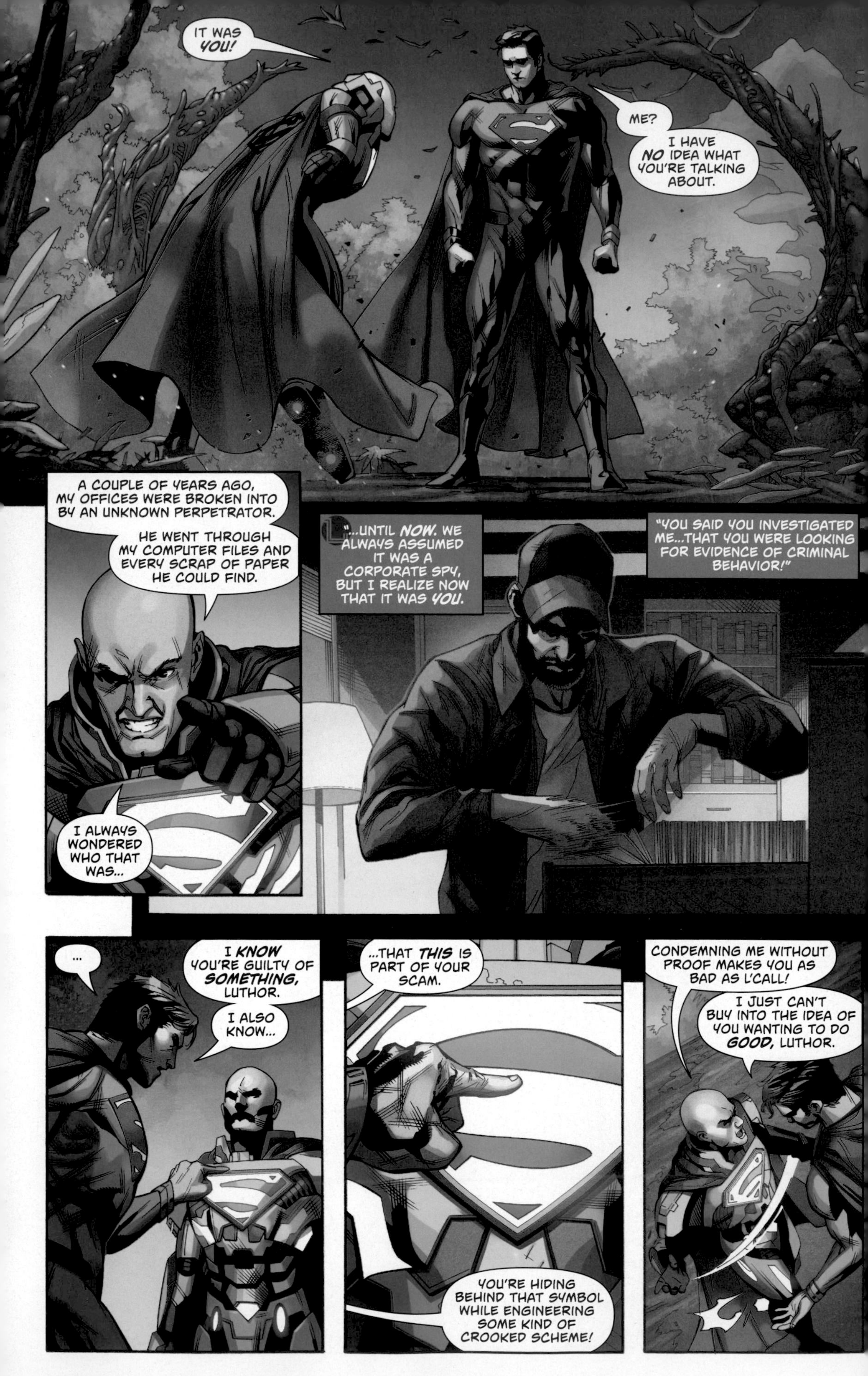
IT WAS YOU!
ME?
I HAVE NO IDEA WHAT YOU'RE TALKING ABOUT.
A COUPLE OF YEARS AGO, MY OFFICES WERE BROKEN INTO BY AN UNKNOWN PERPETRATOR.
HE WENT THROUGH MY COMPUTER FILES AND EVERY SCRAP OF PAPER HE COULD FIND.
I ALWAYS WONDERED WHO THAT WAS...
"...UNTIL NOW. WE ALWAYS ASSUMED IT WAS A CORPORATE SPY, BUT I REALIZE NOW THAT IT WAS YOU.
"YOU SAID YOU INVESTIGATED ME...THAT YOU WERE LOOKING FOR EVIDENCE OF CRIMINAL BEHAVIOR!"
...
I KNOW YOU'RE GUILTY OF SOMETHING, LUTHOR.
I ALSO KNOW...
...THAT THIS IS PART OF YOUR SCAM.
YOU'RE HIDING BEHIND THAT SYMBOL WHILE ENGINEERING SOME KIND OF CROOKED SCHEME!
CONDEMNING ME WITHOUT PROOF MAKES YOU AS BAD AS L'CALL!
I JUST CAN'T BUY INTO THE IDEA OF YOU WANTING TO DO GOOD, LUTHOR.

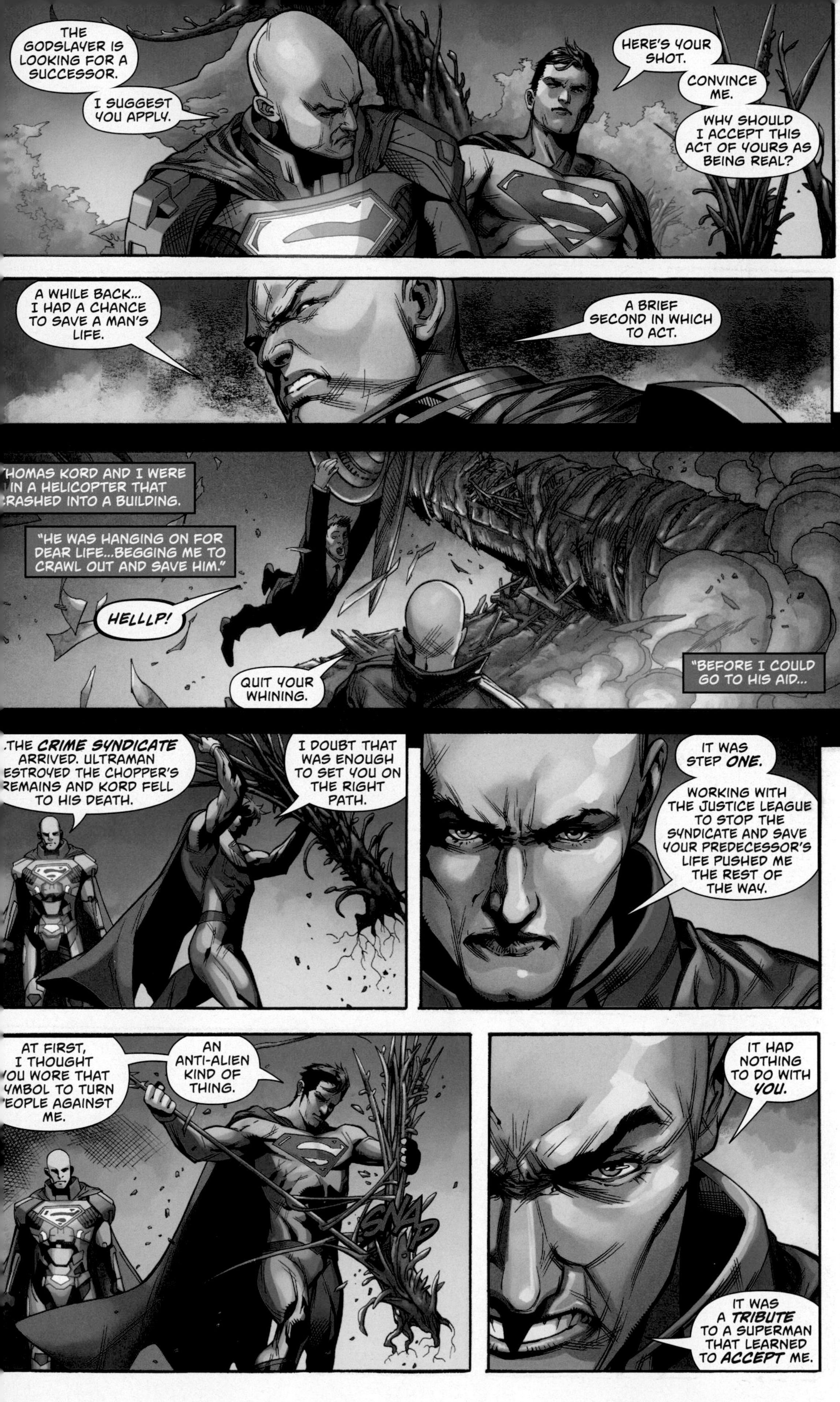
THE GODSLAYER IS LOOKING FOR A SUCCESSOR.
I SUGGEST YOU APPLY.
HERE'S YOUR SHOT.
CONVINCE ME.
WHY SHOULD I ACCEPT THIS ACT OF YOURS AS BEING REAL?
A WHILE BACK... I HAD A CHANCE TO SAVE A MAN'S LIFE.
A BRIEF SECOND IN WHICH TO ACT.
THOMAS KORD AND I WERE IN A HELICOPTER THAT CRASHED INTO A BUILDING.
"HE WAS HANGING ON FOR DEAR LIFE...BEGGING ME TO CRAWL OUT AND SAVE HIM."
HELLLP!
QUIT YOUR WHINING.
"BEFORE I COULD GO TO HIS AID...
...THE CRIME SYNDICATE ARRIVED. ULTRAMAN DESTROYED THE CHOPPER'S REMAINS AND KORD FELL TO HIS DEATH.
I DOUBT THAT WAS ENOUGH TO SET YOU ON THE RIGHT PATH.
IT WAS STEP ONE.
WORKING WITH THE JUSTICE LEAGUE TO STOP THE SYNDICATE AND SAVE YOUR PREDECESSOR'S LIFE PUSHED ME THE REST OF THE WAY.
AT FIRST, I THOUGHT YOU WORE THAT SYMBOL TO TURN PEOPLE AGAINST ME.
AN ANTI-ALIEN KIND OF THING.
SNAP
IT HAD NOTHING TO DO WITH YOU.
IT WAS A TRIBUTE TO A SUPERMAN THAT LEARNED TO ACCEPT ME.

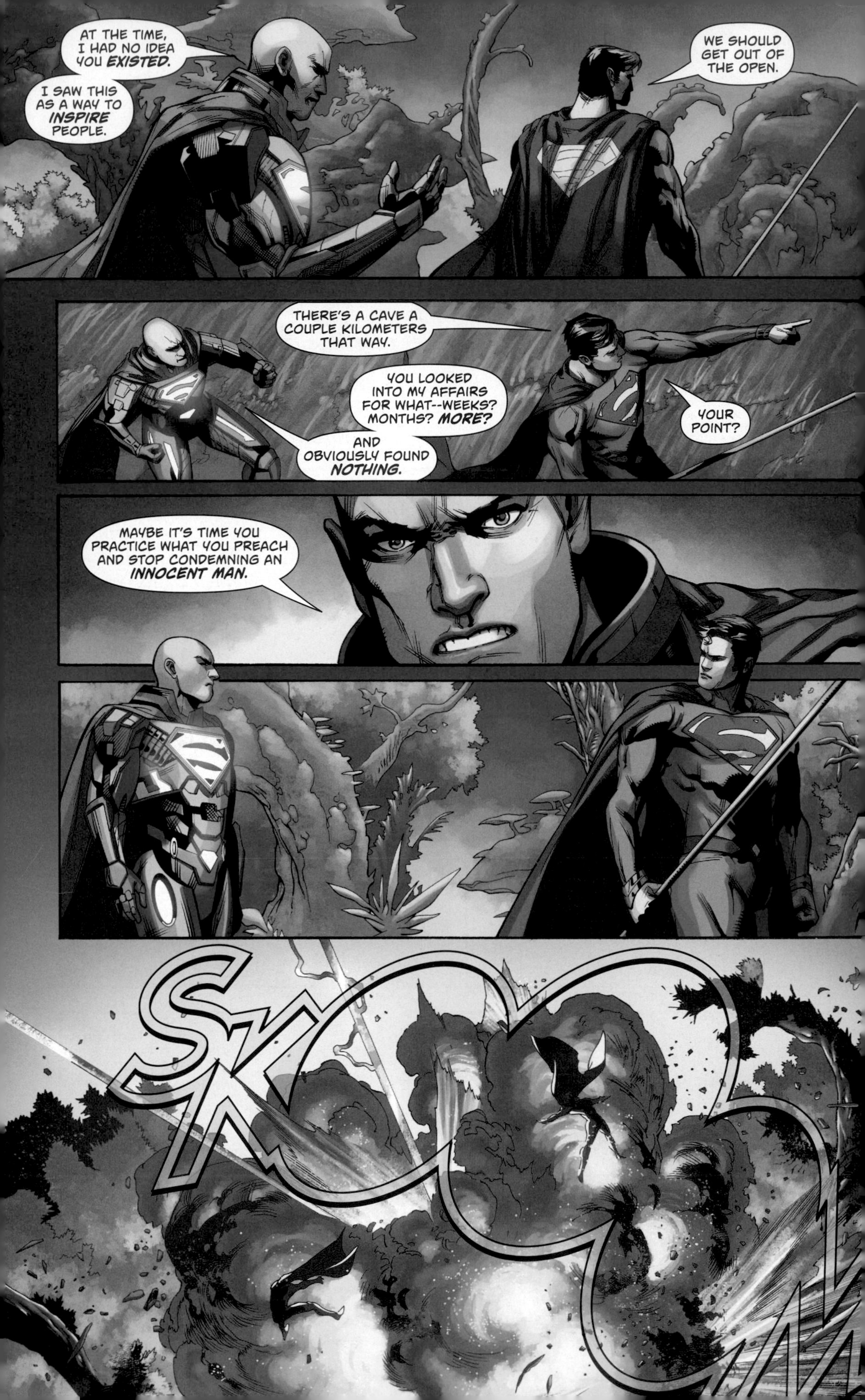
AT THE TIME, I HAD NO IDEA YOU EXISTED.
I SAW THIS AS A WAY TO INSPIRE PEOPLE.
WE SHOULD GET OUT OF THE OPEN.
THERE'S A CAVE A COUPLE KILOMETERS THAT WAY.
YOU LOOKED INTO MY AFFAIRS FOR WHAT--WEEKS? MONTHS? MORE?
AND OBVIOUSLY FOUND NOTHING.
YOUR POINT?
MAYBE IT'S TIME YOU PRACTICE WHAT YOU PREACH AND STOP CONDEMNING AN INNOCENT MAN.
SKOOM

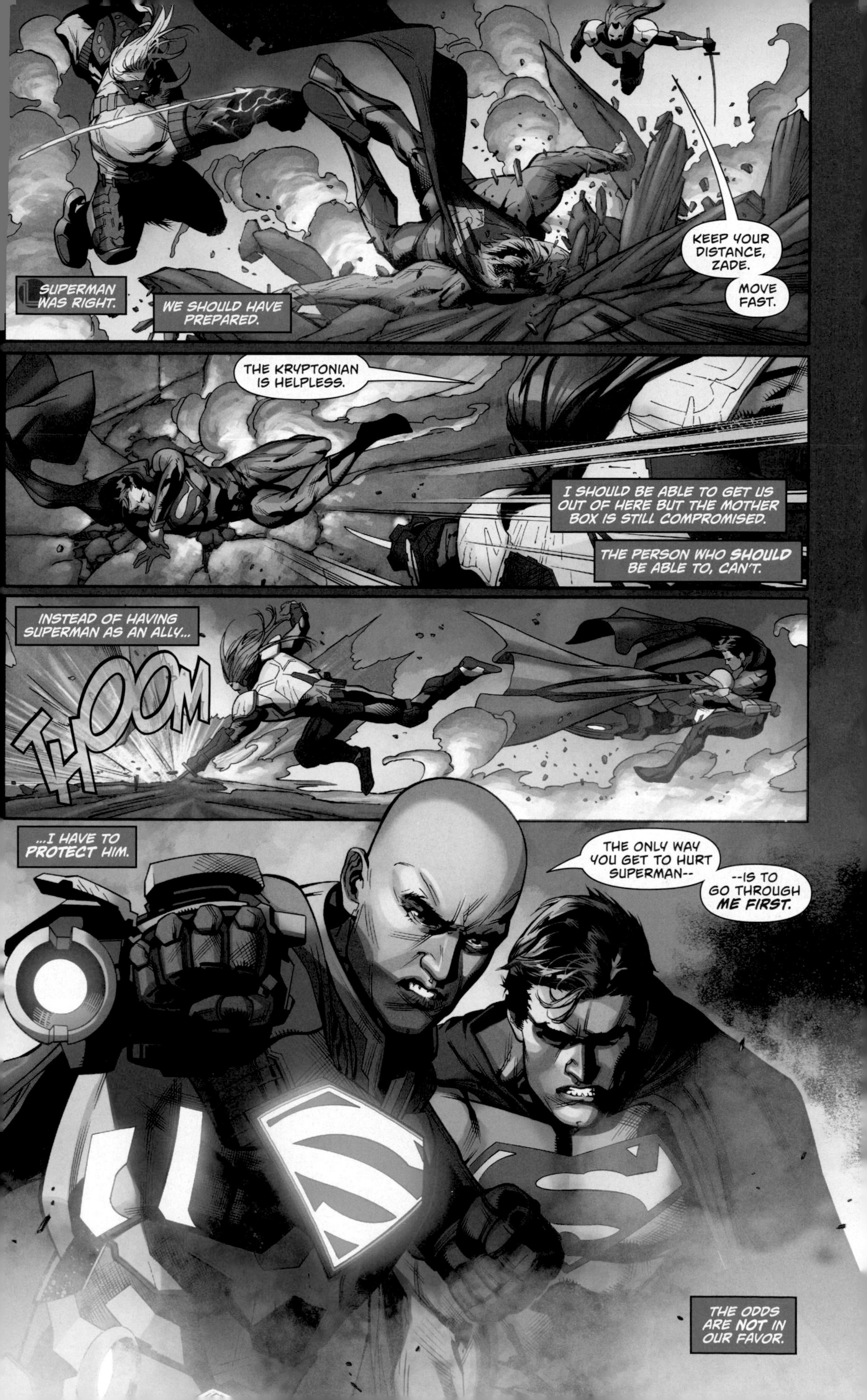
SUPERMAN WAS RIGHT.
WE SHOULD HAVE PREPARED.
KEEP YOUR DISTANCE, ZADE.
MOVE FAST.
THE KRYPTONIAN IS HELPLESS.
I SHOULD BE ABLE TO GET US OUT OF HERE BUT THE MOTHER BOX IS STILL COMPROMISED.
THE PERSON WHO SHOULD BE ABLE TO, CAN'T.
INSTEAD OF HAVING SUPERMAN AS AN ALLY...
THOOM
...I HAVE TO PROTECT HIM.
THE ONLY WAY YOU GET TO HURT SUPERMAN--
--IS TO GO THROUGH ME FIRST.
THE ODDS ARE NOT IN OUR FAVOR.

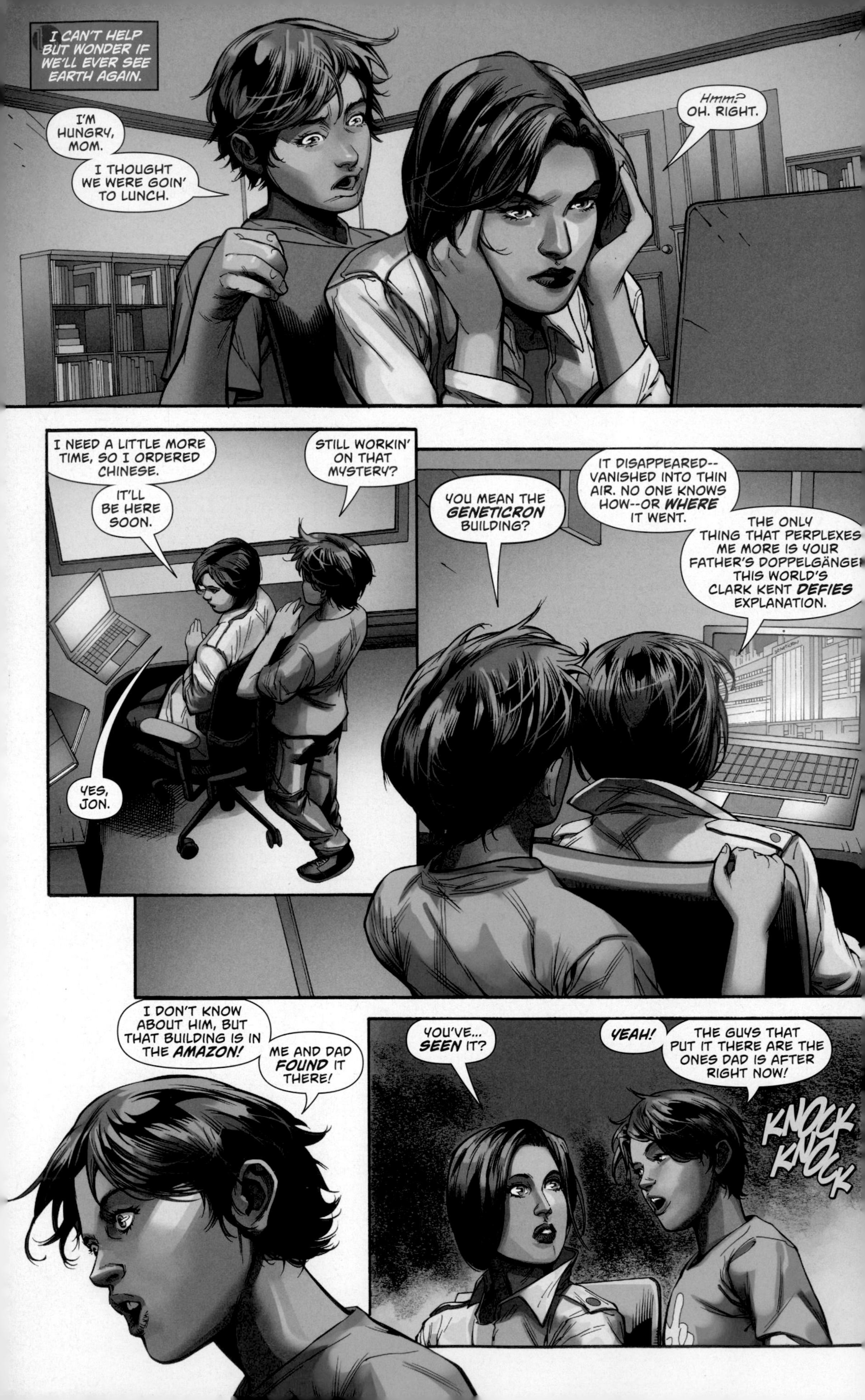
I CAN'T HELP BUT WONDER IF WE'LL EVER SEE EARTH AGAIN.
I'M HUNGRY, MOM.
I THOUGHT WE WERE GOIN' TO LUNCH.
Hmm? OH. RIGHT.
I NEED A LITTLE MORE TIME, SO I ORDERED CHINESE.
IT'LL BE HERE SOON.
STILL WORKIN' ON THAT MYSTERY?
YES, JON.
YOU MEAN THE GENETICRON BUILDING?
IT DISAPPEARED-- VANISHED INTO THIN AIR. NO ONE KNOWS HOW--OR WHERE IT WENT.
THE ONLY THING THAT PERPLEXES ME MORE IS YOUR FATHER'S DOPPELGÄNGER. THIS WORLD'S CLARK KENT DEFIES EXPLANATION.
I DON'T KNOW ABOUT HIM, BUT THAT BUILDING IS IN THE AMAZON!
ME AND DAD FOUND IT THERE!
YOU'VE... SEEN IT?
YEAH!
THE GUYS THAT PUT IT THERE ARE THE ONES DAD IS AFTER RIGHT NOW!
KNOCK KNOCK

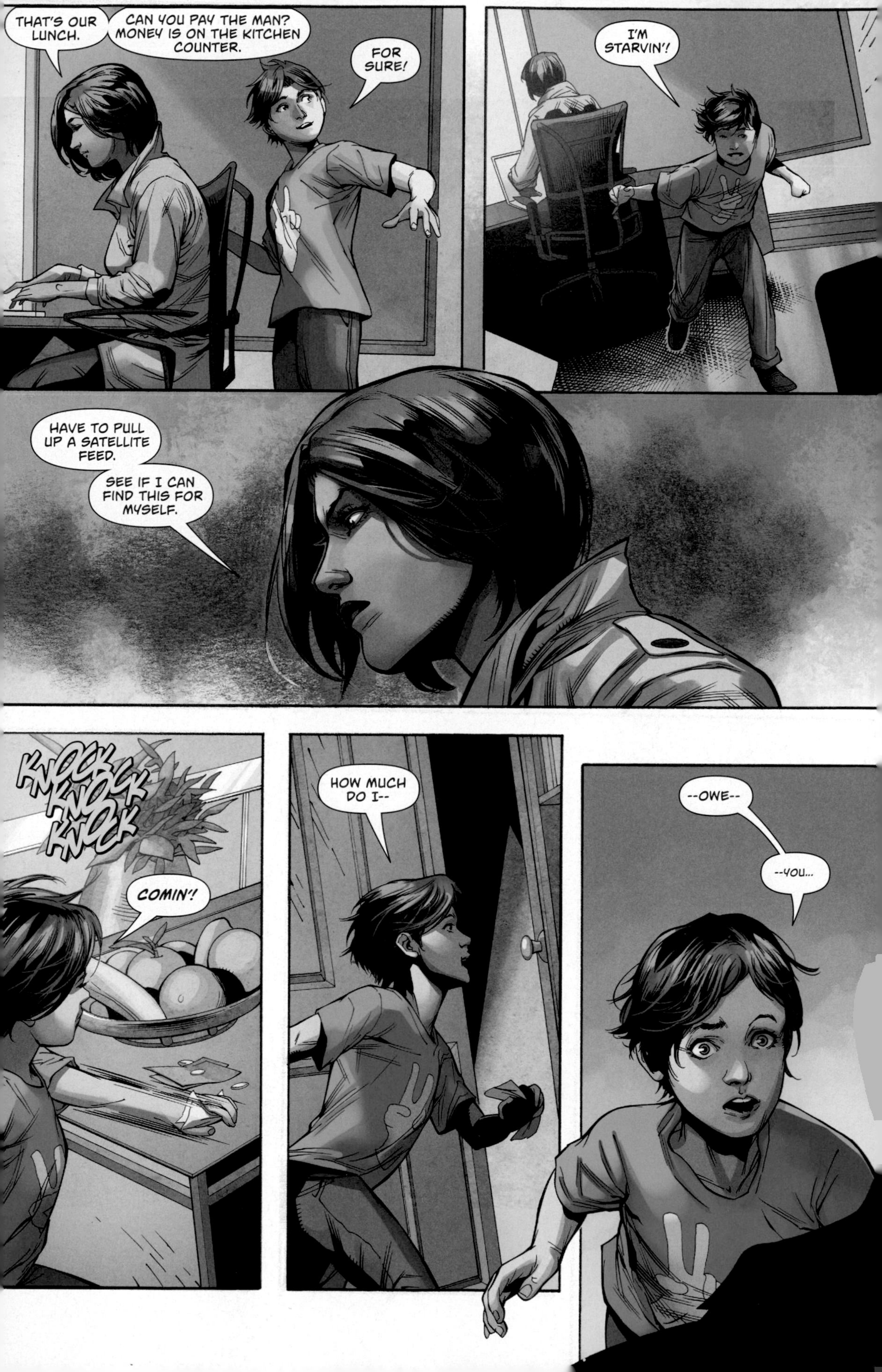
THAT'S OUR LUNCH.
CAN YOU PAY THE MAN? MONEY IS ON THE KITCHEN COUNTER.
FOR SURE!
I'M STARVIN'!
HAVE TO PULL UP A SATELLITE FEED.
SEE IF I CAN FIND THIS FOR MYSELF.
KNOCK KNOCK KNOCK
COMIN'!
HOW MUCH DO I--
--OWE--
--YOU...

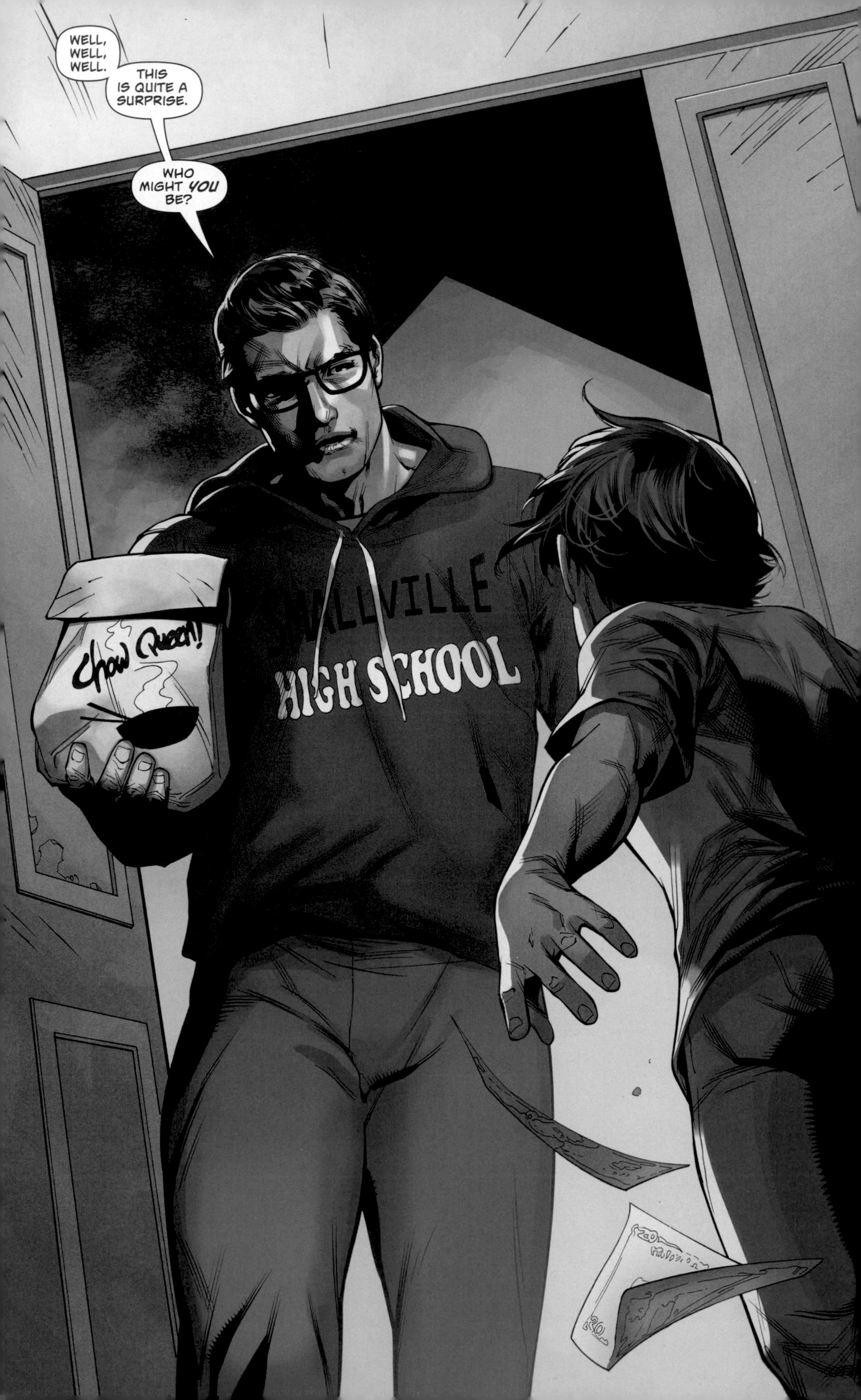
WELL, WELL, WELL.
THIS IS QUITE A SURPRISE.
WHO MIGHT YOU BE?
Chow Queen!
HIGH SCHOOL

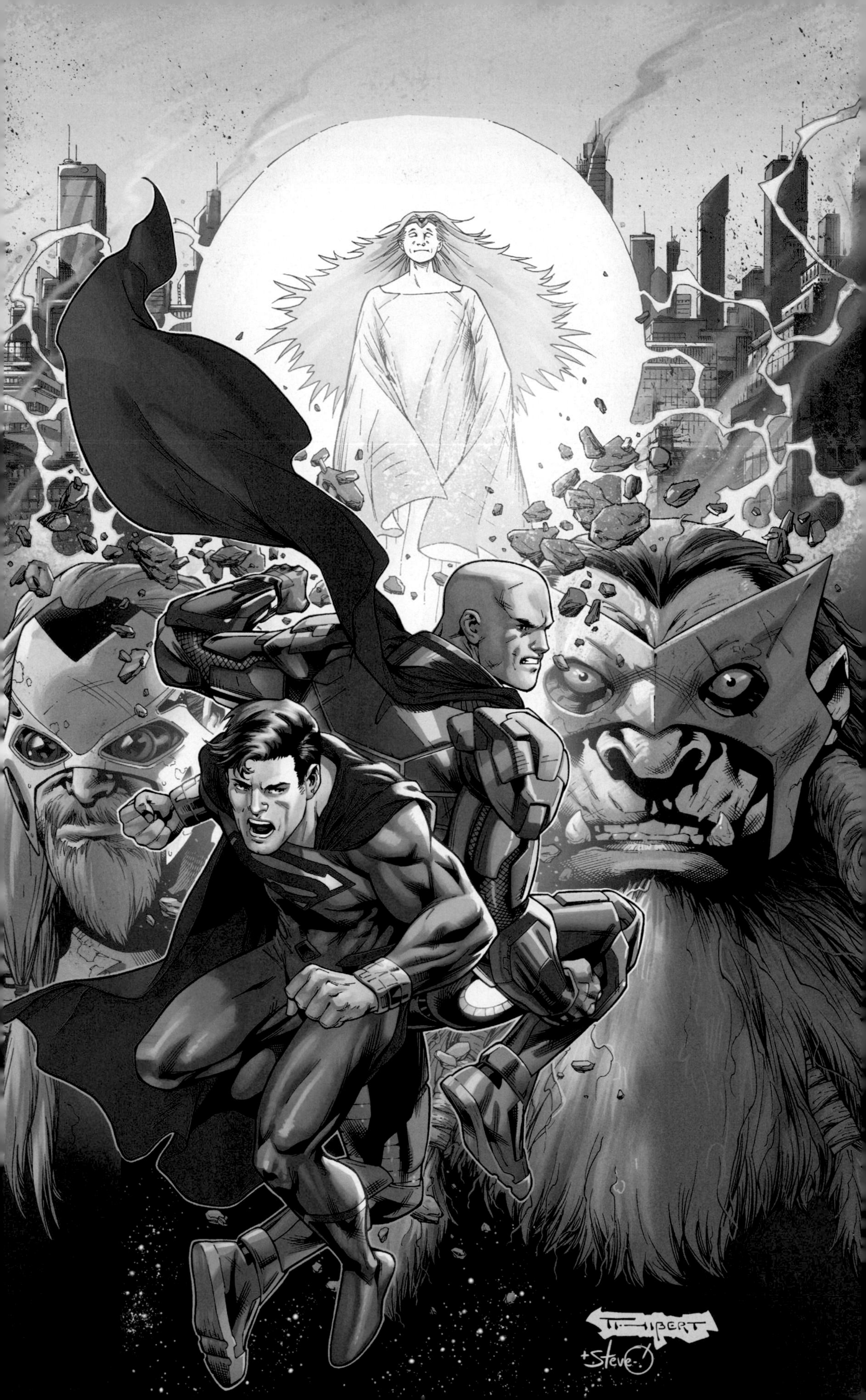

MEN OF STEEL PART 6

STEPHEN SEGOVIA penciller * ART THIBERT inker * ULISES ARREOLA colorist
ART THIBERT STEVE DOWNER cover artists

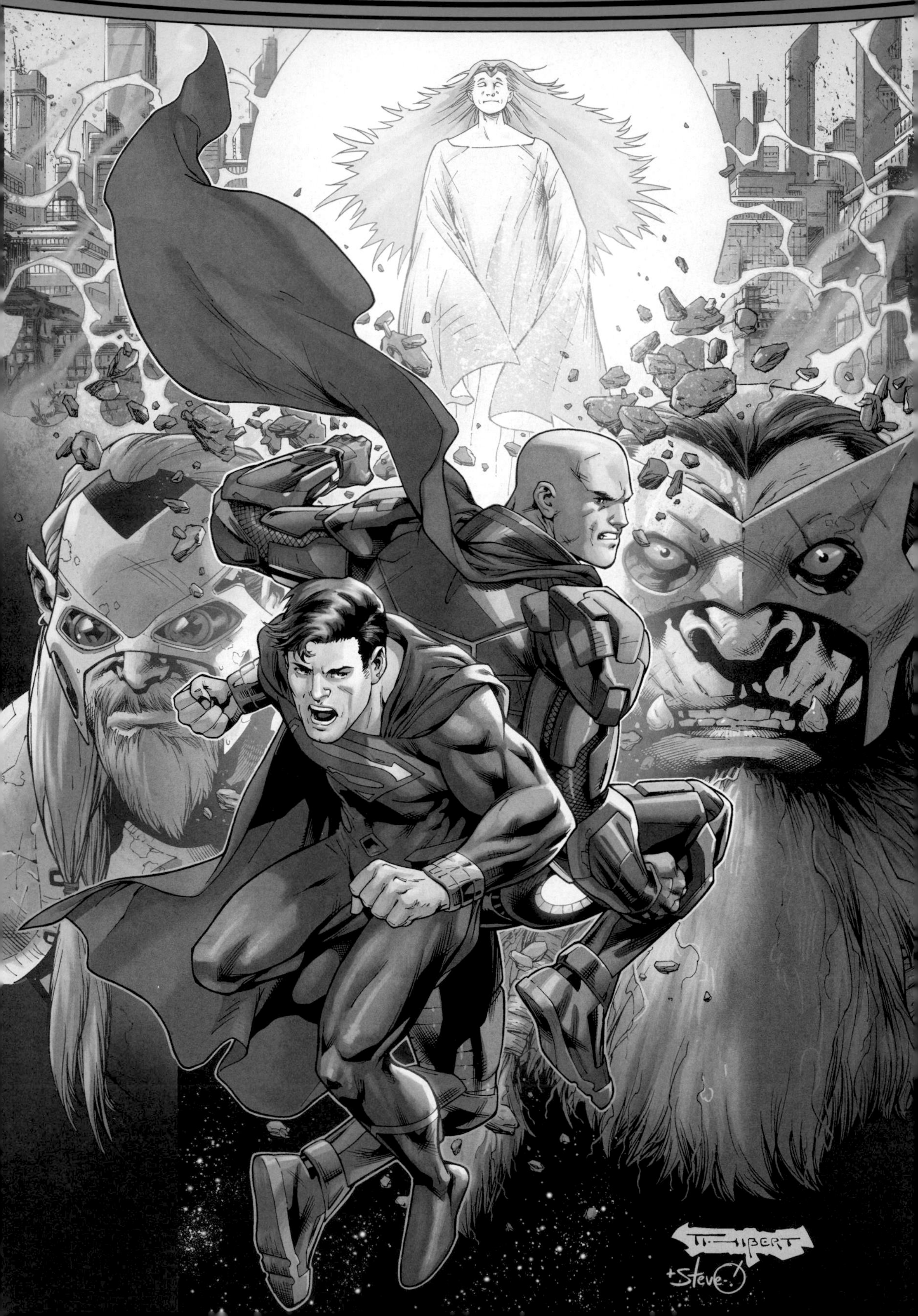

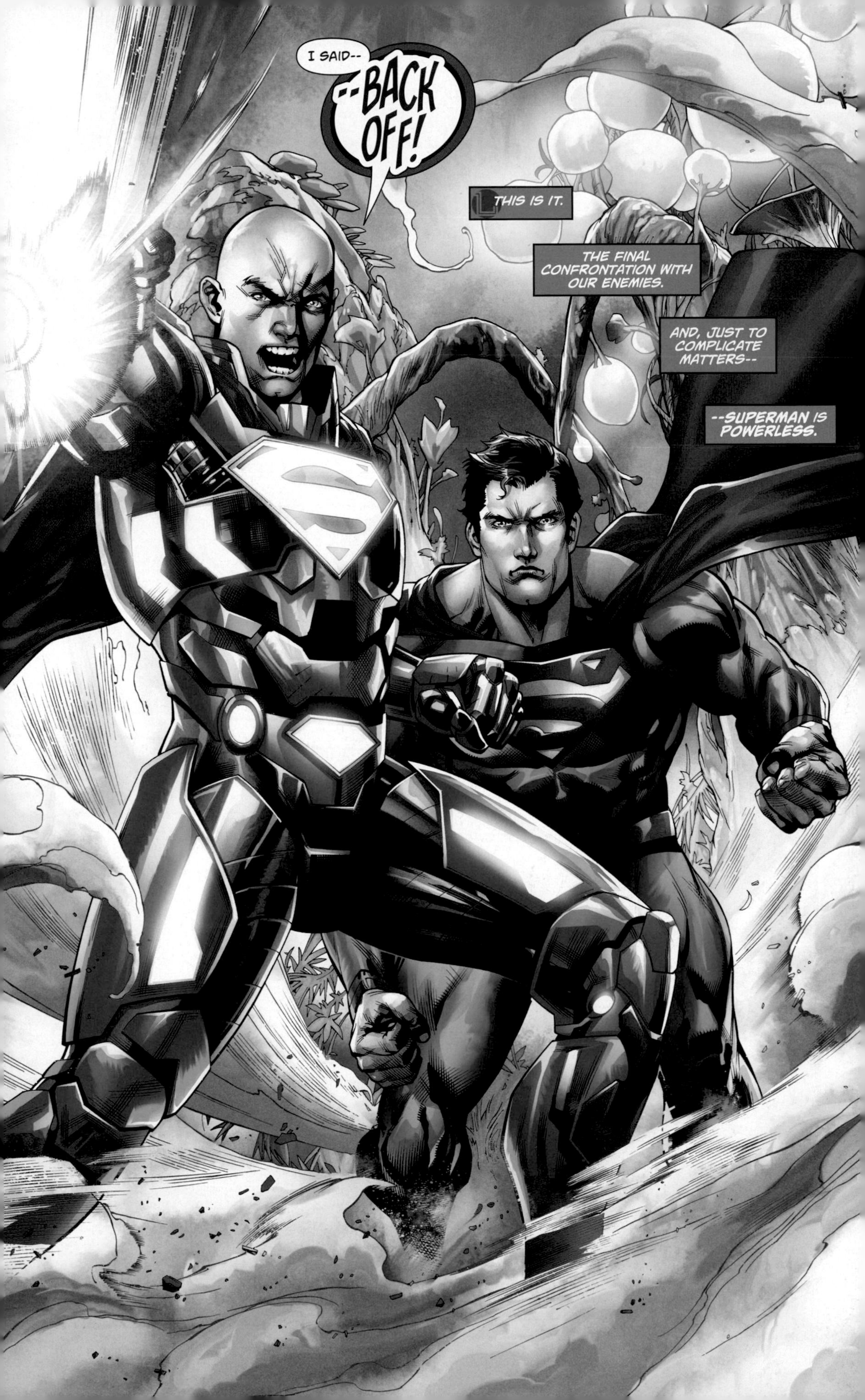
I SAID--
--BACK OFF!
THIS IS IT.
THE FINAL CONFRONTATION WITH OUR ENEMIES.
AND, JUST TO COMPLICATE MATTERS--
--SUPERMAN IS POWERLESS.

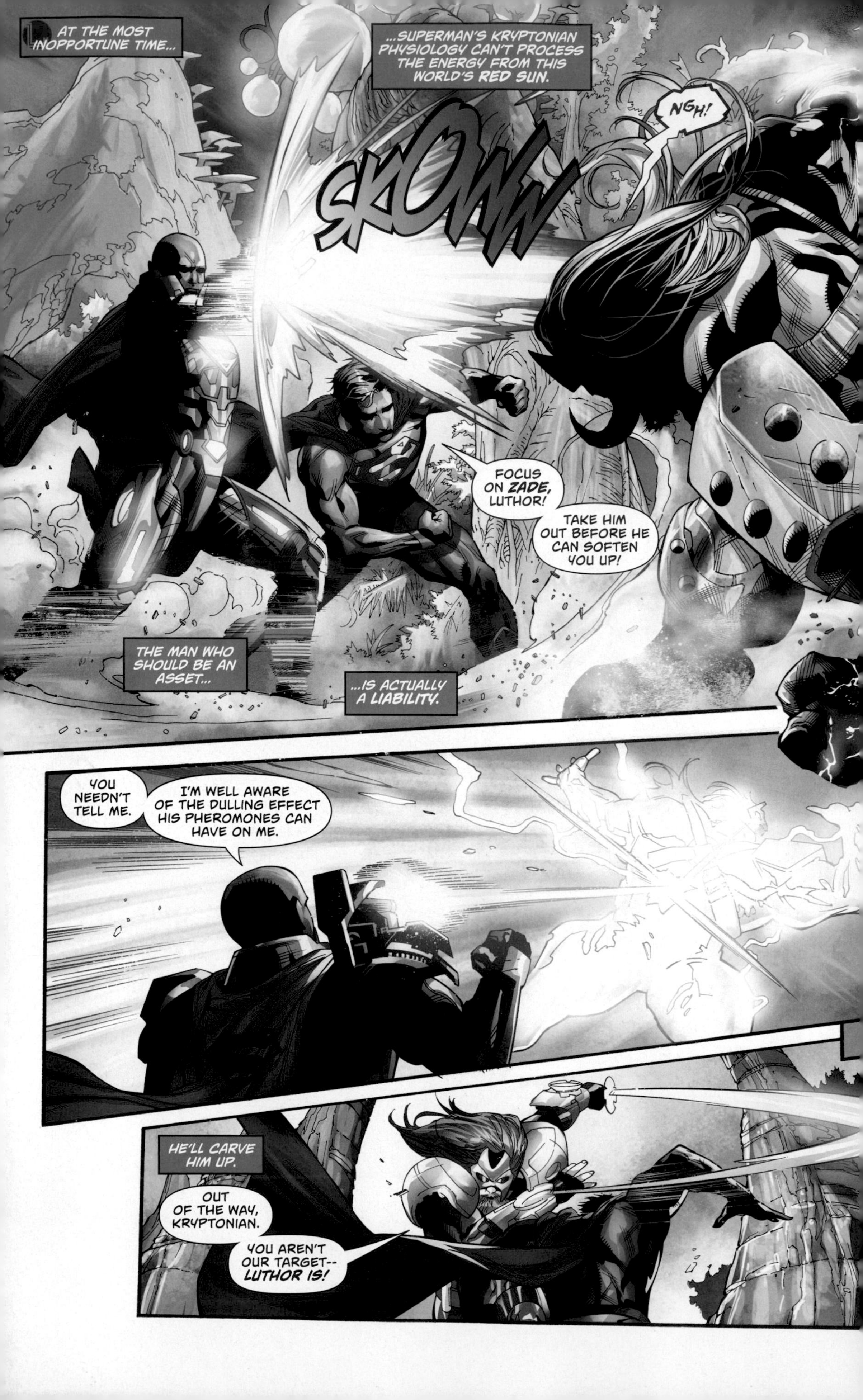
AT THE MOST INOPPORTUNE TIME...
...SUPERMAN'S KRYPTONIAN PHYSIOLOGY CAN'T PROCESS THE ENERGY FROM THIS WORLD'S RED SUN.
SKOWW
NGH!
FOCUS ON ZADE, LUTHOR!
TAKE HIM OUT BEFORE HE CAN SOFTEN YOU UP!
THE MAN WHO SHOULD BE AN ASSET...
...IS ACTUALLY A LIABILITY.
YOU NEEDN'T TELL ME.
I'M WELL AWARE OF THE DULLING EFFECT HIS PHEROMONES CAN HAVE ON ME.
HE'LL CARVE HIM UP.
OUT OF THE WAY, KRYPTONIAN.
YOU AREN'T OUR TARGET-- LUTHOR IS!

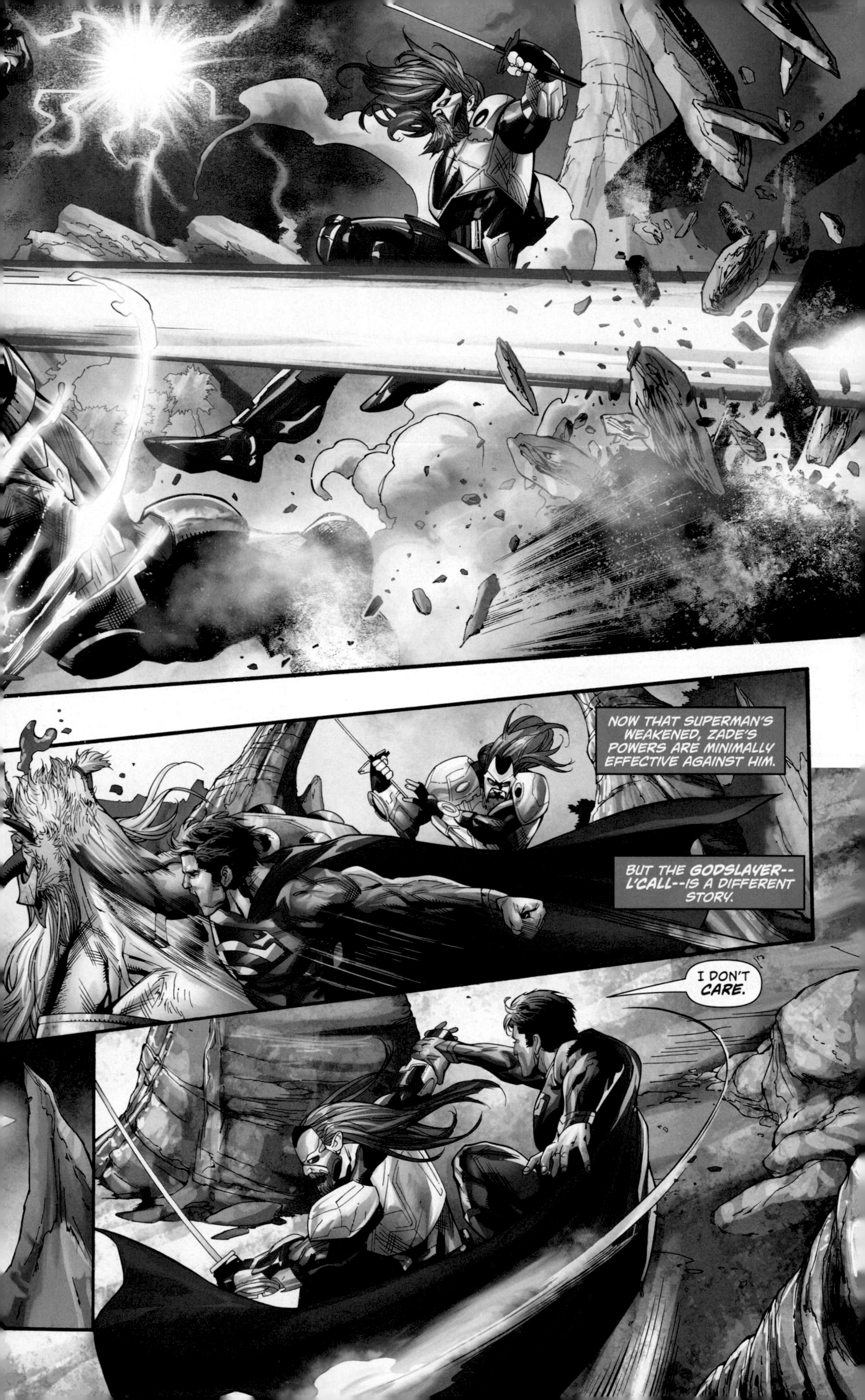
NOW THAT SUPERMAN'S WEAKENED, ZADE'S POWERS ARE MINIMALLY EFFECTIVE AGAINST HIM.
BUT THE GODSLAYER--L'CALL--IS A DIFFERENT STORY.
I DON'T CARE.

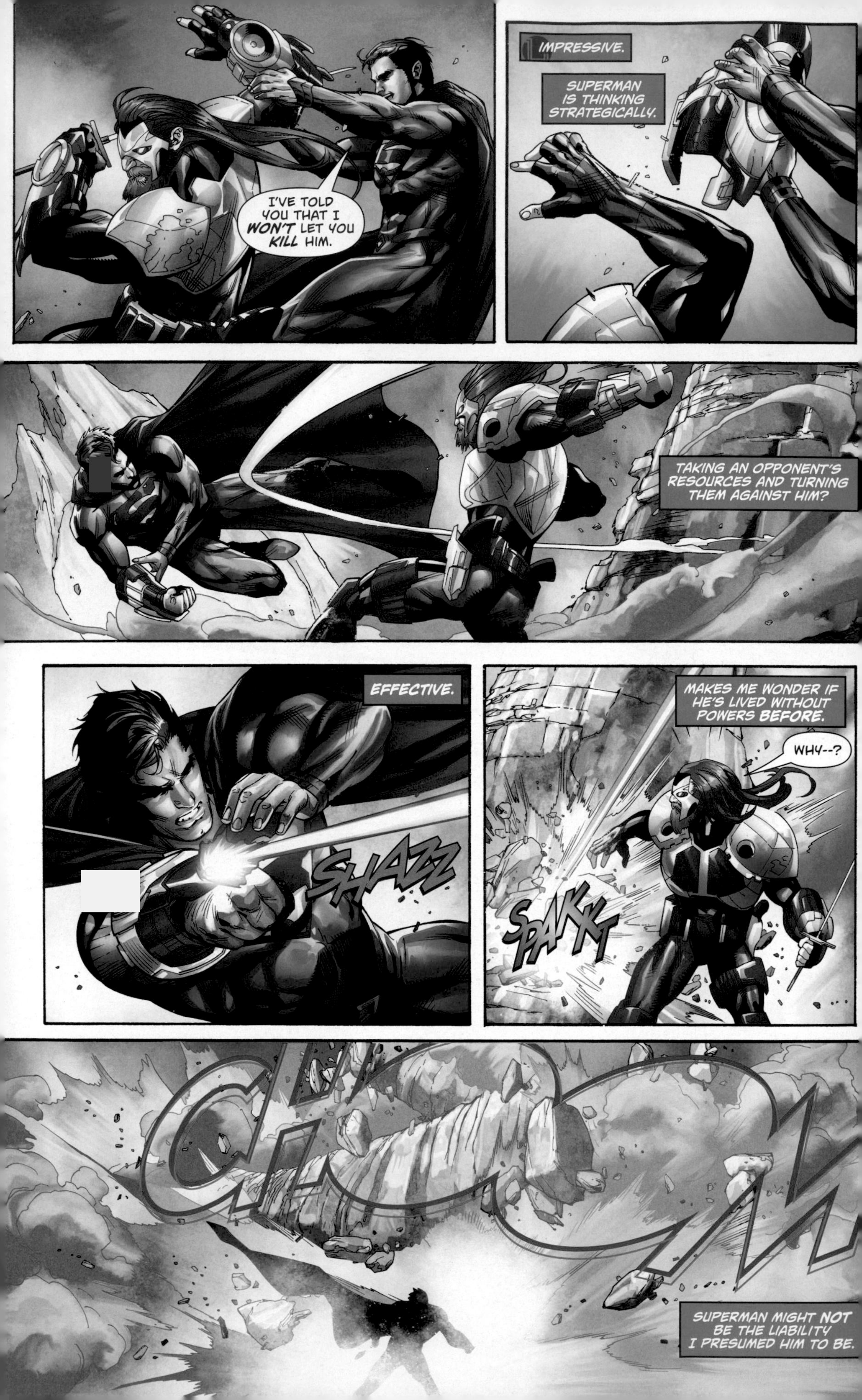
I'VE TOLD YOU THAT I WON'T LET YOU KILL HIM.
IMPRESSIVE.
SUPERMAN IS THINKING STRATEGICALLY.
TAKING AN OPPONENT'S RESOURCES AND TURNING THEM AGAINST HIM?
EFFECTIVE.
SHAZZ
MAKES ME WONDER IF HE'S LIVED WITHOUT POWERS BEFORE.
WHY--?
SPAKKT
SUPERMAN MIGHT NOT BE THE LIABILITY I PRESUMED HIM TO BE.

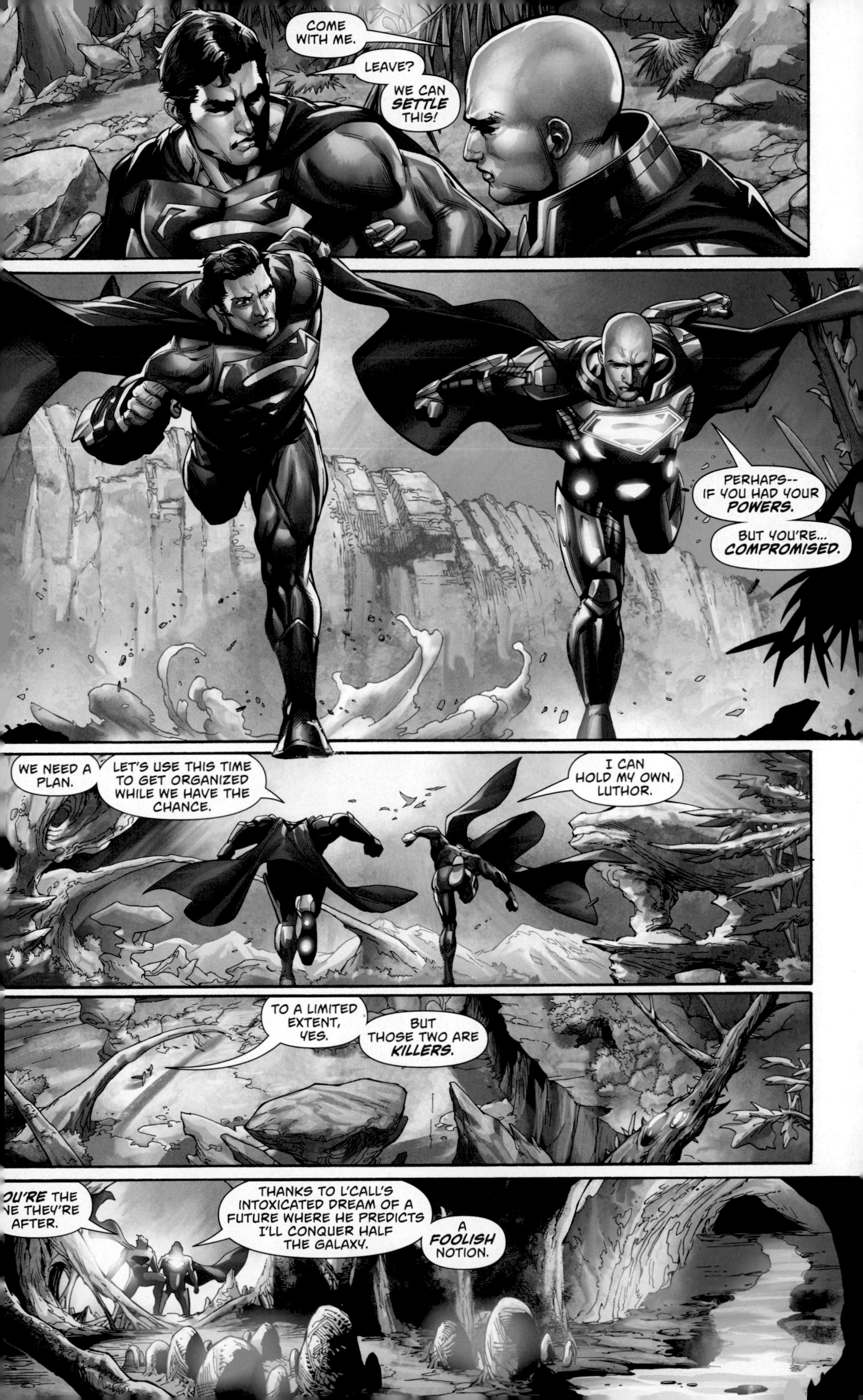
COME WITH ME.
LEAVE?
WE CAN SETTLE THIS!
PERHAPS-- IF YOU HAD YOUR POWERS.
BUT YOU'RE... COMPROMISED.
WE NEED A PLAN.
LET'S USE THIS TIME TO GET ORGANIZED WHILE WE HAVE THE CHANCE.
I CAN HOLD MY OWN, LUTHOR.
TO A LIMITED EXTENT, YES.
BUT THOSE TWO ARE KILLERS.
AFTER.
THANKS TO L'CALL'S INTOXICATED DREAM OF A FUTURE WHERE HE PREDICTS I'LL CONQUER HALF THE GALAXY.
A FOOLISH NOTION.

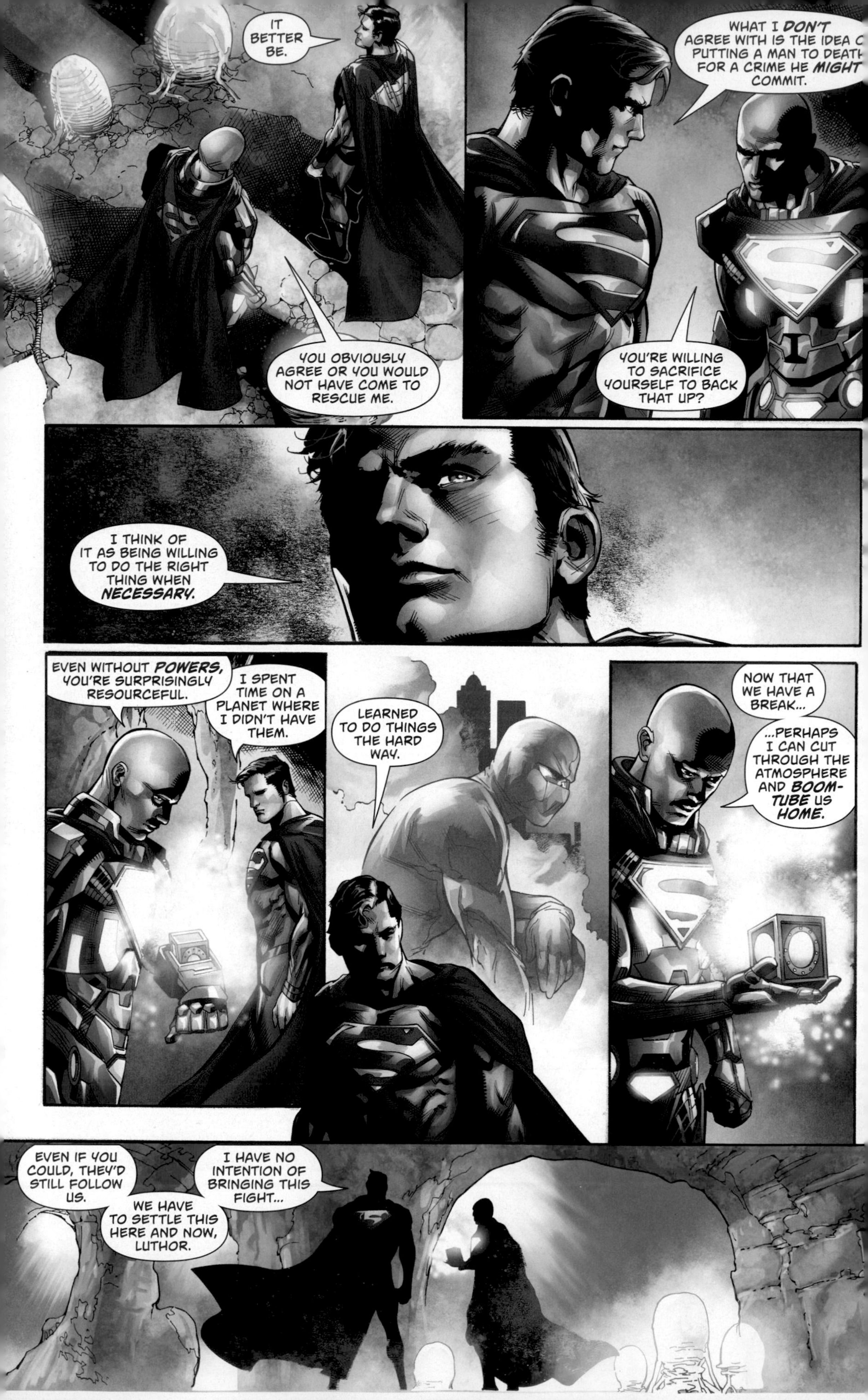
IT BETTER BE.
YOU OBVIOUSLY AGREE OR YOU WOULD NOT HAVE COME TO RESCUE ME.
WHAT I DON'T AGREE WITH IS THE IDEA OF PUTTING A MAN TO DEATH FOR A CRIME HE MIGHT COMMIT.
YOU'RE WILLING TO SACRIFICE YOURSELF TO BACK THAT UP?
I THINK OF IT AS BEING WILLING TO DO THE RIGHT THING WHEN NECESSARY.
EVEN WITHOUT POWERS, YOU'RE SURPRISINGLY RESOURCEFUL.
I SPENT TIME ON A PLANET WHERE I DIDN'T HAVE THEM.
LEARNED TO DO THINGS THE HARD WAY.
NOW THAT WE HAVE A BREAK...
...PERHAPS I CAN CUT THROUGH THE ATMOSPHERE AND BOOM-TUBE US HOME.
EVEN IF YOU COULD, THEY'D STILL FOLLOW US.
WE HAVE TO SETTLE THIS HERE AND NOW, LUTHOR.
I HAVE NO INTENTION OF BRINGING THIS FIGHT...

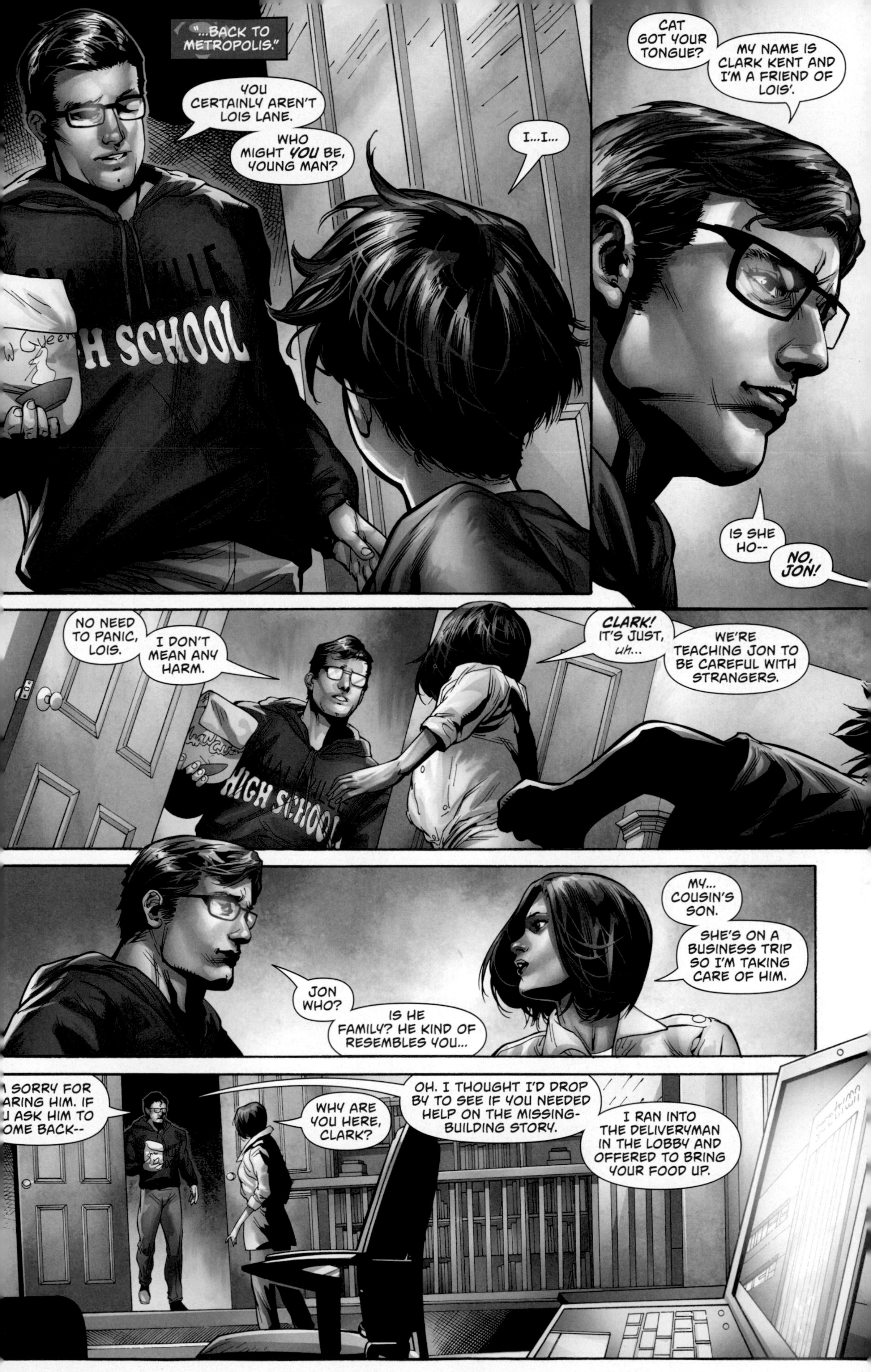
"...BACK TO METROPOLIS."
YOU CERTAINLY AREN'T LOIS LANE.
WHO MIGHT *YOU* BE, YOUNG MAN?
I...I...
CAT GOT YOUR TONGUE?
MY NAME IS CLARK KENT AND I'M A FRIEND OF LOIS'.
IS SHE HO--
NO, JON!
NO NEED TO PANIC, LOIS.
I DON'T MEAN ANY HARM.
CLARK! IT'S JUST, *uh...*
WE'RE TEACHING JON TO BE CAREFUL WITH STRANGERS.
HIGH SCHOOL
JON WHO?
IS HE FAMILY? HE KIND OF RESEMBLES YOU...
MY... COUSIN'S SON.
SHE'S ON A BUSINESS TRIP SO I'M TAKING CARE OF HIM.
SORRY FOR
ARING HIM. IF
U ASK HIM TO
OME BACK--
WHY ARE YOU HERE, CLARK?
OH. I THOUGHT I'D DROP BY TO SEE IF YOU NEEDED HELP ON THE MISSING-BUILDING STORY.
I RAN INTO THE DELIVERYMAN IN THE LOBBY AND OFFERED TO BRING YOUR FOOD UP.

THAT'S VERY THOUGHTFUL OF YOU, CLARK.

SURE! I--

BUT RIGHT NOW, I'M HELPING JON WITH HIS HOMEWORK.

MATH? I'M GREAT AT--

THANKS. WE HAVE IT UNDER CONTROL.

ANOTHER TIME, OKAY?

SEE YOU IN THE OFFICE!

BUT--THE GENETICRON BUILDING--!

CAN WAIT UNTIL MONDAY.

BYE!

BUT--!

THAT WAS CREEPY, MOM!

HE'S JUST LIKE DAD--BUT NOT LIKE DAD--ALL AT THE SAME TIME!

I KNOW, JON. AND WE NEVER, EVER WANTED HIM TO SEE YOU.

SHE'S LYING TO ME.

I CAN FEEL IT.

THE QUESTION IS...

...WHY?

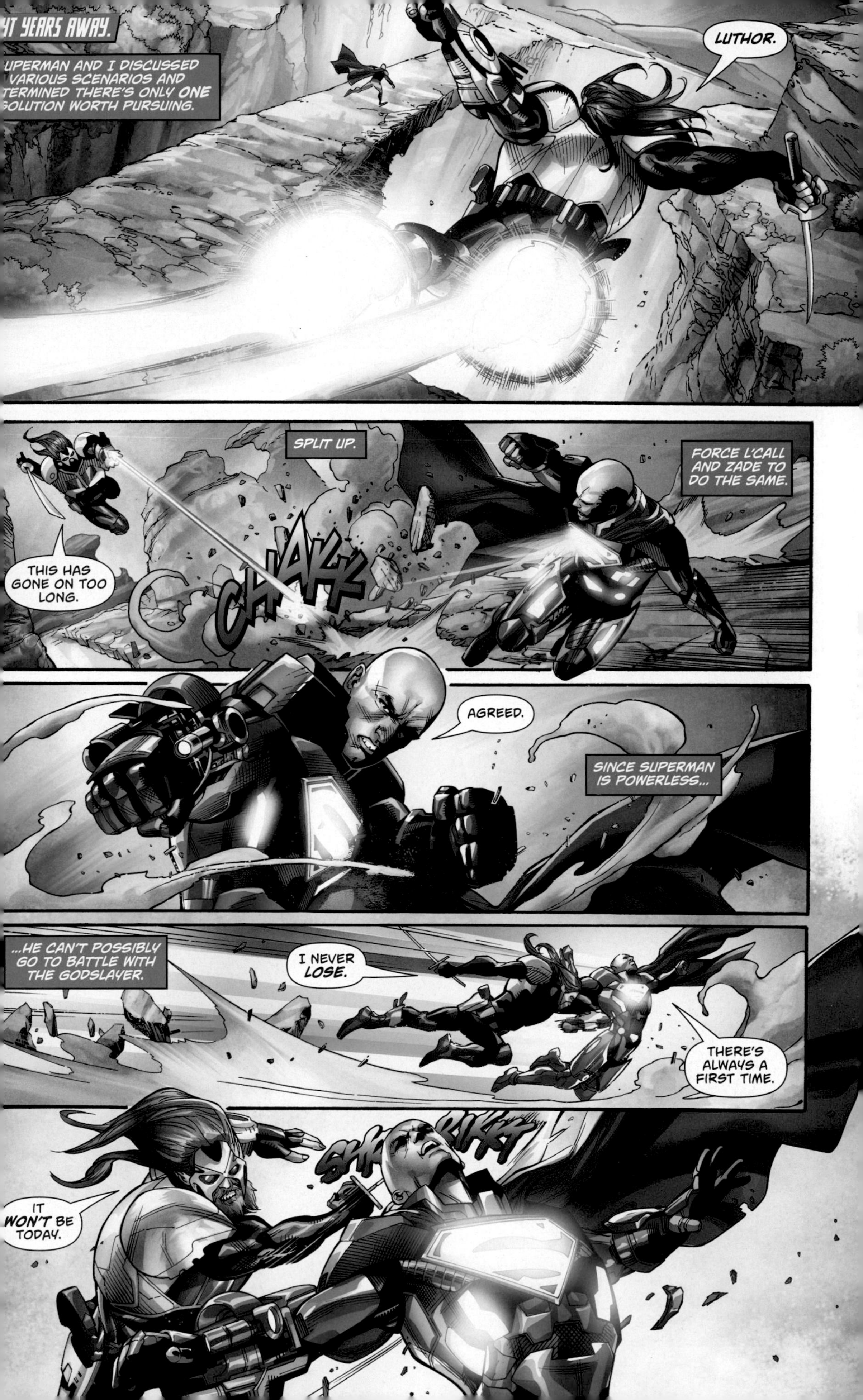
HT YEARS AWAY.
UPERMAN AND I DISCUSSED VARIOUS SCENARIOS AND TERMINED THERE'S ONLY ONE SOLUTION WORTH PURSUING.
LUTHOR.
SPLIT UP.
FORCE L'CALL AND ZADE TO DO THE SAME.
THIS HAS GONE ON TOO LONG.
CHAKK
AGREED.
SINCE SUPERMAN IS POWERLESS...
...HE CAN'T POSSIBLY GO TO BATTLE WITH THE GODSLAYER.
I NEVER LOSE.
THERE'S ALWAYS A FIRST TIME.
IT WON'T BE TODAY.

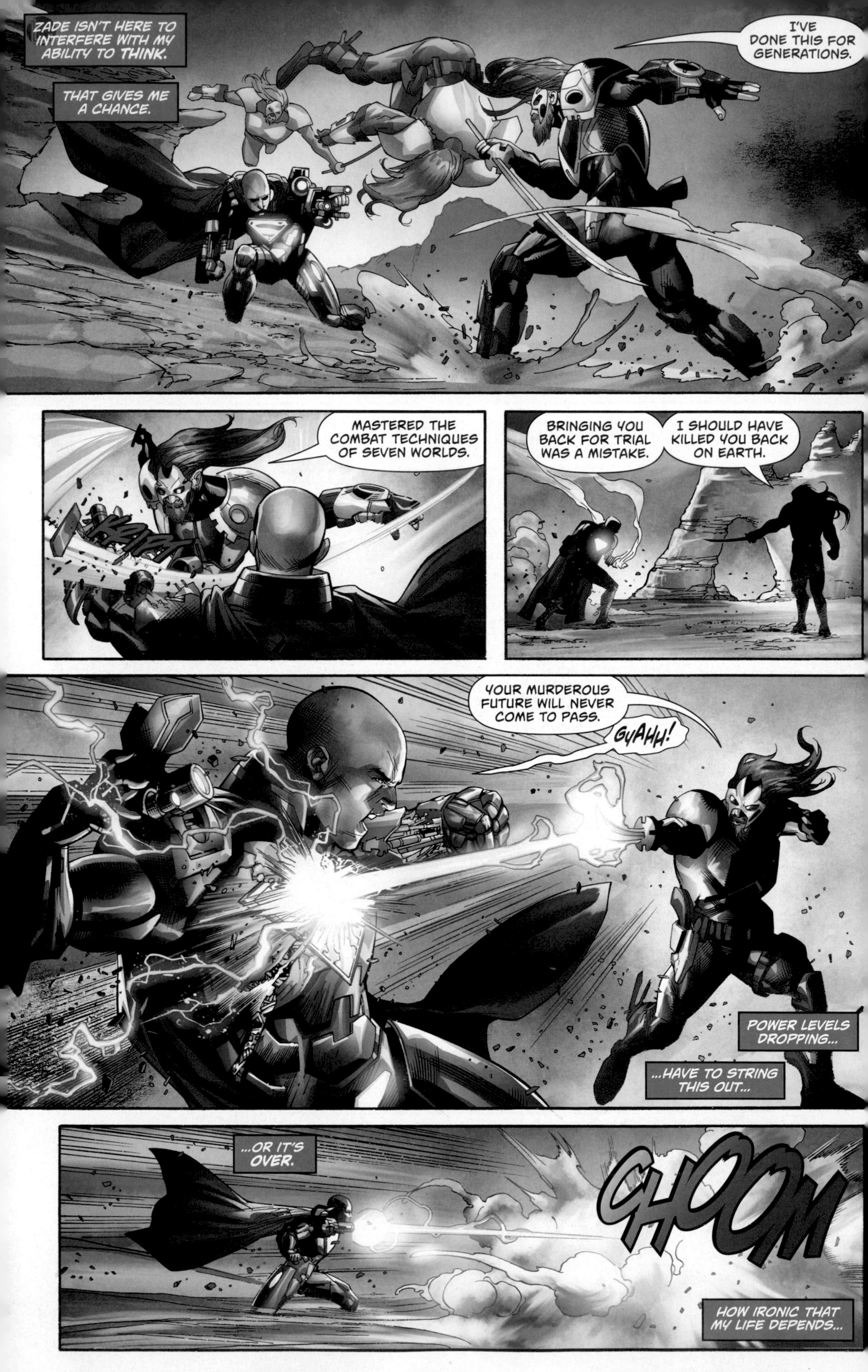
ZADE ISN'T HERE TO INTERFERE WITH MY ABILITY TO THINK.
THAT GIVES ME A CHANCE.
I'VE DONE THIS FOR GENERATIONS.
MASTERED THE COMBAT TECHNIQUES OF SEVEN WORLDS.
BRINGING YOU BACK FOR TRIAL WAS A MISTAKE.
I SHOULD HAVE KILLED YOU BACK ON EARTH.
YOUR MURDEROUS FUTURE WILL NEVER COME TO PASS.
GYAHH!
POWER LEVELS DROPPING...
...HAVE TO STRING THIS OUT...
...OR IT'S OVER.
CHOOM
HOW IRONIC THAT MY LIFE DEPENDS...

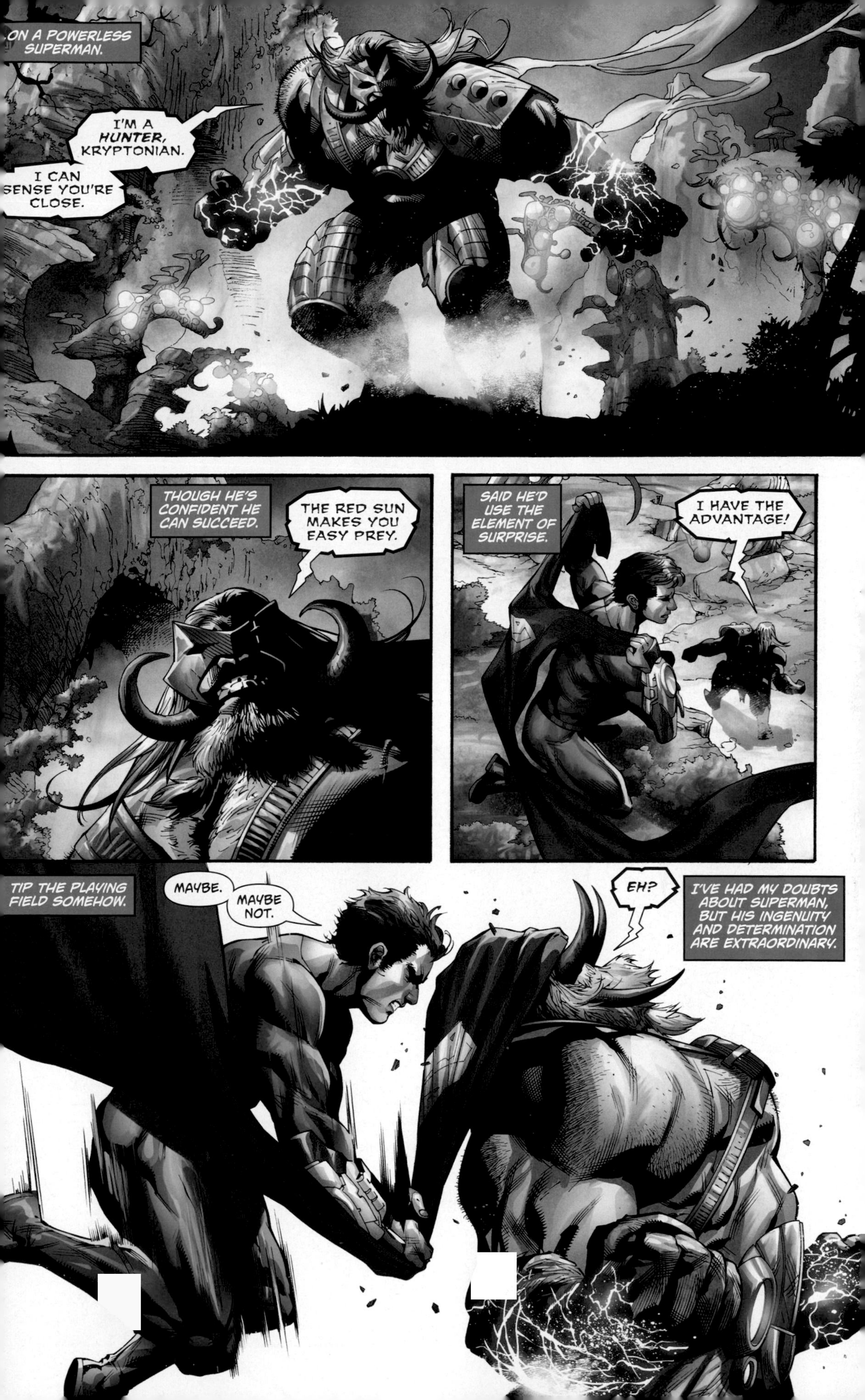
ON A POWERLESS SUPERMAN.
I'M A HUNTER, KRYPTONIAN.
I CAN SENSE YOU'RE CLOSE.
THOUGH HE'S CONFIDENT HE CAN SUCCEED.
THE RED SUN MAKES YOU EASY PREY.
SAID HE'D USE THE ELEMENT OF SURPRISE.
I HAVE THE ADVANTAGE!
TIP THE PLAYING FIELD SOMEHOW.
MAYBE.
MAYBE NOT.
EH?
I'VE HAD MY DOUBTS ABOUT SUPERMAN, BUT HIS INGENUITY AND DETERMINATION ARE EXTRAORDINARY.

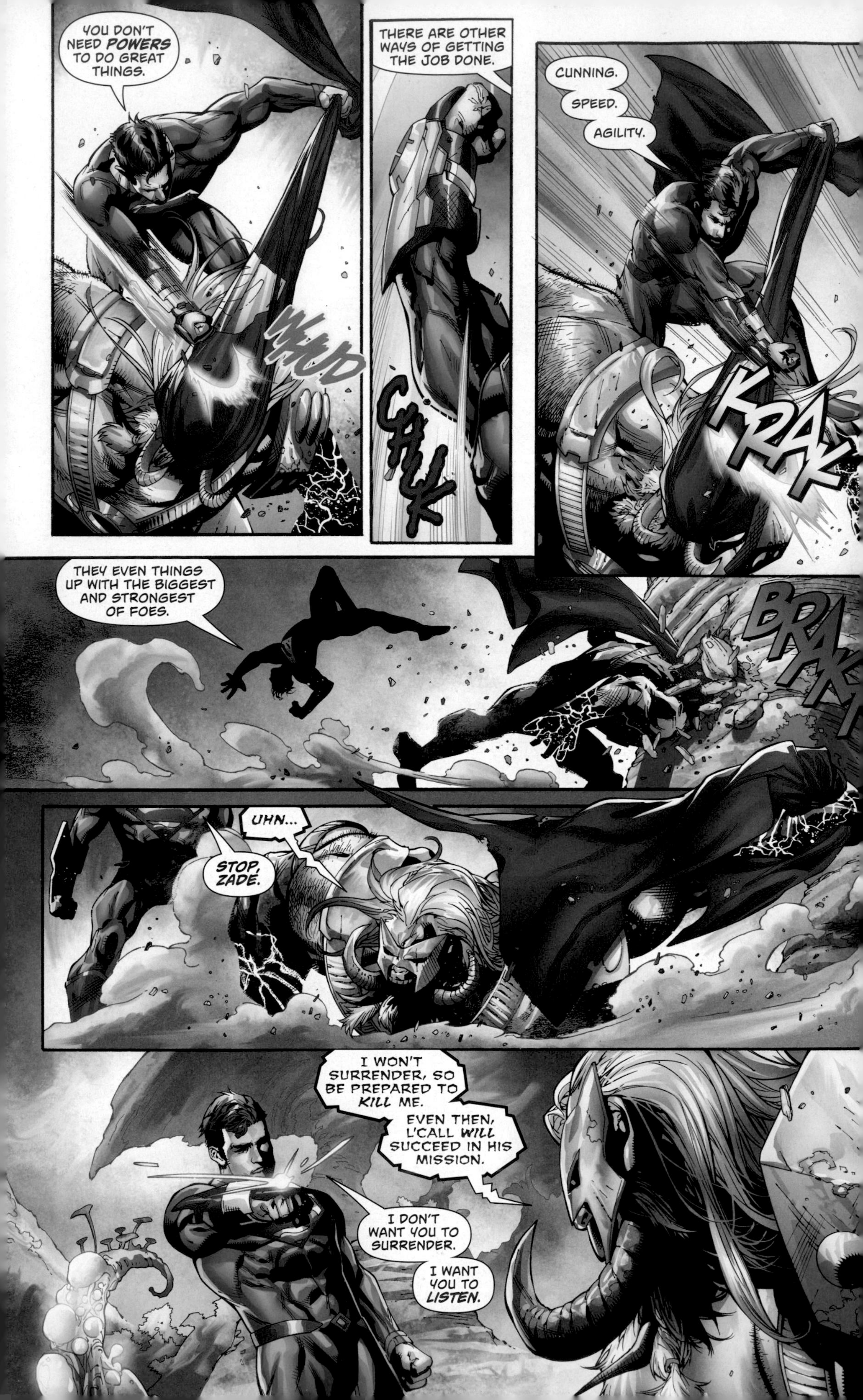

YOU DON'T NEED **POWERS** TO DO GREAT THINGS.
WHUD
THERE ARE OTHER WAYS OF GETTING THE JOB DONE.
CHUK
CUNNING.
SPEED.
AGILITY.
KRAK
THEY EVEN THINGS UP WITH THE BIGGEST AND STRONGEST OF FOES.
BRAK
UHN...
STOP, ZADE.
I WON'T SURRENDER, SO BE PREPARED TO *KILL* ME.
EVEN THEN, L'CALL *WILL* SUCCEED IN HIS MISSION.
I DON'T WANT YOU TO SURRENDER.
I WANT YOU TO ***LISTEN.***

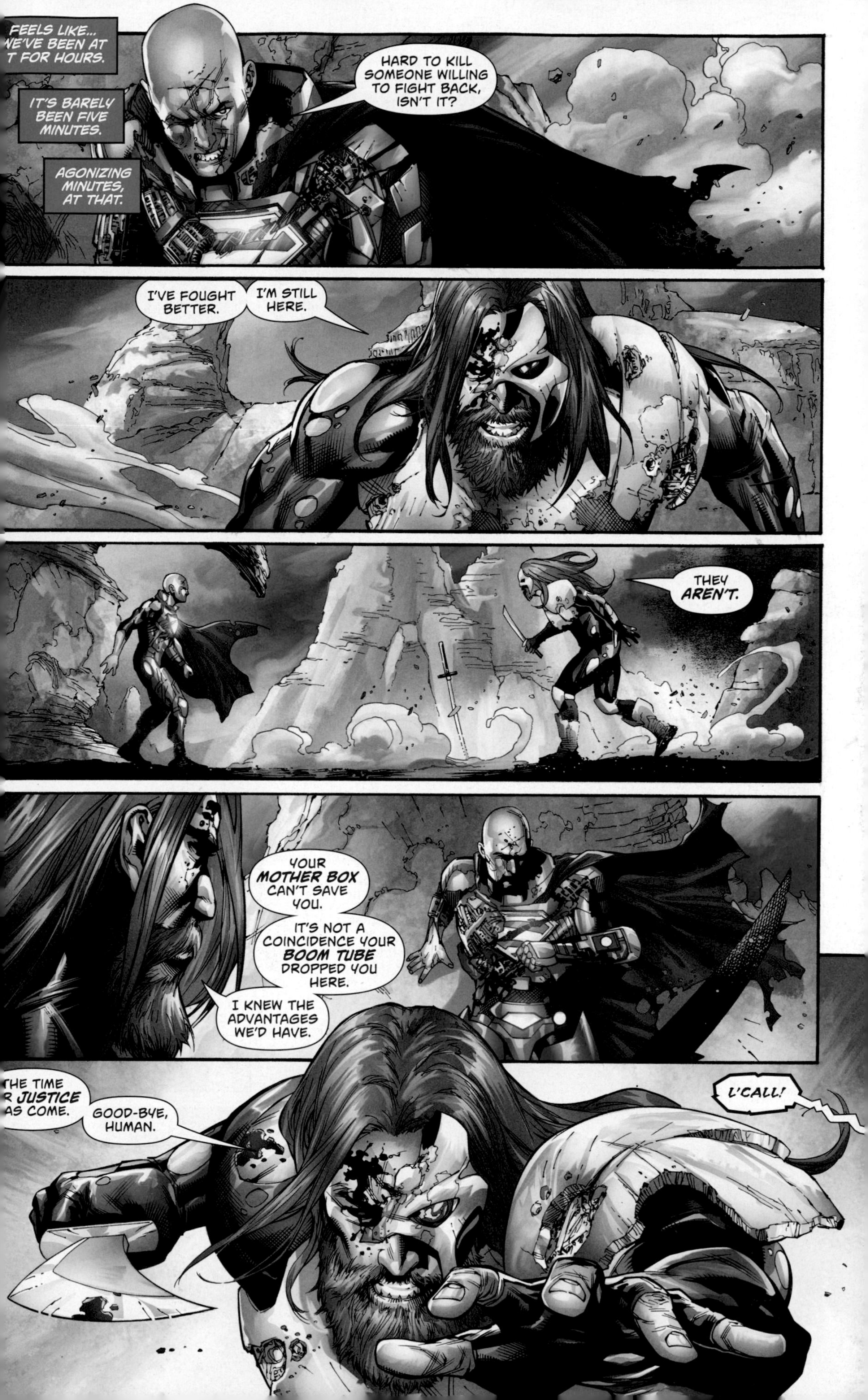
FEELS LIKE... WE'VE BEEN AT IT FOR HOURS.
IT'S BARELY BEEN FIVE MINUTES.
AGONIZING MINUTES, AT THAT.
HARD TO KILL SOMEONE WILLING TO FIGHT BACK, ISN'T IT?
I'VE FOUGHT BETTER.
I'M STILL HERE.
THEY AREN'T.
YOUR MOTHER BOX CAN'T SAVE YOU.
IT'S NOT A COINCIDENCE YOUR BOOM TUBE DROPPED YOU HERE.
I KNEW THE ADVANTAGES WE'D HAVE.
THE TIME JUSTICE AS COME.
GOOD-BYE, HUMAN.
L'CALL!

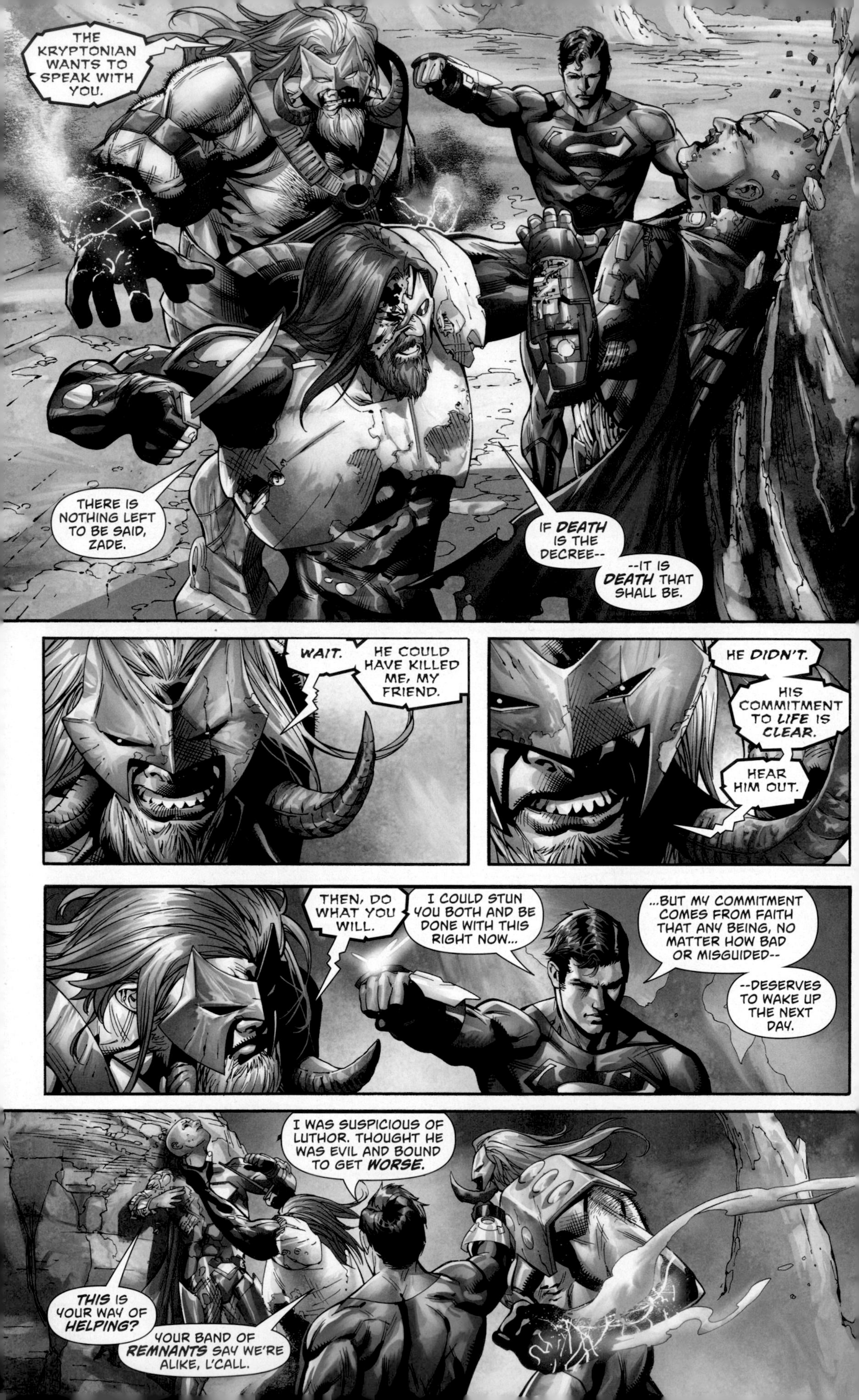
THE KRYPTONIAN WANTS TO SPEAK WITH YOU.
THERE IS NOTHING LEFT TO BE SAID, ZADE.
IF DEATH IS THE DECREE--
--IT IS DEATH THAT SHALL BE.
WAIT.
HE COULD HAVE KILLED ME, MY FRIEND.
HE DIDN'T.
HIS COMMITMENT TO LIFE IS CLEAR.
HEAR HIM OUT.
THEN, DO WHAT YOU WILL.
I COULD STUN YOU BOTH AND BE DONE WITH THIS RIGHT NOW...
...BUT MY COMMITMENT COMES FROM FAITH THAT ANY BEING, NO MATTER HOW BAD OR MISGUIDED--
--DESERVES TO WAKE UP THE NEXT DAY.
I WAS SUSPICIOUS OF LUTHOR. THOUGHT HE WAS EVIL AND BOUND TO GET WORSE.
THIS IS YOUR WAY OF HELPING?
YOUR BAND OF REMNANTS SAY WE'RE ALIKE, L'CALL.

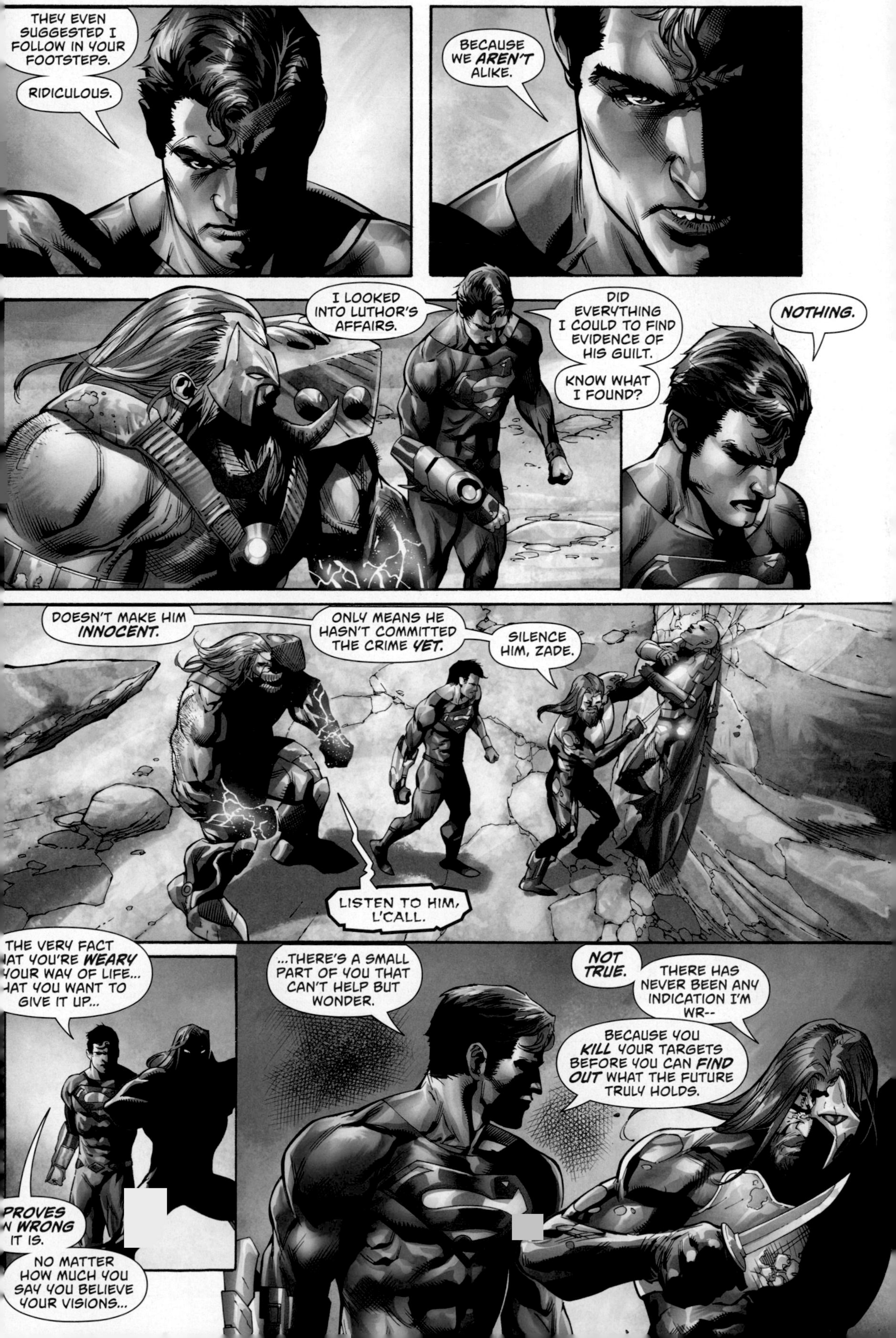
THEY EVEN SUGGESTED I FOLLOW IN YOUR FOOTSTEPS.
RIDICULOUS.
BECAUSE WE *AREN'T* ALIKE.
I LOOKED INTO LUTHOR'S AFFAIRS.
DID EVERYTHING I COULD TO FIND EVIDENCE OF HIS GUILT.
KNOW WHAT I FOUND?
NOTHING.
DOESN'T MAKE HIM *INNOCENT.*
ONLY MEANS HE HASN'T COMMITTED THE CRIME *YET.*
SILENCE HIM, ZADE.
LISTEN TO HIM, L'CALL.
THE VERY FACT
HAT YOU'RE *WEARY*
YOUR WAY OF LIFE...
HAT YOU WANT TO
GIVE IT UP...
...THERE'S A SMALL PART OF YOU THAT CAN'T HELP BUT WONDER.
NOT TRUE.
THERE HAS NEVER BEEN ANY INDICATION I'M WR--
BECAUSE YOU *KILL* YOUR TARGETS BEFORE YOU CAN *FIND OUT* WHAT THE FUTURE TRULY HOLDS.
PROVES
N *WRONG*
IT IS.
NO MATTER HOW MUCH YOU SAY YOU BELIEVE YOUR VISIONS...

CONSIDER THIS.

YOU THOUGHT ME WORTHY OF BEING YOUR SUCCESSOR.

KEEP THINKING OF ME THAT WAY.

A **PROTECTOR** OF LIFE.

I PLEDGE TO YOU, HERE AND NOW, THAT I WILL NEVER LET LEX LUTHOR--

--OR ANYONE ELSE--**EVER**--

--GET TO THE POINT WHERE THEY DESTROY EARTH OR ANY OTHER WORLD.

LOOK INTO **MY** FUTURE INSTEAD OF LUTHOR'S--

--AND I THINK YOU'LL SEE I'M **RIGHT.**

Hmph.

L'CALL CLOSES HIS EYES.

I WILL NEVER KNO THE WONDERS O WHAT THE GODSLA SAW IN THAT MOME

ALL I KNOW IS THAT HE SOFTENED. AND MAY HAVE EXHIBITED...

...THE SLIGHTEST OF SMILES.

IT APPEARS THE LIGHT OF SUPERMAN'S FUTURE--

--OVERWHELMS THE PERCEIVED THREAT OF MY OWN.

THIS...HAS BEEN AN **HONOR,** KRYPTONIAN.

PREPARE YOURSELVES.

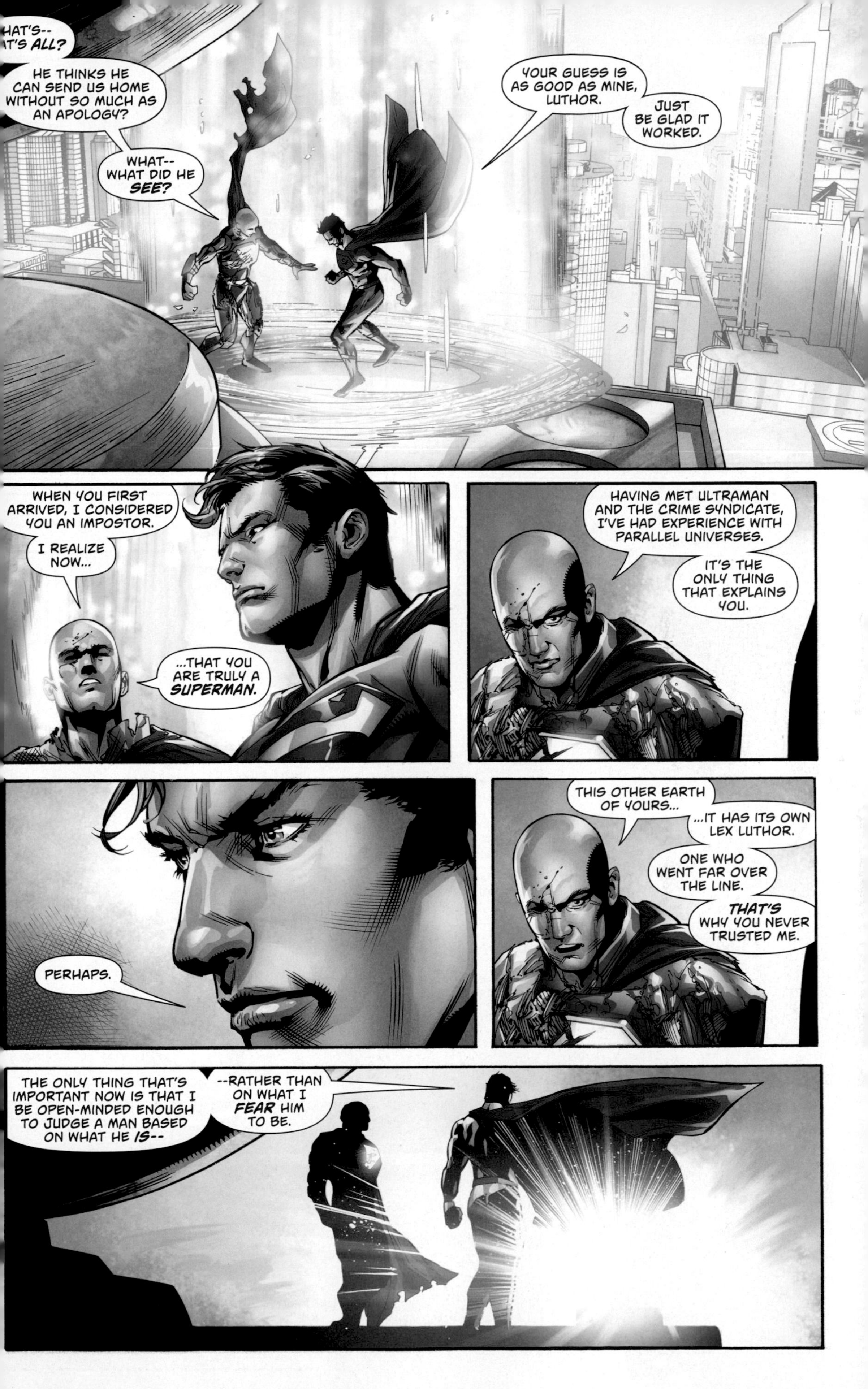
HAT'S--
AT'S ALL?
HE THINKS HE CAN SEND US HOME WITHOUT SO MUCH AS AN APOLOGY?
WHAT-- WHAT DID HE SEE?
YOUR GUESS IS AS GOOD AS MINE, LUTHOR.
JUST BE GLAD IT WORKED.
WHEN YOU FIRST ARRIVED, I CONSIDERED YOU AN IMPOSTOR.
I REALIZE NOW...
...THAT YOU ARE TRULY A SUPERMAN.
HAVING MET ULTRAMAN AND THE CRIME SYNDICATE, I'VE HAD EXPERIENCE WITH PARALLEL UNIVERSES.
IT'S THE ONLY THING THAT EXPLAINS YOU.
PERHAPS.
THIS OTHER EARTH OF YOURS...
...IT HAS ITS OWN LEX LUTHOR.
ONE WHO WENT FAR OVER THE LINE.
THAT'S WHY YOU NEVER TRUSTED ME.
THE ONLY THING THAT'S IMPORTANT NOW IS THAT I BE OPEN-MINDED ENOUGH TO JUDGE A MAN BASED ON WHAT HE IS--
--RATHER THAN ON WHAT I FEAR HIM TO BE.

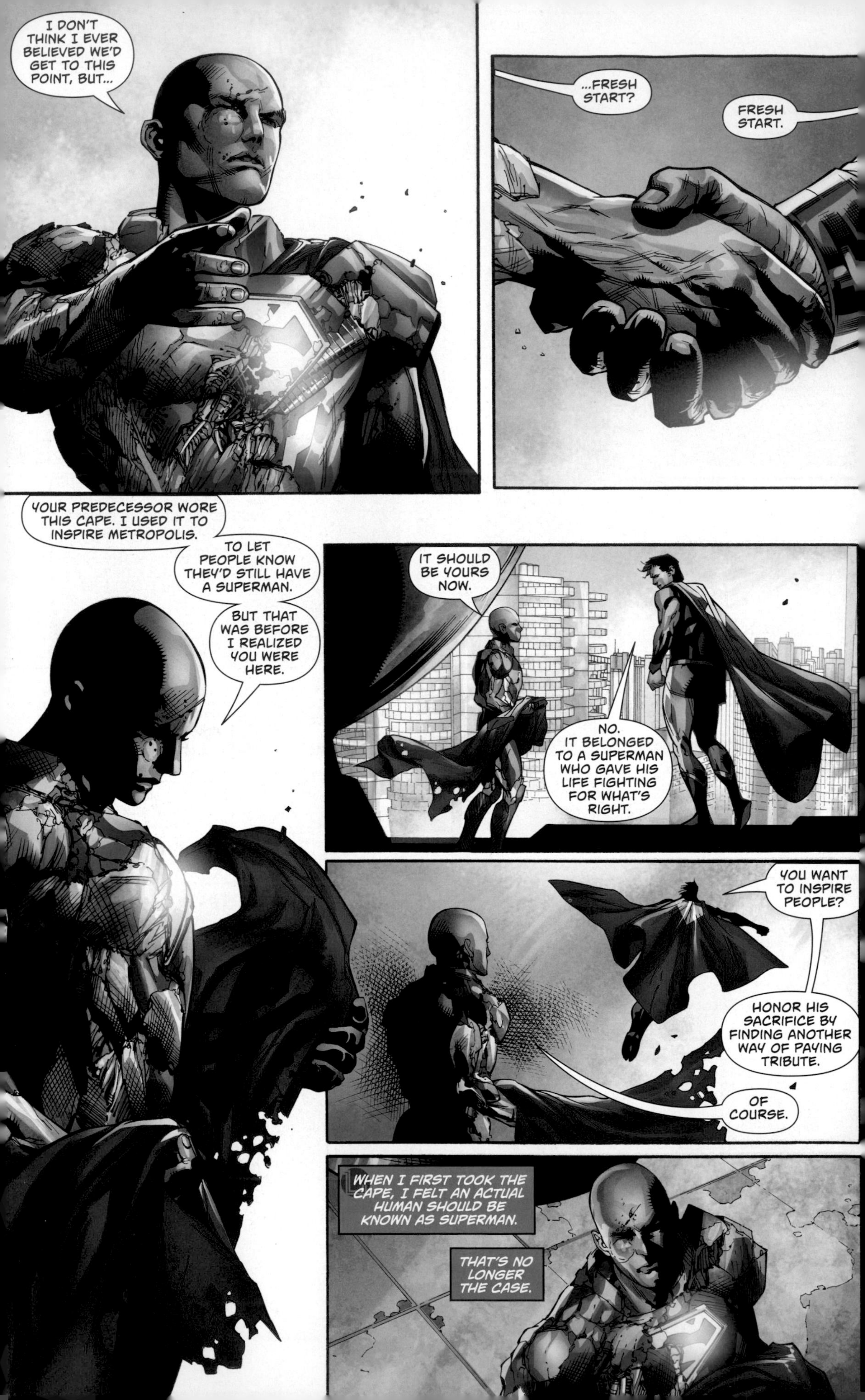
I DON'T THINK I EVER BELIEVED WE'D GET TO THIS POINT, BUT...
...FRESH START?
FRESH START.
YOUR PREDECESSOR WORE THIS CAPE. I USED IT TO INSPIRE METROPOLIS.
TO LET PEOPLE KNOW THEY'D STILL HAVE A SUPERMAN.
BUT THAT WAS BEFORE I REALIZED YOU WERE HERE.
IT SHOULD BE YOURS NOW.
NO. IT BELONGED TO A SUPERMAN WHO GAVE HIS LIFE FIGHTING FOR WHAT'S RIGHT.
YOU WANT TO INSPIRE PEOPLE?
HONOR HIS SACRIFICE BY FINDING ANOTHER WAY OF PAYING TRIBUTE.
OF COURSE.
WHEN I FIRST TOOK THE CAPE, I FELT AN ACTUAL HUMAN SHOULD BE KNOWN AS SUPERMAN.
THAT'S NO LONGER THE CASE.

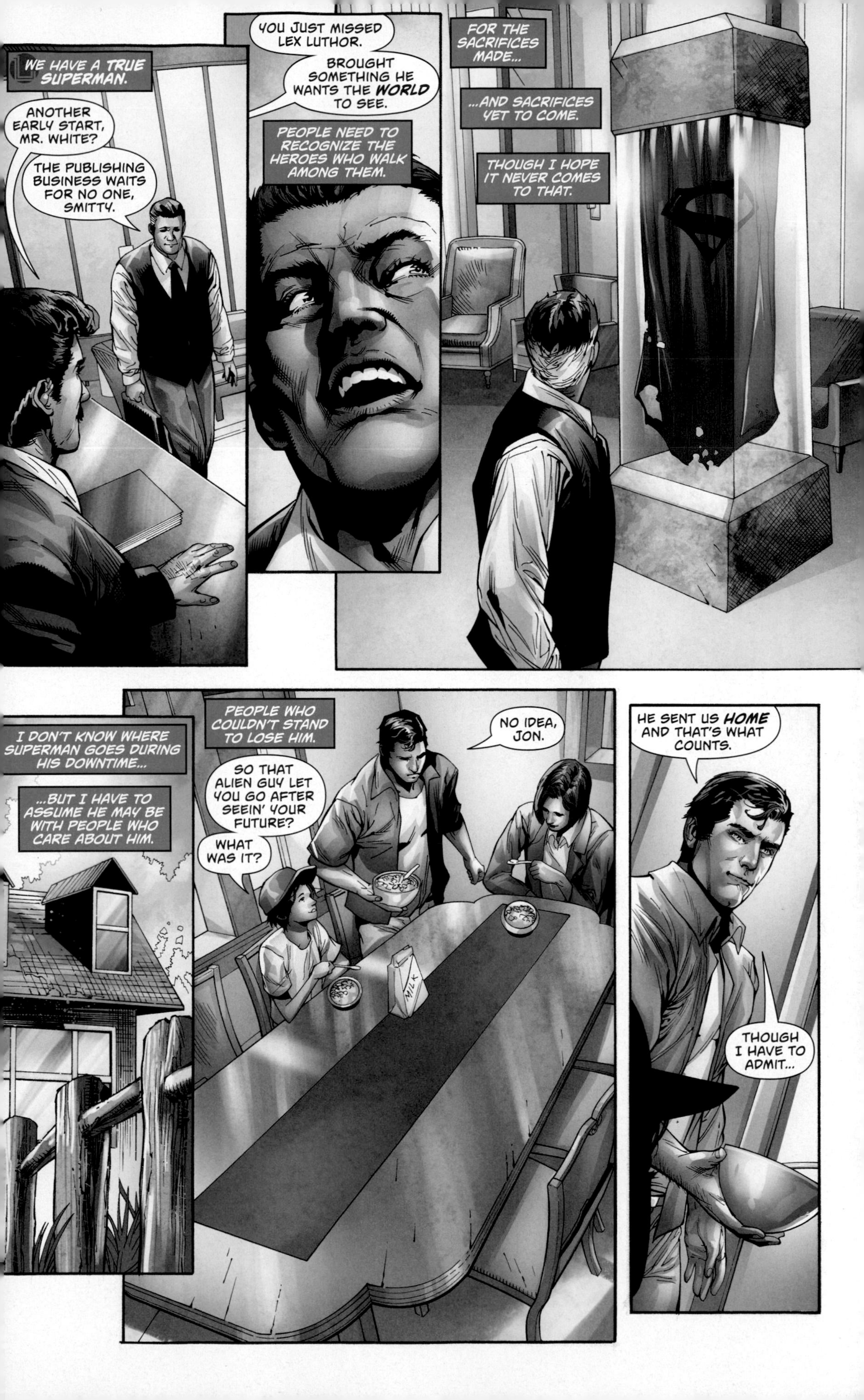
WE HAVE A TRUE SUPERMAN.
ANOTHER EARLY START, MR. WHITE?
THE PUBLISHING BUSINESS WAITS FOR NO ONE, SMITTY.
YOU JUST MISSED LEX LUTHOR.
BROUGHT SOMETHING HE WANTS THE WORLD TO SEE.
PEOPLE NEED TO RECOGNIZE THE HEROES WHO WALK AMONG THEM.
FOR THE SACRIFICES MADE...
...AND SACRIFICES YET TO COME.
THOUGH I HOPE IT NEVER COMES TO THAT.
I DON'T KNOW WHERE SUPERMAN GOES DURING HIS DOWNTIME...
...BUT I HAVE TO ASSUME HE MAY BE WITH PEOPLE WHO CARE ABOUT HIM.
PEOPLE WHO COULDN'T STAND TO LOSE HIM.
SO THAT ALIEN GUY LET YOU GO AFTER SEEIN' YOUR FUTURE?
WHAT WAS IT?
NO IDEA, JON.
MILK
HE SENT US HOME AND THAT'S WHAT COUNTS.
THOUGH I HAVE TO ADMIT...

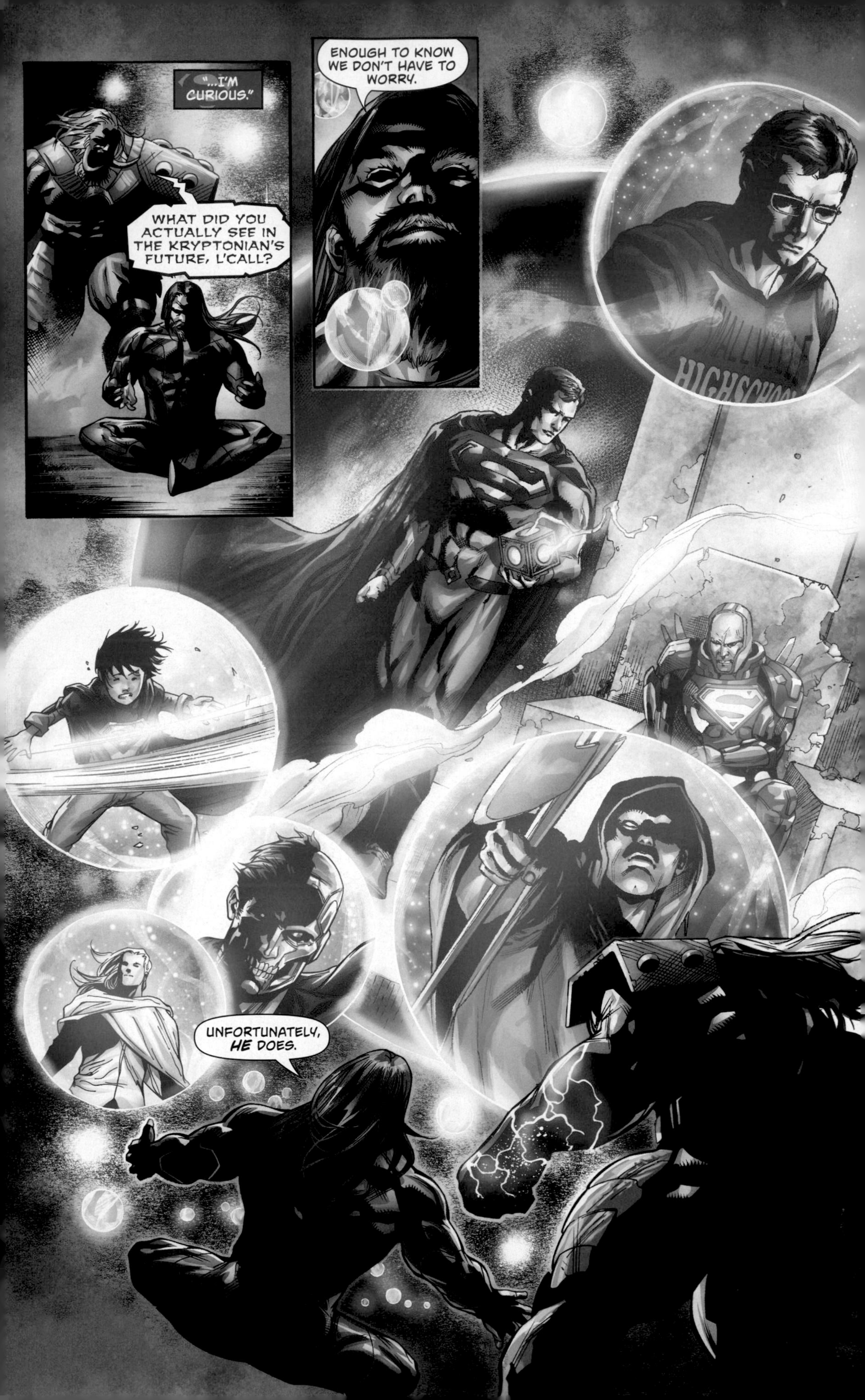
"...I'M CURIOUS."
WHAT DID YOU ACTUALLY SEE IN THE KRYPTONIAN'S FUTURE, L'CALL?
ENOUGH TO KNOW WE DON'T HAVE TO WORRY.
HIGHSCHOOL
UNFORTUNATELY, HE DOES.

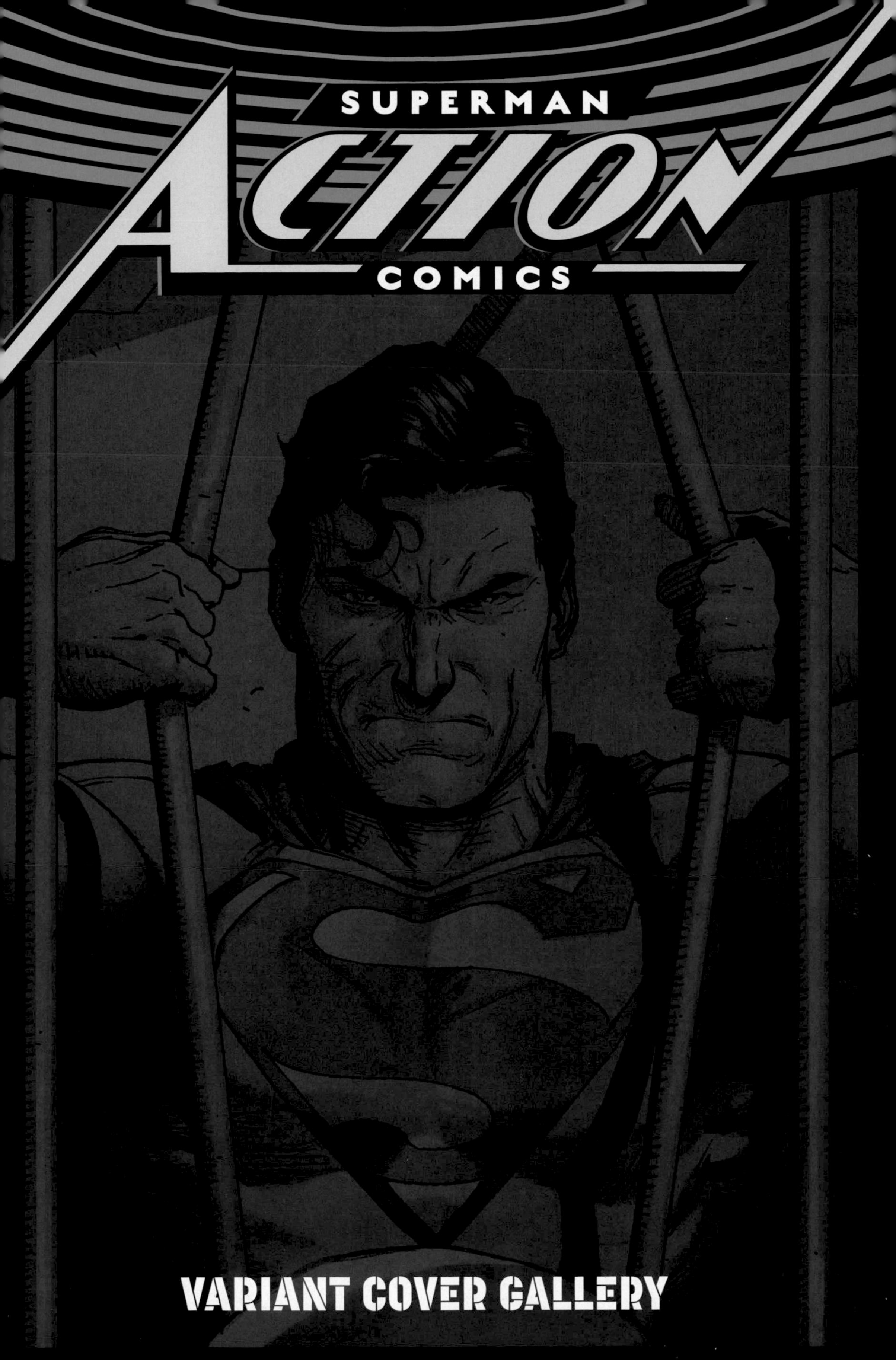
SUPERMAN
ACTION
COMICS
VARIANT COVER GALLERY

Variant cover art for ACTION COMICS #967 by GARY FRANK and BRAD ANDERSON

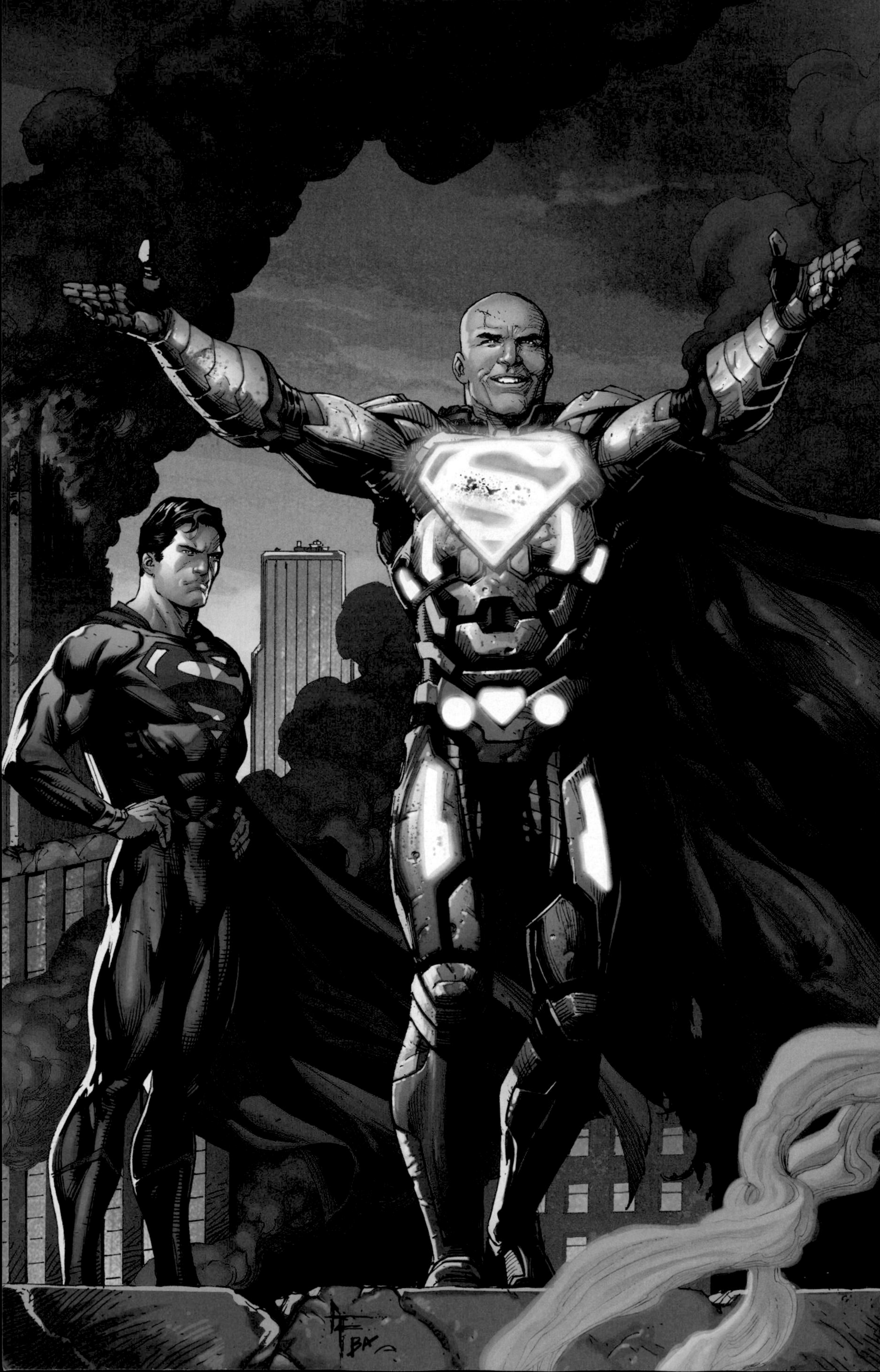

Variant cover art for ACTION COMICS #968 by GARY FRANK and BRAD ANDERSON

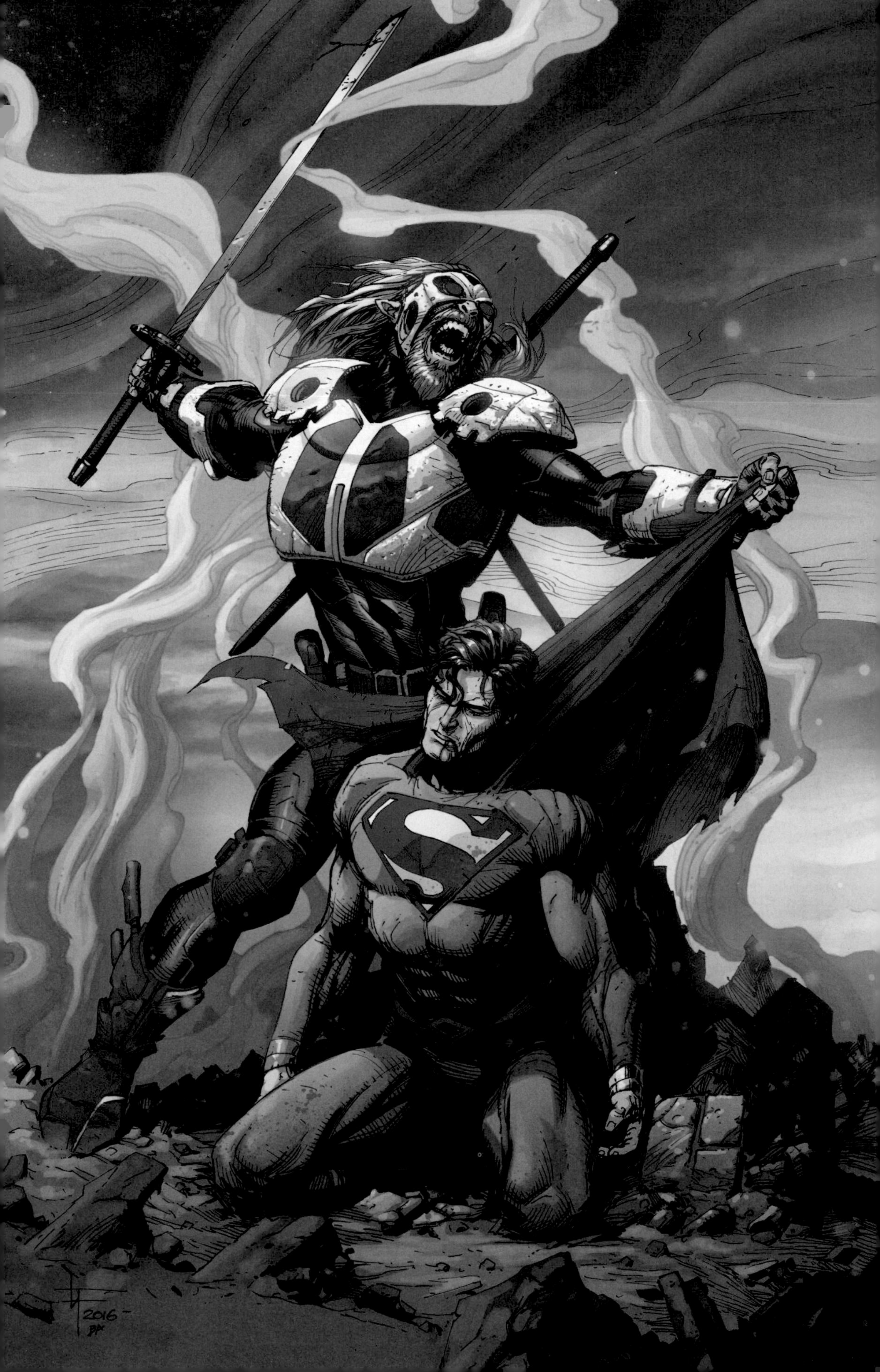
2016

Variant cover art for ACTION COMICS #969 by GARY FRANK and BRAD ANDERSON

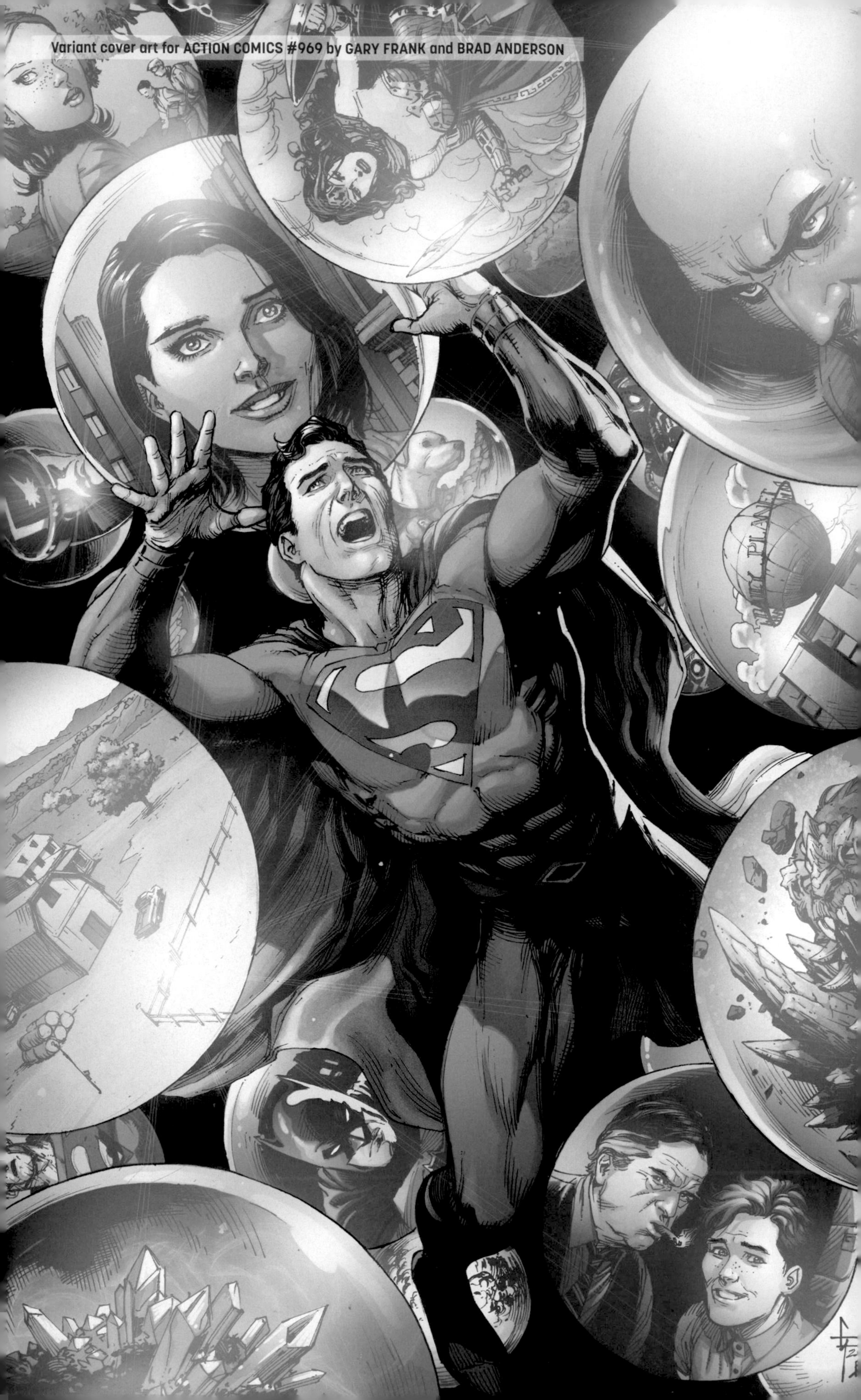

Variant cover art for ACTION COMICS #970 by GARY FRANK and BRAD ANDERSON

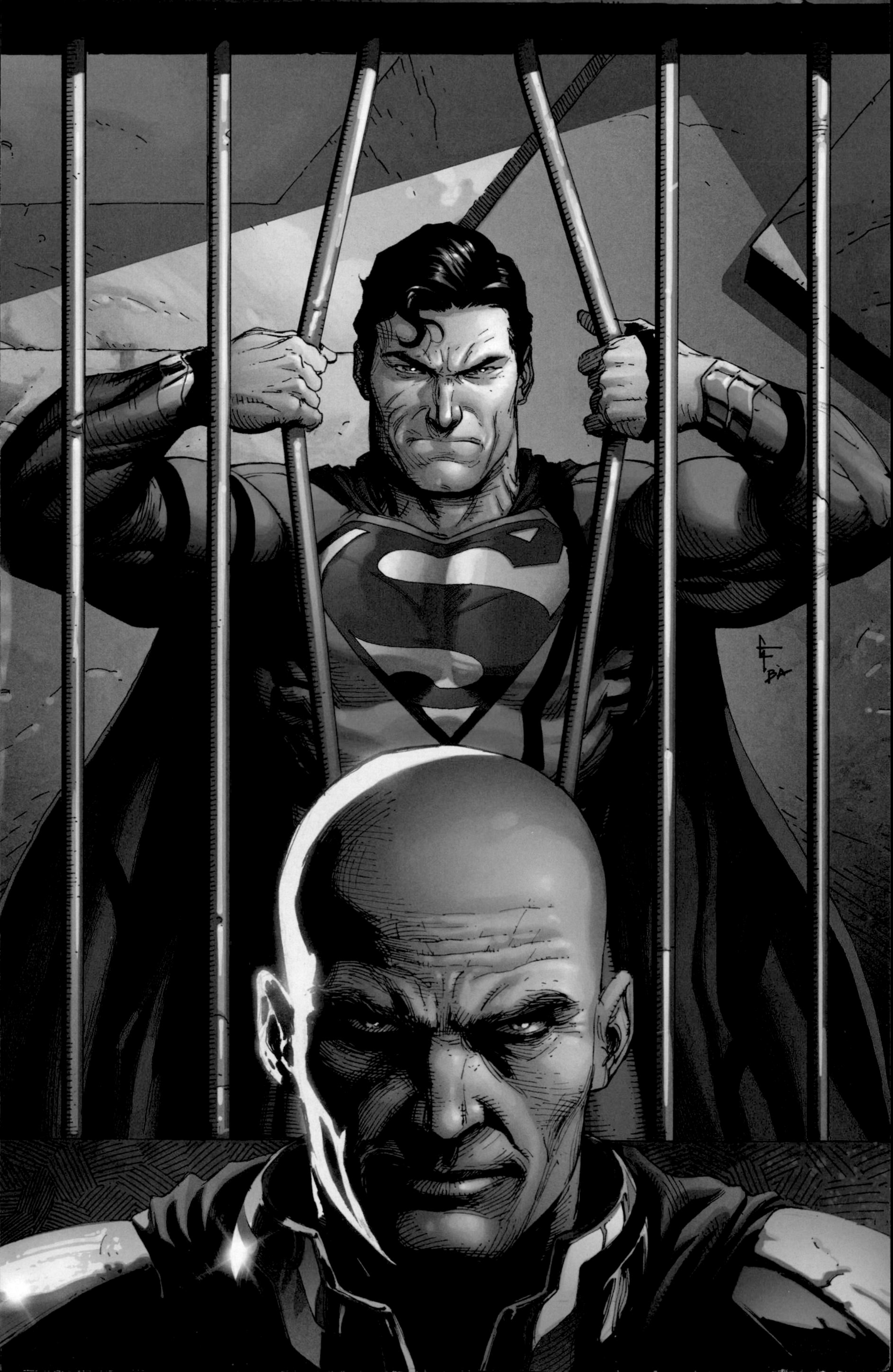

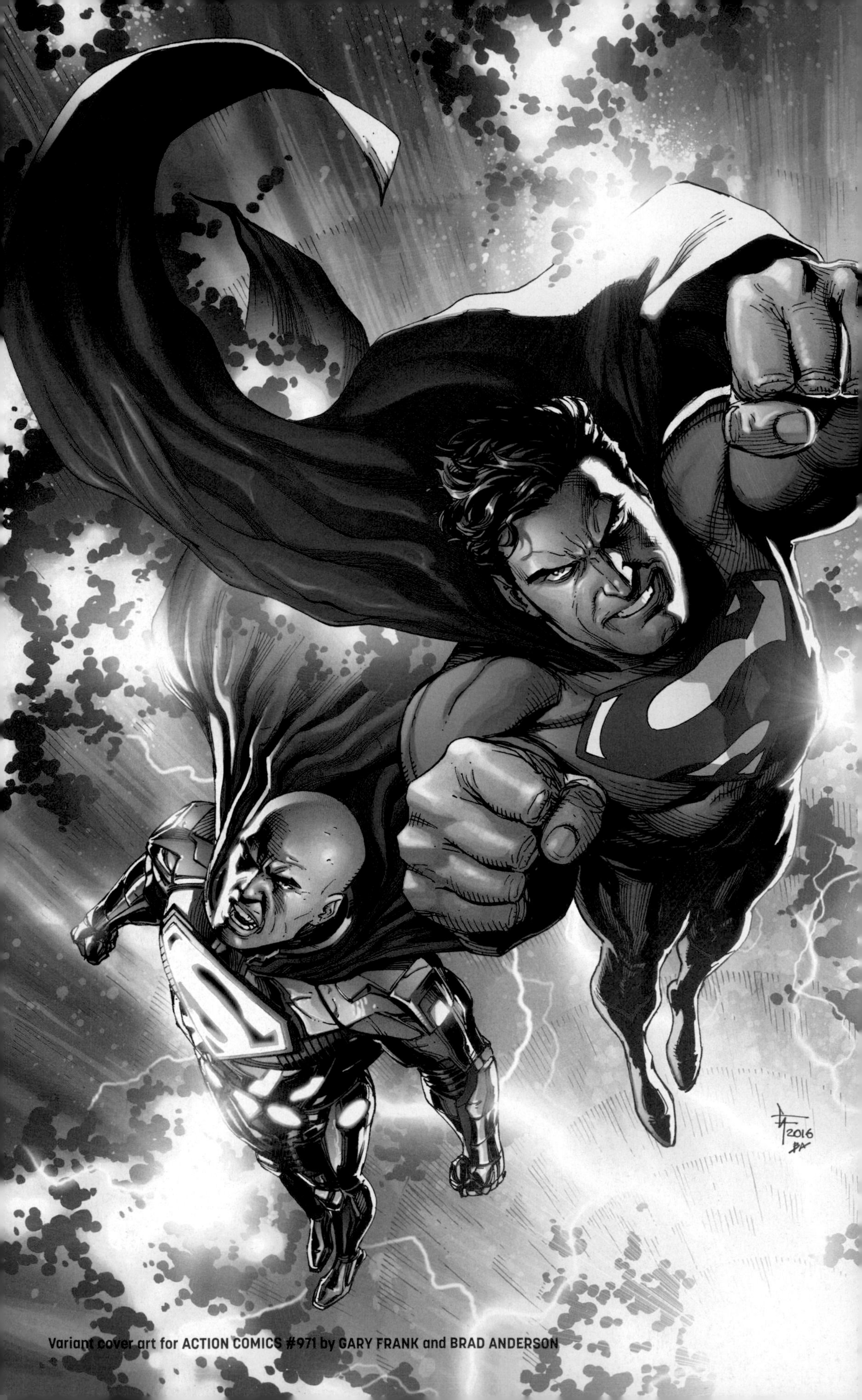

Variant cover art for ACTION COMICS #971 by GARY FRANK and BRAD ANDERSON

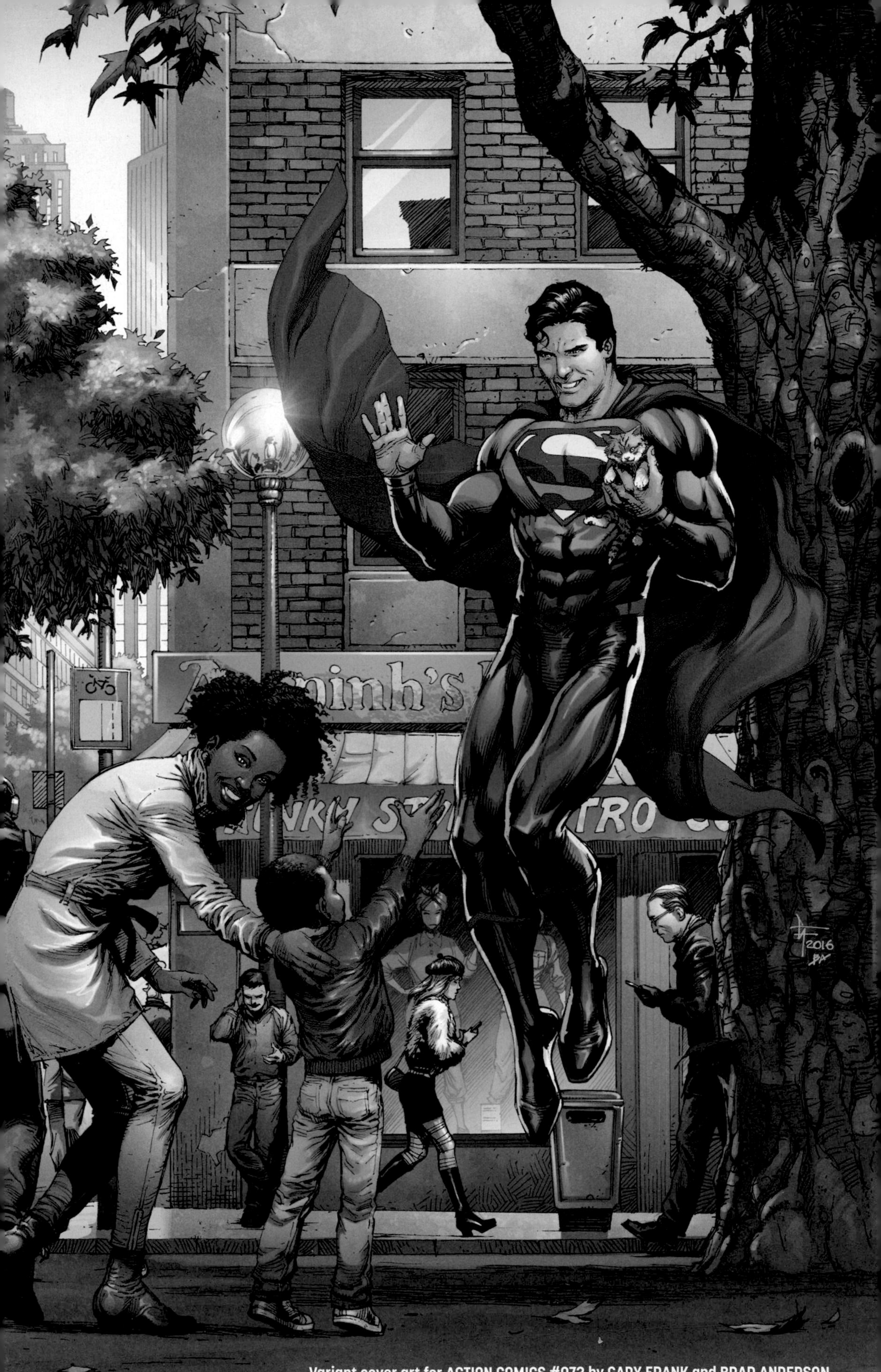

Variant cover art for ACTION COMICS #972 by GARY FRANK and BRAD ANDERSON

"That gorgeous spectacle is an undeniable part of Superman's appeal, but the family dynamics are what make it such an engaging read."
– A.V. CLUB

"Head and shoulders above the rest."
– NEWSARAMA

DC UNIVERSE REBIRTH
SUPERMAN
VOL. 1: SON OF SUPERMAN
PETER J. TOMASI with PATRICK GLEASON,
DOUG MAHNKE & JORGE JIMENEZ

VOL.1 SON OF SUPERMAN
PETER J.TOMASI ∗ PATRICK GLEASON ∗ DOUG MAHNKE ∗ JORGE JIMENEZ ∗ MICK GRAY

**SUPERGIRL VOL. 1:
REIGN OF THE SUPERMEN**

**ACTION COMICS VOL. 1:
PATH OF DOOM**

**BATMAN VOL. 1:
I AM GOTHAM**

"Tyler Kirkham draws some fine doom and destruction." **IGN**

"Delivers a fun and exciting story." **COMIC BOOK RESOURCES**

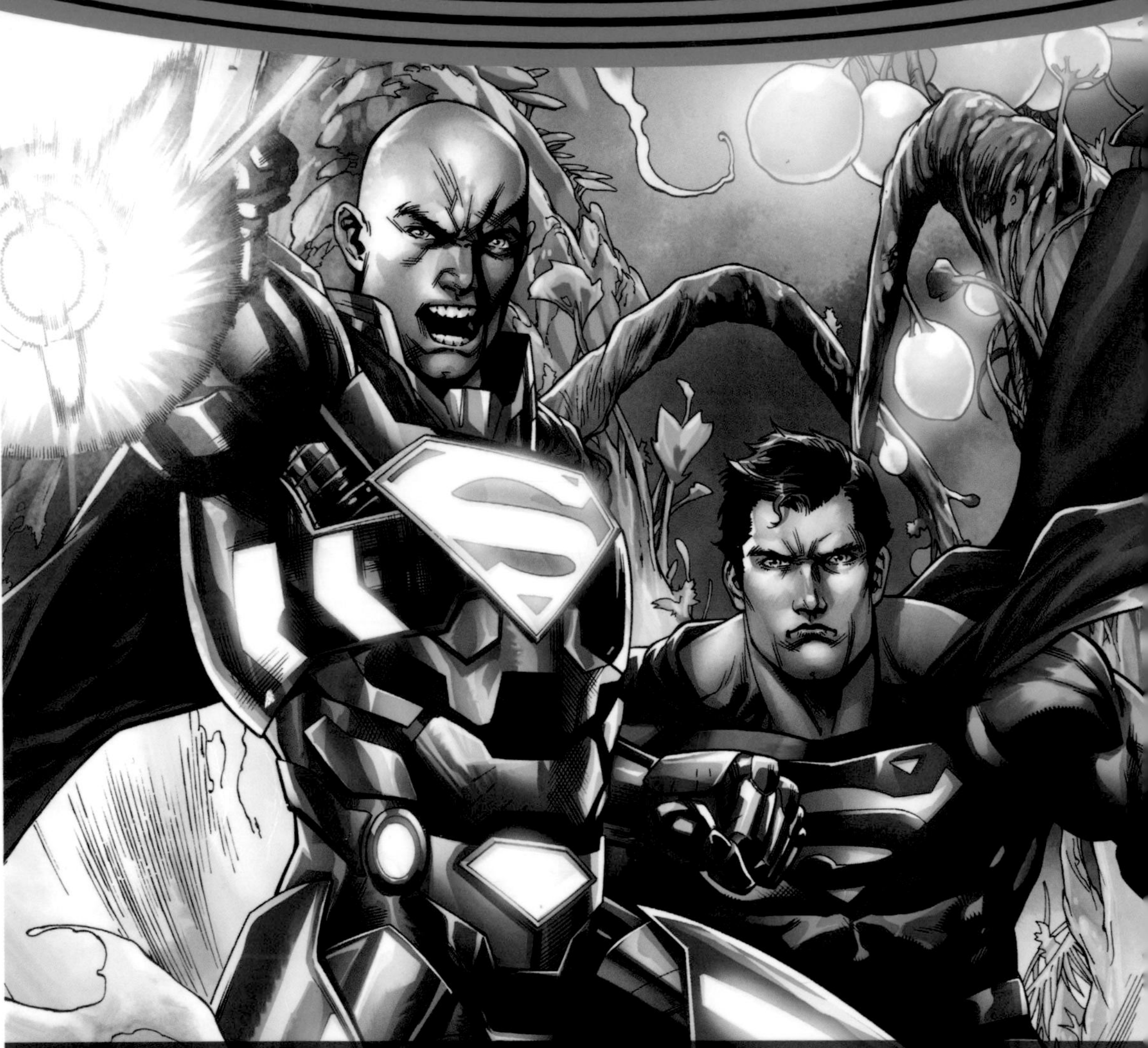

LEX LUTHOR TEAMS UP WITH SUPERMAN?!

Lex Luthor says he's a hero. He's even taken to wearing the Superman "S" on his armor. And so far, though he's unable to trust him, Superman can't find any evidence that Lex is anything but what he claims to be.

But for the mysterious alien warrior who calls himself the God Killer, evidence isn't necessary. He's been granted a vision of the future where Lex ascends to Darkseid's throne on Apokolips and crushes Earth beneath his heel. For the terrible crimes he is destined to commit, the only sentence can be death!

Now Superman finds himself in the unlikely positio of having to defend his greatest enemy from cert death...even if it means enduring the wrath of God Killer himself!

Can Superman possibly save Lex from overwhelmi odds? Or would the universe be better off if he let t God Killer complete his mission?

The smash-hit Rebirth of Superman continues, from classic Superman writer **DAN JURGENS** and artists **TYLER KIRKHAM**, **PATCH ZIRCHER** and **STEPHEN SEGOVIA**. Collecting ACTION COMICS #967-972.

51699 >

9 781401 273576

$16.99 USA $22.99 CAN ISBN: 978-1-4012-7357-6 dccomics.com